# Thoughts

by Mattie F. Gaskins

**RoseDog❀Books**
PITTSBURGH, PENNSYLVANIA 15238

The contents of this work including, but not limited to, the accuracy of events, people, and places depicted; opinions expressed; permission to use previously published materials included; and any advice given or actions advocated are solely the responsibility of the author, who assumes all liability for said work and indemnifies the publisher against any claims stemming from publication of the work.

All Rights Reserved
Copyright © 2017 by Mattie F. Gaskins

No part of this book may be reproduced or transmitted, downloaded, distributed, reverse engineered, or stored in or introduced into any information storage and retrieval system, in any form or by any means, including photocopying and recording, whether electronic or mechanical, now known or hereinafter invented without permission in writing from the publisher.

RoseDog Books
585 Alpha Drive, Suite 103
Pittsburgh, PA 15238
Visit our website at *www.rosedogbookstore.com*

ISBN: 978-1-4809-7518-7
eISBN: 978-1-4809-7541-5

# Acknowledgements

Giving honor praise and glory to our heavenly father God, his son Jesus Christ whom is all our savior. I thank you very much for life all our lives my family. My book is dedicated to my wonderful parents, even though you're gone! You're not forgotten. I miss and love you very much. Also my book is dedicated to my beautiful and intelligent daughter Ja'Near Kiamesha. You are my Shero. My everything. Your courage strength and determination is beyond exemplary. Inspiring me and all of us. Good job keep up the good work. I pray wishing hoping and believing God continues giving you life and longevity.

—Love, Ma

# Prologue

Where has time gone? In my lifetime, I began to write this story in the fall of 1977, which was thirty-nine years ago. Throughout the years, I tried rewriting some of the chapters; trying to find the right words and phrases. Just a few minutes ago, before I started writing this first sentence, I didn't quite know what my first line would be, but now I do. My mind is bearing too much; so many heavy burdens. Some of these burdens are beyond my control. Out of my hands. Acts of God, but still I must hold on and bear the burdens. I'm not confused, but I'm terribly depressed. My physical body is recuperating from major surgery a month ago. I can even deal with this body pain and the aches; what I can hardly bear is my heartaches, pain, and loneliness. I try not to believe in superstitious sayings that things comes in threes. For me right now, at my point in life, it's true. First it was my emergency major surgery. Secondly, two weeks later my sister died. This hurts terribly bad, almost like Hell. I've never had a sister or a brother who died before, who I knew of and lived with. Although, before I was born, I was told that my parents had lost four babies to death. So, to me, those babies' deaths were before my time. I really didn't know them, and therefore, their death didn't leave an impact on me. Thirdly, after burying my older sister this same day, I finally had to face the facts that the man I loved and wanted for thirty-five years is also dead to me; even though he is still very much alive and kicking. Right now, writing these words, I must take a breather from the awful hurt and misery from these revelations. Once more resuming, as I remain at home recuperating these next months, I now have time to reflect upon my life and future as well as my past and present;

from the turmoil inside of me. This time, I'm going to make it all the way or die trying. I have to do this for my survival. I need peace within, for the remainder of my life, however long this may be—hours, days, weeks, months, or years. I now know that I deserve better and more to have peace within myself, if not true happiness, because life is too short, and for some, it's even shorter. I'm fifty years old—that's half of a century. All my life, I've been a dreamer and a fantasizer, but I never, not ever, thought that someday I'd be this old. Don't get me wrong. Yes, I want to live a life of longevity. In some ways, life has flown quickly flown by. Actually, in reality I guess that I really didn't help myself much, especially with relationships of love, only now I'm going to live out the remainder of my life for my family, and more importantly, for yours truly, namely, me. Months ago, before I turned fifty years old, I began to wonder what was and is my purpose in life. Why have I been hurt so much by love? To me, love is many definitions, and it's unconditionally free. With those words said, when it comes to love, I was left out, short changed, and wrongly done. I no longer want to know why love passed me by; what I need is closure from love so that I can at long last finally be free and have peace within. Therefore, I'm giving up on me ever having love. In all my fifty years, it hasn't happened. I now doubt that it ever will. Even at this time in life, if by some miracle I did find love, this wouldn't erase or compensate for all the misery, hurt, loneliness, heartache, and pain I've suffered. I grew up in a religious family, believing in God our father and our savior his son Jesus Christ; now that I'm older, I've witnessed a lot in life; been through many trials and tribulations from my own experiences. These experiences have left me very doubtful and truthfully without faith. My mother once told me that she had religion since she was sixteen years old. I honestly and truly believe that if anyone had religion, it was my mother. My mother lived her life believing in God and being a righteous person, having tremendous faith and prayer belief. For me, her daughter, to now for years to have doubts and no faith, it's sad and pitiful, but I must tell the truth. I'm a truthful person; not a liar. I don't think God will hold this against me for speaking my mind; at least I hope not. I'm not a hypocrite. I've also heard the saying, "God forgives up to seven-hundred and seventy-seven (777) times a day." Don't get me wrong when I say I have no faith. This doesn't mean that I don't believe God exists. I also do think Gods exists. Otherwise, how else would our lives, the world, and this universe exist? Now, what I don't believe is that God wanted us humans on the other planets. If he did, he would have put us there instead of placing us on planet Earth. I must say truthfully and frankly, speaking bluntly, that in my opinion, we as people down here on this earth can't and don't live in peace and harmony, especially not with freedom. Instead, we have all of this hatred, prejudice, and discrimination. Now, to think about life on another planet, it's comical and so very sad, because we people can't live here on earth together in peace. Yet, to me, to now try and understand and comprehend life on an unchartered planet is totally unrealistic as well as unacceptable. How unbelievable is that some people are rich enough to buy land up on the moon? Yet so many others of us are poor and hungry. We don't have enough food to eat or a roof over our head to live. To this, I say take one day at a time. Tomorrow is not here yet, so don't worry about it. Yes, we can plan and look forward to tomorrow, but tomorrow, again, is not here yet.

Resuming back to my state of mind of not having faith in God—because after years and years of praying and trying for love—my prayers are still unanswered. My pain and hurt is just as deep. In my conclusion, it doesn't take forever for prayers to be answered. Even though my mother always said, "God may not come when you want him, but he's right on time." I now say to myself, if my prayers and hopes were going to come true, it would have happened by now. Therefore, it's way past time I stop trying and just simply give up completely and forever. Besides, I now realize, why want a man that doesn't want me? He never really wanted me. I really do deserve better, without anyone's help. I'm going to get my peace of mind. For fifty years, I have survived. Only, now I'm finally passing the grades. Graduating from love's closures. From this statement I say hallelujah. Girl, do it. Correction: not girl. The word is, "Woman, you're on your way." No, it won't be as easy as it sounds, but still, I know I can do it. For I must—for myself. My questions again are, where has my life gone, and what's my purpose in life?

Read this book and you'll find out. I'm not a writer. Maybe beyond the completion of this book I might be. However, whether I am or not, writing this book is and will be psychologically therapeutic for myself. No one else can help me now. I must help myself by ending my pains and hurt. Here's to me for closure.

# Chapter One
# Life on the Farm

*Thoughts* is the name of my story. In this story, some events and occurrences are fictitious and some are autobiographical; only the writer knows what's true or false. *Thoughts* is about the life and times of a young black girl who eventually became a mature woman. Her name is La'friska Tashanti. Describing her, she has medium-length black hair, dark skin, a smooth complexion with two deep dimples, large breasts, and a dynamite shapely figure. A true fact is that her figure is one of her best attributes. The other attribute is the greatest—her eyes, which are exotic, far-away-looking, dreamy, and beautiful brown. La'friska is cute and attractive looking on the outside; inwardly, she is truly beautiful. She was born in the winter month of February, 1951. She was born in the county of Florence, South Carolina, a farming community in the high hill area section. Her parents had fourteen children, ten of whom survived, and two sets of twins that died at birth. These sets of twins were way before La'friska came along. Her parents were farmers. Even though her parents were very poor, they somehow kept them fed and clothed and kept a roof over their heads. Her parents were very hard working and honest people. They were also kind and considerate. Her parents taught them to be hard working and honest too. Her parents' honestly was a trademark. As a true fact, her father was well respected by blacks, and especially whites. They would say, "That old man is hard working, and he teaches those children to do the same and to be honest." La'friska never knew what it was like to have grandparents, because they died before she was born. Even though she never knew what it was like to have grandparents, she was very glad and happy that she had both her parents alive, because she knew some kids who didn't have both parents alive, or parents to call their own. La'friska's ancestral heritage extended from Africa as well as the West Indies. On her mother's side came the West Indies. Her ancestors on both family sides extended back hundreds of years. They were large, numerously plentiful families. On her father's side, the family tree traced back eight generations, including Cherokee Indian. Also, her mother's family tree traced back several generations. Many of them were slaves, so poor and hardworking, with honesty and pride. Yet, they somehow survived. As this story is being told and written, it's so terribly very sad that, with all those generations of ancestors on both sides of the families, they are dead and buried now, all the older people who could have really told us about our ancestral heritage which would have greatly enlightened us younger generations. Now it's too late. Even though we do know some of our heritage, our ancestors knew it better, because now younger generations get things mixed up and just plain wrong. So it's truly sad that we don't know our family trees a lot better. Back in the old days, these ancestors worked so hard toiling the soil trying to survive. Then to having babies after babies, they probably couldn't get socializing much. They were tired and worn out from working hard in the fields, plus raising their many offspring. They didn't have time or sense enough to make sure vital information about their heritage was passed down, grilled into us generation after generation. So as to one day we somebody could backtrack, tracing our heritage, writing it down on paper or film, revealing and exposing our families' roots. As far as our ancestors go, the crux of the point is that we all should have gotten to know and understand our family heritage; now, instead, we'll always wish and wonder about many things, because the older people are, again, dead, and can't answer our now-too-late questions. Even though La'friska's parents, grandparents, and ancestors didn't know about their earlier generations' ancestors, they did know about their latter generations. La'friska remembered her parents many times talking about their parents and grandparents. La'friska's parents were born in the Florence County, South Carolina area. Her parents are now both deceased, *God rest their souls.* Describing La'friska's parents, her father's name wasn't quite so common. There aren't many men named Anderson. Anderson was somewhat tall, at five feet seven inches, weighing 145 pounds. Dark-skinned complexion with a head full of hair even up until the day he died at seventy-one years of age. He still had all of his hair, with absolutely no baldness at all. He never put grease or oils in his hair. The comb would just glide smoothly through his hair. It's a true fact that when he died, La'friska's brother trimmed his hair for the burial. When La'friska saw that

## Thoughts

her father's hair had been cut, she asked, "Who cut his hair?" Her father's hair comb was long and green. It's also true that after her father's funeral, La'friska made sure that she took her father's comb as a sentimental keepsake. Through the years after his death, she treasured that comb. Back to describing her father, he was very friendly and talkative. For a man who couldn't write, he was very wise and intelligent. He also taught himself to read the Bible, and he would read it sometimes before going to sleep at night. Right now, La'friska vividly recalls in her mind seeing her father lying in his bed in his pajamas, reading his Bible before going to sleep. She would hear him trying to pronounce his words, dissecting them and sounding them out. In addition to having all of those qualities, her father had to have a priceless gift, which was his beautiful, natural smile. To see that smile as his face lit up with such a wonderful grin—her father didn't smile all the time, but when he did—it was magic. To this day, that's where La'Friska got her smile—from her dad. To advance ahead in this story, let's describe La'Friska's smile, because she didn't believe in forcing fake smiles. So, when she did smile, it was natural, pure from the heart, showcasing two deep dimples. Her smile could light up a world. Let's now describe La'Friska's mother; her name was Madlyn. She had light brown skin with a smooth complextion, weighing a hundred and fifty-five pounds at five foot five, with hair that she kept during the duration of her life in seven parted twists. When she untwisted those seven twists, her hair was automatically curled into a Shirley Temple-type of hairdo. All she had to do was run her fingers through them to cover up the parts. Although Madlyn was five feet five inches tall, and what some would consider as somewhat overweight, she still had a beautiful figure. This is also where La'friska and her six sisters inherited their dynamite shape. As a matter of fact, Madlyn looked better than her children, for she was a very attractive woman, with brown eyes.

Madlyn had a remarkable personality. She was always pleasant, kind, and so very nice. She was somewhat on the quiet side, but yet, she had a unique quality about herself. She was considerate of others' feelings, ensuring that she wouldn't try to hurt others' feelings. She didn't gossip about others. It was a true fact that she did not entertain the gossip of others. She simply didn't believe in partaking in gossip. She was also known as an honest person. People admired and respected Madlyn. To stress this point, I must skip forward just for a minute to the end of Madlyn's life at the age of seventy-six. Upon Madlyn's death, at her funeral, a church member stood up and spoke out loudly regarding what a beautiful person she was. In conclusion of the said church member's speech, it was said "Madlyn wasn't a woman of many words, but her words had meaning." From that woman's quote, La'friska and her whole family knew this was true. They were glad, proud, and extremely happy that others knew and recalled this trait that their mother embodied. Another incident at the funeral in the church was when La'friska's older sister, Ester, cried out in her grief, saying, "What a wonderful mother." She was so much more than just a devoted wife and a wonderful mother, especially to God and Jesus Christ. For Madlyn was a very devoted Christian woman. She had much faith and belief in God. Her faith was phenomenal. She had religion since the age of sixteen. Madlyn would many times be heard quoting such sayings as, "God he may not be there when you want him, but he's right on time." Looking back, La'friska always recalled her mother saying that if someone doubted God's existence. Another saying Madlyn would use when it concerned people gossiping was, "They talked about Jesus Christ, and he died for us, therefore you know they'll talk about us."

Yes, La'friska's parents were poor, but through their determination and struggling they still managed to survive raising their ten children, teaching them determination, honesty, and especially independence. Life on the farm, work is never ending. From sun up to sun down, hectic and back-breaking, it was heavy and hard manual labor. La'friska's father farmed all twelve months of the year. Most farms stopped farming in the fall when all the crops had been harvested out of the fields for that year. But not La'friska's father. He had to find something to keep busy at, plus make the entire family busy along with him too. For example, when such crops as tobacco, cotton, corn, and beans had been harvested for the fall season, her father then planted fall vegetables such as collard, turnip, and mustard greens and peanuts. After these fall vegetables were harvested, some were sold to the fruit market, and the rest her mother prepared and froze for their winter survival. La'friska's parents never brought vegetables from the supermarket, since her parents grew their own. It's a fact that her father sold vegetables to the food markets. Sometimes he practically gave the vegetables to the food market owners because the owners had too much on hand, or so they said. Therefore, her father wasn't paid much that day or time for his vegetables. Even in the hard cold winter months of January and February, La'friska's father planted more winter vegetables. You see, she recalls this because she remembers how very cold her hands were from cleaning the debris from the vegetables and washing them. Her hands were frozen from the ice cold water. Also in the winter, her father made them clean up the fields. After coming home from school, dinner was eaten at 3:30 pm, clothes were changed, and then they proceeded to the fields to complete said chores. Chores consisted of picking up the wood stalks (tobacco, cotton, corn, and bean stalks) and even dried weeds and bush stalks. As I now write this story I'm taking a breather because the world's most gifted singer is playing. Who? Mr. Jon Lucien

# Thoughts

from the U.S. Virgin Islands. I love him platonically. Right now, listen, love has never sounded so good. Jon is like a potato chip; you just can't eat one. With Jon, just one song won't do. So now I'm having my own party. As I listen to Jon, his way with words inspires me. For I am not a writer yet. I hope to have the skills to complete this writing. Okay, party over.

Back to describing picking up the stalks. Stalks had to be piled up in piles and then burned up. Even though we worked in the winter, the work wasn't hard like in the summer and fall months. In the spring months like May and June we planted different types of vegetables—veggies such as yellow and white squash, cucumbers, pickled baby cucumbers, and string beans. That was called truck season time. These veggies were picked every day except Sundays. Sunday, the Sabbath, was too holy a day, so nobody worked. In her family, they were always taught God worked six days building the world, and on the Sabbath day he rested. Also on Saturdays, in their family, they worked a half day in the mornings. Back to Sundays, the Sabbath in July and August when it was gathering tobacco time after midnight, which is technically a new day, Monday, her father would take the children and unload the tobacco barn cured out tobacco from the previous week. This had to be done before morning light came, because the tobacco for that week had to be harvested that same day, which was Monday morning You see, farmers in tobacco season time looked out for each other. They had to, so they worked out a system amongst themselves, each one gathering their tobacco crop on a different day, six days of the week. They hired day people to work either half a day, or they worked all day, depending on the size of the farmer's crop. These same people were promised to be hired out to six different days to other farmers harvesting their crops. Back to La'friska's father and the children unloading the tobacco barn after midnight. Her mother wouldn't help out working; she wouldn't lift a helping hand because it was still Sunday night. Even though it was way past midnight, to her, it was still a holy day, the Sabbath, and on that day God rested from working. Her mother would be outside with them watching and looking around, but she wouldn't lift a working hand. La'friska's father knew how her mother thought and felt about what he was doing, so he didn't asked her to help. In fact, her father would tell her mother that, "God said when the ox is in the ditch, you have to get him out." So her father felt he was doing what he had to do, therefore he was justified in his actions. Another topic her parents differed on was her father telling his business. Her mother would often say "Anderson, you talk too much, telling people too much of your business." La'friska's father would reply right back saying, "Madlyn you have to tell people some of your business in order to get theirs." Now to this La'friska thought they both have a point. None the less her father was a great talker he talked so much that sometimes he'd ask the same thing twice during conversation. Sometimes her father would be quite for a while, when he was tired and worn out from working. She remembers this because her father would yell at her to sit down, saying she was walking too much. La'friska would be angry all she was doing was trying to get where she was going to do what she needed to do. Now on the other hand her father yelled at her, but yet he put up with her younger brother Joseph asking him fifty million questions. Such as daddy you ever seen cheetah that plays on Tarzan, or daddy you ever seen an elephant? Her father would say "boy shut up I'm tired". Well her brother would be **quiet** for a second then he'd be off again talking running his mouth. To this La'friska would really be mad because he yelled at her and yet he let her brother Joseph get away with to her murder talking too much. Mind the word murder is just a figure of speech to describe her brothers talking. To La'friska her brother Joseph whom is four years younger than her, plus he is the baby boy in the family. La'friska is the baby girl. Again Joseph got away with a lot he didn't have to work hard because he was the baby. She too didn't work as hard as her sisters and brothers because she too was also one of the babies in the family. It wasn't until after their older sisters and brothers left home that she and her brother Joseph had to work hard. They were the only two children now left at home. Some of their sisters and brothers are so much older than they are, seventeen and eighteen years older than them. Her and her brother Joseph can't remember them being at home when they grew up. La'friska can't remember the older five of their sisters and brothers living at home, but she can recall the last five of them at home together for a while. As a child La'friska grew up healthy normal and happy, yes they worked hard in the fields and chores around the house inside and outside. Outside chores such as carrying water and feed too feed the live stocks hogs, cows, horses, mules, goats, chickens, ducks and also the dogs. They had to carry this water two to three blocks. Their hands would be so tired from switching the tubs or buckets from hand to hand. These buckets held at least six gallons of water. They had to pump the water from a pump and this pumping was tiresome. Years earlier they had no pump, instead they had a well. Reminiscing back this well was scary and even now recalling this it's still is. It's a miracle no one was killed in that well from possibly falling in it and drowning. Describing this, well, it had a square wall built around it about five feet high. La'friska's parents taught them not to go near the well, so they wouldn't fall in. Let's skip forward a minute. Last year, her sister Betsy had them fallen out down on the floor laughing plus crying at her about this very same well. They were down home reminiscing about the good old days, how it was when they grew up well Betsy revealed something to them about herself that they never knew, she said that one day their father

## Thoughts

had beat her about something and she had gotten so mad that she was going to jump into the well, but when she looked down into the well there was a black snake wrapped around the little tree that was growing down in the well and that snake changed her mind from killing herself. They could vividly picture this scene in their mind's eyes, because that well was scary and dangerous. Back to life on the farm, in addition to chores on the outside they had chores inside to such as chopping wood outside them carrying the wood inside. They had to cut a lot of wood to fill the wood box. They had a wood heater to heat the kitchen and also a wood stove to cook on. This wood stove had six burner lids to place pots on. It had an oven to bake in and it had two cabin storage unit on top to keep food in plus they also had an electric stove that her father brought especially for her mother to cook on, so she wouldn't have to do long cooking on the wood stove after coming from the fields working hard. This stove wasn't brought until years later, as time got better at the end of harvesting the crops, although it had taken her father years to buy this stove because of being poor. He finally did and to this day the stove is still like new and working good. This stove had five different temperatures and a red light to indicate when the oven is on This in itself is amazing that in all this space and time this very same stove over forty years later is still good and working. In this day and time it only proves that in the old days, years ago, things were made of quality standards. This stove also had a long pull out drawer to store pans and pots in. La'friska's mother was a marvelously wonderful cook, she remembers her mother doing all the cooking, even though two of her older sisters that's ahead of her was still home, her mother still did the cooking. They said her father didn't want to eat their cooking. Her mother would attend church every other Sunday which was on preaching Sundays. The minister in those days didn't preach every Sunday, on the other two Sundays out of the month the church would have Sunday school, no preaching on those days. Sunday school is where you read from the bible and then have open discussions about what you read and try to interpret its meaning. Anyone who wants to can voice their opinion expressing their thoughts.La'friska remembers on those Sunday school days, how she and her mother would be home in the kitchen cooking and baking cakes or pies. Her mom would bake from scratch which would consist of her using flour, sugar, yellow color, butter, milk etc together to make the cakes. One of the cakes they would make would be a chocolate cake. The chocolate frosting in the old days was made by mixing cocoa, milk or water and sugar. Then boiling it on the stove. She remembers how the chocolate would stick to the pot and she'd be sticking her fingers in the pot when her mother was finished frosting the cake. Her mother always left some scraps or fragments so she could make her own little something, whether that something was cake or cookies or even sweet potato pie. If enough scraps weren't left her mother would let her mix up more ingredients from scratch. They also made other cakes such as butter pound cake, apple jelly cake, coconut cake, sweet potato pies and pumpkin pies. In La'friska's house there was always some kind of sweets ever Sunday. Even if her mother didn't bake every week, she'd have some hidden from the week before. She recalls when she was in her teens, one of her cousins said, "I always like coming to aunt Madlyn's house because I know she has cake." Another incident La'friska remembers concerning her mother's wonderful cooking was when the preacher's wife said on one of their visits "Mrs. Tashanti, I love your jelly cake." The neighbors also knew that whenever they stopped by at the Tashanti's, that they were always made to feel welcome by way of food offering and refreshments. Yes on Sundays, dinner was extra special. If the preacher and his wife came to dinner the food was even more elaborate and plentiful. In those days, the preacher and his wife would go to a member's home for dinner. That's the way the church members decided to do things since the preacher traveled over 25 miles to come to church. So on preaching service Sunday's the preacher and his wife went to different member's homes for dinner. So once or twice a year the preacher had dinner with them. La'friska recalls these dinners because she or her sister Betsy had to stand at the table holding newspaper fanning and swatting the flies away. They fanned the flies away before the preacher and his wife arrived, as their mother set the table with the food and other tableware arrangements. Her mother would use the good dishes. The food would look so festive in their serving bowls. Even though her parents kept them fed, somehow or another when the preacher came to have dinner to food seemed better. Her mother would dig down deeper into the freezer and bring out meats and vegetables that was frozen only for some special occasion. Speaking of freezers, the same freezer is still good and working. Forty years ago products were made of better quality. La'friska remembers how in the summer they had to pick the butter beans, string beans, corn, tomatoes, and peas and cleanse and prepare them for freezing. They had a lot of beans to shell. Even though the beans were easy to shell, there were a lot of them. Sometimes, La'friska was glad to have to prepare the vegetables for freezing because that kept her from having to work in the fields. Working in the fields was very hot, especially in the middle of the day into the evenings. In the summer months the temperatures were very high. Sometimes temperatures reached 119 degrees and that was within the shaded areas. Imagine out in the open how hot it was. La'friska remembers going to the fields after breakfast which was seven o'clock in the morning. Sometimes the morning dew which is nothing but water wouldn't be dried yet. Just walking alone would leave them damp almost wet.

## Thoughts

When the sun came out they would dry off from the hot heat. The field work she hated the most was working in the tobacco field. They had to suckle the tobacco to protect it. Suckling the tobacco means breaking the unnecessary little baby stalks off the stalk from the stems of the tobacco leaf. This baby stalk grows between the stems and it has to be removed every week because it grows back all over the stalk. If suckling the tobacco isn't completed it damages the farmers crops. Also worms grow on the tobacco leaf. These worms made La'friska's skin crawl and they scared her. Each week they had to turn the leaf over on both sides checking to see if any worms were on it. If there was a worm or worms on the tobacco they had to pull the worm off and break it in half. Thus, making sure the worm was dead. This procedure scared and frightened her so very much. Even though she was so scared she eventually devised her own strategy without telling the others what she was doing. She would hide a piece of stick in her clothes so when she found a worm on her row and no one was looking, she'd tear the part off where the worm was and drop it on the ground, then take the stick and jug it into the middle of the worm killing it. She'd be squeamish doing it but she knew that she had to. After killing the worm she'd throw dirt on top of it so no one would find it. That's how she learned to cope with dealing with the tobacco worms. There was one time she remembers working on her mother's row when she was younger. She found a worm; her mom saw it and made her kill it. La'friska had to take the worm off with her bare hands and tear it into two. Touching that thing killed her on the inside. To describe a tobacco worm, it is long and green with short fin legs that helps it cling to the leaf. You really have to pull it off and then it still true to continue to cling on. To fast forward a bit, remembering the worms were the reason why she would not eat shrimp after she came to live up north. Shrimps reminded her of a tobacco worm. When the shell is peeled off it looks like a worm with the legs curled up and the little fin's showing. Another type of worm with a hurtful sting is the cotton worm. It is white and furry and resembles a caterpillar. These grow on the cotton stalks. Everyone knows how cotton looks but most people don't know the procedure done to bring about the finished product we all know as cotton. First cotton seeds have to be planted in the late spring months or May of early June. The field has to be cleaned of weeds or grass. Then the field has to be plowed in rows. If a farmer has the right equipment his planting time will be cut in half. The right equipment such as a tractor and tractor plows are used to plow the field in neat rows. If a farmer doesn't have this equipment then the job becomes longer and harder meaning it has to be done manually with a mule or a horse and a single wood plow. The mule is hooked up to the plow and someone has to walk with their hands holding onto the plow as the mull pulls it through the field. Now with the field cleaned and plowed, the cotton seeds are then sowed into the row soil and covered so the birds and crows can't eat it. As the weeks pass by the seed is now grown into a plant. As these plants continue to grow they have to be pruned and weeded out. Some of the plants are pruned out and eliminated so the rest of the cotton plants can have room to grow better. Cotton work is simple but yet it's so hard because the field is big and wide and the rows are long. The work is time consuming. Every week the grass and weeds have to be cleaned out. Weeks later the finished product is as we know it cotton.

Farming is a cycle, from one cycle to the next. June is vegetable truck season. July and August are tobacco gathering time. People look forward to tobacco time because this is mainly where the money it. Six days of the week some farmers are gathering their crops which means he needs help. So people have schedule days to help others out. This method goes on from six to eight weeks. Although, the farmers do not receive their money until August after selling their tobacco, it's definitely a process. Until this process is finished those eight weeks the ones making the money are the day laborers. Years ago people worked all day and may have made all of three dollars. This was in the sixties and early seventies. In the eighties, the amount made moved up to twenty and twenty five dollars a day. The farmers had to pay this amount if they wanted their crops gathered because people said it was too hot to work in the field. They wouldn't work in the hot field for chump change. Of course by this time in the eighties all La'friska and her brothers and sisters had already left home. They felt they had really been short-changed because when they live down south they did not make that kind of money. What made matters worse was they had to give their parents most of their money and even if they were allowed to keep some they had to buy their school clothes.

In late August and September it was time to pick cotton. Talk about it being hot. It was and is still hot. If hell was any hotter, then La'friska couldn't imagine and doesn't want to be there. They couldn't go to school some days because they had to stay home and pick cotton. When the weather was dry, they stayed out of school 2-3 days a week at the beginning of school. In the south, school starts in late August. So in the beginning of the school year they weren't able to attend every day. Now if it rained they went to school because cotton cannot be picked when it is wet. It must be stored on the out barn dry. La'friska remembers her mother and her family mainly picking the cotton. Her father was not always in the fields with them because he was busy doing some other kind of work. There was one incident that sticks out in her mind. It was late in the evening and the sky was clouding up getting dark and a few drops of rain came. Well La'friska thought to herself that she would go home for the day. She glanced at her father and he in

# Thoughts

turn read her mind by responding, "Don't look at me, we're not going anywhere." Actually the rain never came that day and they continued in the field working. To work a cotton field, you must wear loose fitting clothes. You must wear a lot of clothes also, especially if you wore a dress. Underneath the dress must be long leg pants to keep the mosquitoes from biting you and also to protect your legs from getting scratched by the cotton bushes and overgrown weeds. To cover and protect your arms a long sleeve shirt must be worn. On your head a wide-brimmed straw hat, and make sure that the hat has a string on it to tie around your head. So when the wind blows the hat won't fly off your head. With those clothes on for protection, let me tell you that it is hot and humid. Add the elements of Mother Nature's weather and it is horrendous. Shoes aren't always worn especially by the children. Southerners go bare feet in the summer months only at home never in public. Even though it was hot the wind would sometimes blow cooling them off. They lived for these moments whenever they worked in the fields especially the fields far away from the house. They brought their own individual water jars. When they returned home at twelve o'clock noon it was then considered dinner time. They took the water jar to be refilled when they returned back to the field after dinner around one o'clock of one thirty p.m. Oh lets clear this dinner time thing up. Southerners still referred to breakfast as breakfast but there was no lunch in these days. If one was smart and had a piece of bread left over from breakfast they took that to the field with them. That was their snack. At twelve o'clock p.m. down south it's call dinner time later that evening whatever the hour time might be it's call supper time. About picking cotton sometimes they'd take a ten minutes breather twice a day, one in the morning around ten o'clock the other in the evening around four o'clock. She remembers at those times some of them would make a shade out of the extra cotton sheets they had. They'd spread the sheets on top of the tallest cotton bushes and crawl underneath it out of the hot sun and rest for a little while. Talk about time passing at those times, time flew by they didn't want to get up. As I write this story it's a Saturday and I'm sitting on my front porch it's amazing all of a sudden it starts to rain for four minutes and I know God is showing me how powerful he is. This rain act reminds me of the saying we have down home south, when it's raining and the sun comes out people said in the old days that is, they said the devil and his wife were fighting. I say to me unbelievable in all my fifty years of life I never once thought to think the devil had a wife. To me I say if he does have a wife she needs to kill the sucker get rid of him, maybe the world wouldn't have all these problems we'd be better off. I won't elaborate any further because I try not to think of the devil; after all, he never helps anyone for the good of things. Look at me, I'm a prime example. If the devil had a done me any good in my life time I wouldn't be writing, correction trying to write this story in order to heal my wounded heart and mind from so much pain. Once again back to this story thoughts and La'friska's farm life. Forty years ago the most dreaded and hardest working job on the farm was picking cotton everyone hated this from the oldest adults down to the children. Even though picking cotton is quite simple, just reach out both hands and pull the cotton out of the burrows on the bushes and put it in the sack you have across your shoulders. This sack is made out of fertilizer material and the color brown it's long and wide square. One sack of cotton could weigh 70 pounds depending how much you pack in it. In those days people got paid by poundage meaning how much their cotton weighed that they pick for the day. Even in the good old days some people knew how to lie and cheat to make money, they'd steal cotton of others sheet when nobody was around. Everyone had their own cotton sheet and as the cotton bag on your shoulder down to the ground got to heavy or full to carry you would then go empty your bag out on your own sheet. These sheets stayed at the end of the cotton rows. Picking cotton was hated because there was a lot of cotton to pull out of these cotton burrows on all those cotton bushes plus the rows were long and seemed like never ending, then also you're bend over the bushes or you get on your knees and walk on the dirt dragging your cotton sack behind as you go picking the cotton. Most people took two rows of cotton at a time. You work on this row and turn around and coming working back on your other row. At the end of the day the cotton of each person is individually weighed so they could know how much they picked. To weigh the cotton La'friska's father had what was called a weigh horse. A weigh horse is made of wood, it's four pieces of wood nailed together the longest piece is about eight feet long and it is in the middle two thick solid pieces of wood about five feet is nailed on each of it post in the middle with the ends extended out wide for support so it can stand up by itself. Then the four pieces is nailed across the two extended wood pieces in the middle, that's a weigh horse now a heavy bell with a long iron ruler scale is hook on the end of this weigh horse head to weigh the cotton or tobacco for that matter. It must be tied up securely in a burlap cotton sheet, describing a cotton sheet. It's the color brown and made out of fertilizer sack material, and this material is made from pine tree wood. There are two kinds of cotton sheets. One is very wide and square shaped, and this one is the biggest of the two. The other is also square shaped, but it's not as wide and big. When cotton is picked out of burrows, it has seeds in it. It's then taken home and stored into a barn some remains tied up in the cotton sheets this depends on how many cotton sheets unused a farmer has because if he doesn't have many sheets this is why the cotton has to be emptied out so the sheets can be reused again and again. When the cotton is

## Thoughts

finished being picked and stored in the barn, it's retied back into the sheets and taken to the cotton mill at the mill it's processed this means the seeds are taken out of the cotton and somehow the cotton is processed into velvety smoothness and softness, that's the process of cotton. La'friska recalls there's one thing she liked about cotton when it was stored in the barn she played on it. The loose cotton that was emptied out of the sheets she would run up on the mound of pile high cotton her legs would sink down into the cotton and even though she could feel the seeds in the cotton sticking her, she didn't pay that no attention instead she'd lay down into the cotton feeling it's softness through those seeds she liked that softness feeling. Also she remembers when they were in the hot cotton fields picking the cotton it would be so hot that sometimes she and her older two sisters Bonnie and Betsy would say to the wind," blow wind blow," another saying they'd used "north wind blow or north sister and ducky blow." Amazingly, this tactic worked 'because the wind did and would blow and they could feel the breeze cooling them off. It's laughable everybody hated cotton picking time but they loved tobacco season time. The process of tobacco gathering, on the farmers gathering day the barn must be emptied out of the previous week crop. The workers go to the field to crop the tobacco which is mostly men or boys. To crop tobacco you start at the bottom of the stalk and break off the ripe leaf's some stalks might have two three or four ripe leafs, you can tell if the leafs are ripe because their color is turning yellow. Tobacco is the color green before it's cured out in the barn after it's cured out it's a light brown or dark brown color, these two colors differ because of the grade quality of the tobacco. Cropping tobacco is easy the leafs break off the stalks easily you crop tobacco with one hand and hold the cropped leafs with the other hand by holding the leaf's under your arm close to your side. Your side can hold a lot of leafs when your arm is too loaded then you leave your row and go put the cropped leafs in the tobacco drag. This tobacco drag is long and square it's made of wood and fertilizer sacks are nailed into it to cover the woods bottom and sides so the tobacco won't fall out. The field has a special row especially made up so the drag can come down. It's every fifth row this row is three rows together made into one, it must be wide. As the worker hands crop tobacco from the field the hands at the barn which is mostly women and children they string up the tobacco on a stick with twine thread. The barn tables are made specially designed with openings to place sticks in. There's a stringer and two hands that completes a set. The two hands, one on each side of the stringer, pick up four or five leaves of tobacco together and hand it to the stringer. The stringer takes from this side and then the other side person. It's repetitious. The stringer starts at the head of the stick and comes down to the end of the stick stringing the tobacco onto the stick with the tobacco thread wrapped around each bundle. One bundle goes on one side of the stick and the other bundle goes on the other side of the stick. When the stick is finished, one of the hands takes the stick into the barn and gives it to the person which is mostly a strong man for them to hang up in the barn on the lower aisles. Once these aisles fill up it takes three men to perform this work. It's called hang the tobacco. The height of a barn is two stories high and the barn is in the shape of a square. The floor is made up of dirt or some farmers put down sand. The barn is leveled without a bottom floor. There are sides and a top but no wood floor. There are four oil burner stoves inside. The burners are lit up with oil and fire to cure out the tobacco for an entire week. When hanging tobacco, two people have to climb up unto the tiers in the particular aisle. One person is at the top while the other remains at the bottom. The third person is on the floor handling the stick of tobacco to the second person on the lower level. The second person hands it up to the first person. Once one tier is filled up you continue onto to fill in the rest of the tiers in the barn.

After finishing the tobacco gathering for the day, La'friska's parents would fire up the oil burners to begin the curing out process for the week. In her family Monday's were always their gathering day. When they were younger her father hired more people to help them and it took a half day to gather the tobacco. Even if there was a little work left to be finished her father paid the workers and then took them back home. La'friska's mother and the rest of her family had to finish up the work that was left over. The next day they had to go to the field and suckle the tobacco. Oh yes, they had to break off the tobacco stalk because the top of the stalk blossomed out into a beautiful flower. This top had to be broken off each week so it didn't get to tough to break off. Plus tops, worms and suckles weren't good for the crop because they were harmful to the quality of the crop. Each day there was something to do. They canned vegetables and tied tobacco. To tie tobacco it has to already be cured out and it smells very good. You have to separate the different qualities of the tobacco, the quality grades being best, good, and worst. The best tobacco is the highest paying. To tie tobacco you put a handful of leaves together and take another leaf and fold it or roll it up and then wrap the folded leaf around the stems of the handful of tobacco about two and a half inches down the stems. The tobacco is tied up and packed neatly then covered with a sheet to keep from drying out. When you've finished grading and tying the tobacco they are placed on sticks and piled up in order to recover the sticks again against drying out too much. That's the process. This tobacco is packed down and covered for four weeks because the market warehouse doesn't open the first four weeks of gathering. When the market does open up the tobacco is taken to the warehouse.

## Thoughts

Once at the warehouse, the farmer has a spot all his own and his tobacco is bid on by the auctioneers. La'friska, her sisters and her baby brother would sometimes go with their parents on bidding day. This day was such a special treat for them because they were able to ride on the roller cot that held the tobacco. The roller cot would be empty and they'd go rolling fast on the floor. The sound that it made was loud and the ride made them excited and happy. The sound of those auctioneers's voices all chanting at the same time that just fascinated them since they'd never heard anyone talk so fast and so loud. Also as children they couldn't comprehend what the auctioneers were saying. After the end of the tobacco sale her father would give them a few dollars. La'friska remembers they'd each buy them some sweet goodies like ice cream, candy, cookies and a 12 pack of biscuit rolls. Plus ten cents brought them three wieners. Those wieners tasted so good that they ate them raw. Some years her father didn't have spare money to give them because he had to pay the harvesting bills for the crops. He'd some years tell them by picking up the left over broken leaves they could have the money from that. One or two days a week they sometimes helped other farmers gather tobacco and the money they made like one dollar and fifty cents for a half a day. They had to sometimes give this money to their parents. The last few weeks of the tobacco season they were allowed to keep their money so they could buy their school clothing. Yes, they worked long and hard on the farm. Then again they also had some fun. Even in the cotton fields they took tobacco thread and caught grasshoppers with their bare hands. They tied strings on these grasshoppers and flew them through the air. They said the word grasshopper backwards saying hopper grass. Speaking of talking they said quinty for the number twenty. The number three was pronounced tree and the number twelve was pronounced queve. Looking back to La'friska the hardest word to say was social security card often pronouncing the word as so-you-cou-cha card. They still now laugh at this word so-you-cou-cha. Oh yes they had lots of fun. They even made some of their play toys. At Christmas time they always received a toy. Even though their parents were poor, yet somehow her parents always managed to get them at least one toy. La'friska recalls how good of condition she kept her toys in. She had a stove that had the temperature button to cut the eyes on the top of the stove. She also had a six room, two story metal tin house with a big porch. This house had furniture in every room. She also had a Ferris wheel that she kept these on the mantel piece shelf. She kept these until she was in her twenties at which time she parted with them by giving them to one of her favorite nieces Ky'ata. La'friska had two dolls that she would take outside in the backyard and sit them at her playhouse she made during playtime. She made this playhouse by taking a brick and putting sticks in the ground. Then she'd take old used tobacco thread that wasn't any good because it had already been used. She'd tie the thread around the sticks and build her house with even sectioned rooms. She'd cook meal pan cakes in old no good pots. The sun would dry these meal cakes up hard. La'friska and two of her older sisters would take a jar of blackberries, mix them with sugar and water in a jar and then place the lid on it and put the jar outside in the weeds for a week. They called themselves making wine. Even though they had never been close to liquor because their parents didn't drink they knew about liquor from passing by the liquor store when they went into town shopping. Her parents would rush them pass the liquor store quickly. Outside of the liquor store they would see some of the no-good, non-working bums hanging around the store sitting on the outside or just standing around. Even as La'friska became older she would rush pass the liquor store when she was by herself. The men wouldn't try to mess with them because they knew who they were and that her father wouldn't have tolerated it.

She had a homemade swing that she made by herself by climbing the big chinaberry tree in the backyard and tying heavy plow ropes and chains up in the tree. This tree they called it chanaya berry instead of chinaberry. Then they'd put a piece of wood on the ropes for their seat. They had moo cho fun on this swing and when the swing broke they would climb the tree and fix it by themselves. The swing broke many times because they would swing high up in the air. They'd bend down and pump and pump to build up momentum making themselves go faster and faster. They had no fear it is a wonder they didn't hurt or kill themselves. La'friska remembers breaking the swing many times and falling on her backside. Even though this fall hurt that didn't stop her. She'd get right back on the swing or if it was broken she'd climb up the tree and fix it herself. Yes, southern girls are called tom boys especially if they are tough and rough. They called themselves swimming by laying down in the big water holes the hogs and pigs made from the rain. These holes would be full of water and at the bottom it was muddy. When they came out of those holes their legs and feet would be muddy. In one of the fields there was another hog pasture with a hole so big it was probably five or six feet deep. It was so deep that they had a wood crate heavy box to stand on in order to get down in and out of the hole. They would take off their clothes and get down in the hole in the water trying to swim even though they couldn't swim. They would hear their mother calling them and they'd get out and grab their clothes putting them on as they ran through the woods and field wiping the mud off their legs and feet with grass. In your mind's eye can't you just picture this scene? Running half naked while pulling up their clothes over their muddy legs and feet. The mud made it harder to get on their clothes and to top it off they were cleaning their legs and

## Thoughts

feet with hands full of grass. They pulled off weed bushes as they continued to run home. As deep as that hole was again, it's a miracle they weren't drowned. Another incident would be them jumping clear across the canal and landing on the edge down in the water hanging onto bushes and trees that they grabbed for support. The canal was wide and had a lot of water in it along with fishes and snakes. They way they'd jumped the canal was they would be a block and a half from the canal and then start to run towards it fast in order to build of speed so that by the time they reached the canal they were at top speed and they'd leap jumping the canal. As they ran their bodies adrenaline was in exhilarating overdrive. They didn't know it then but now today looking back reminiscing about how fast they ran they could have been Olympic medalists.

They walked through the woods exploring the quiet peacefulness. They thought of Tarzan, Jane and the jungle boy. Their favorite Tarzan actors were and still are today Johnny Wissmuller and Maureen Sullivan. For no other actor and actress could touch these two's portrayal of La'friska and her sisters Marilynn, Bonnie and Betsy every Saturday afternoon their expedition entailed walking the road from one end all the way around the back to the house picking up soda bottles to make money, They were paid two cents per bottle. Most of the bottles they found were on the shoulders of the highway after people threw them from their car windows. She and her sisters would race to get the bottles. Walking around the highways and the dirt roads was at least two and a half miles. There were three different country stores to go to. They carried rice sacks or flour sacks to put their bottles in. When they got to the store, they'd trade in their bottles. Each of their sacks were kept separate. For example, if La'friska had ten bottles at two cents each bottle, that was twenty cents. She'd spend her money wisely by buying a ten-cent Baby Ruth candy bar and five cents worth of two-for-a-penny butter cookies, which was ten cookies. She'd have a nickel left and would buy one penny candy (a Mary Jane, squirrel nut, and everyone's favorite, red hot candy balls). The hot candy balls were very hot like fire, and it would feel as though your mouth was burning off. They'd be oohing and ahhing at the same time, but still it was so good. On Sunday evenings they'd walk the opposite direction on the dirt roads and go to the clay hole. Clay is dirt, but it's a different type of dirt. It's hard and white and it tasted good. They would dig clay out of the hole and eat it. The clay never made them sick. Sometimes when they went to a particular store, Ms. Witting's, they took the short cut through the woods. La'friska, when she got older and her sisters were gone from home, she took this shortcut by herself. She'd be scared, but she wanted to go to the store and sell her bottles and buy herself something. So off she went half-scared. She'd run through the woods all the way to the store. She would be so scared because she knew that hunters hunted in the woods with their dogs, and they had guns and rifles. Speaking of guns, they all grew up around guns, and they never bothered with them unless their father would give them the gun to take back to the house to place back where it belonged. Yes, the guns scared La'friska, but she never told anyone. Her father and her older brother Esmond would go hunting. Most of the times they brought something back, whether it was birds, rabbits, squirrels, or possums. She remembered that she and her sisters or her mother had to clean the animals that were caught. Her mother cleaned and cooked those wild animals, but she didn't eat them. Her mom didn't drink milk or eat eggs. La'friska once asked her mother why she didn't drink milk, and her mother said that when she was younger she did drink milk, but then she became tired of milk. Speaking of milk, her father had one to two cows. Therefore, they never had to buy milk from the store. Milk was always plentiful in their home. The milk they drank was always from the day before. This was done because that's how they made cream for butter. After the milk from the day before was skimmed for cream, they could then drink the milk. The cream was kept in a jar and stayed in the refrigerator until the jar was almost full or half full, at which time the cream was taken out and someone, mainly the children, had to make the butter. They had to shake the jar constantly or they sat down with a cloth on their lap and beat the jar on their legs. Other methods they used were standing up and shaking the jar or walking around shaking the jar until the cream finally turned into butter. This butter process was repetitious and tiresome. It would take half an hour to make the butter. They made so much butter that their mother would weigh it and pack it up for sale by putting it in the freezer. The milk bowl was big and orange in color, covered with a clean white soft cloth. La'friska recalled how they made snacks for themselves. They'd take coffee grains or cocoa and sugar, mixing it together and putting it in a piece of newspaper and then carrying it to the fields. Later they'd eat it. Sometimes they would place it in their lips and pretend it was tobacco or snuff. They would eat raw onions and cornbread or biscuits and sugar. When they were working in the fields, they pulled up certain weeds and ate the nut root. The nut looked like an acorn or a peanut, and this nut would have dirt on it. They would wipe the dirt off on their clothes and on their hands and then eat it. They called the name of this nut "a he chew." What a word! Another weed they ate was green sweet and sour grass. It was sweet and sour tasting at the same time. They picked briarberries and huckleberries, put sugar on them, and then ate them. Their favorite was briarberries and dumplings with biscuits. Some nights in the summer, their supper meal was briarberries and dumplings. This tasted so good because it had sugar mixed in it. Other tasty treats were cornbread with milk poured over it and crackling cornbread. La'friska had another way of making crackling cornbread. She'd take cornbread that had already been fried on the top of the stove in the skillet and add grease to the pan and refry the bread and push cracklings into it; then she would cook it on both sides.

In December it was killing-hog-day and they had to stay home from school because the work process was an all day into night ordeal. They all would get up early that morning and have breakfast; then they would start the work process. Her father would shoot the hogs out in the pasture away from the house. They'd hear the shots. He'd then haul the hogs up closer to the house, but he'd leave them out in the field near the tree at the edge of the backyard. Her father would put the hog in a big long iron drum. He'd put the hot water that had already been boiling in the drum over the hog. He'd turn the hog over and over until it was well soaked. He'd pull the hog out of the drum by its legs and turned it around with its head down in the drum. This is how the hog's hair got wet in order to scrape the hairs off easily. Her father and mother mainly did the hair scraping part; they had sharp knives and were fast workers. She and her sisters helped scrape the little hair fragments that were left. She hated this part; as a matter of fact, she hated everything about killing-and-cleaning-hogs day. It was a lot of work, and to see her father cut the hog's throat with the knife after the hog had been scraped and washed was too gruesome for her. The blood would be running out. Her father would have a hole dug down in the ground so the blood ran into it. The hog would be tied on one of the farm equipment plows called a single tree. This would be holding the hog on it while it was up in the tree being washed down and cut opened. To watch her father cut open the hog—being careful not to miss and touch the intestines, which is the guts, known as chitterlings—was a work of art. If by chance he had ruptured a gut, the hog manure would have run out, making an awful big mess to clean up. When her father had finished cutting the hog into different pieces, for example, two hams, two shoulders, two sides, head, and feet, his work was done except for taking the meat that was being cured to the meat market. He'd do that, and when he returned back home, he went working on another task of some kind. That left the rest of the work up to her mother and them. Her two older married sisters, Victoria and Marilynn, their job was to clean the chitterlings. This job was the worst, hardest, and smelliest. Smelling the chitterling manure; what an awful mess. They had to first riddle the chitterlings, meaning separate the big guts and the small guts. They had a hole already dug down into the ground to pour the manure in. They cut long pieces off the guts and went over to the hole. One sister would hold the gut in her hand while the other one poured lukewarm water into the gut to loosen up the manure inside of it so it would run out more easily as she ran her hands down the gut, pushing out the foulest-smelling manure. They then poured more water into the gut, rinsing it out. They'd get another gut and repeat the same process until the job was done. La'friska was so very glad that she was younger and didn't have to do much of that part of the job. Oh, she did help a little, but not too much. Sometimes, cleaning the guts, they'd miss and rupture a gut. They had to hurry and take care of that particular gut so it wouldn't leak out manure all over the rest of the guts. Another job was cutting up the meat into chunks for making the hog crackling. After the meat was cut, it was put in the wash pot and cooked, frying into brown-colored cracklins. The pot naturally had fire surrounding it, and the cracklins were stirred as they cooked with a clean, long tobacco stick. The hog's head was boiled in another wash pot. By that time, her mother had prepared dinner. They ate the liver and lights that came out of the hog they'd killed that morning. They had rice to go with the liver and lights, and onions and gravy—plus corn bread and Kool-Aid. They liked to eat the liver but not the lights, although at dinnertime they weren't too hungry because they'd already snacked around the wash pot fire by putting sweet potatoes in the fire and roasting them. They also roasted pieces of the liver and even pieces of the chitterling guts their sisters had just cleaned. They put water in a can with the guts and put the can in the fire around the wash pots. The sweet potatoes would be half roasted, cooked on the outside and burned black—the inside wouldn't be cooked. As a fact, their mother would say to them, "You'll be sick baiting up on those half cook potatoes." Her mother was right too, because by the time they'd finished working and went to bed for the night, their stomachs were hurting, but before they went to bed, the hog head cheese had to be made. Her mother did that. The sausage had to be made; some was stuffed into the guts and some was made into hamburger. The hamburger was packed into freezer bags and put in the freezer. The other sausage was hanged up in the outside corn house barn to dry out. Dried out sausage was delicious. The cracklins were salted and stored in a five-gallon aluminum can and stored in the corn house. Cracklins were good, too. Basically, that's the hog-killing process. What a job; it'll make you sick. Speaking of sick, in the backyard they'd planted flower bushes that made them well if they got sick. The plant was green with wide, big long leaves, and had a red buds on top. It was beautiful and still is, because it's still in existence even as this story is being written; only now in this day and age, it's new name is prayer leaf plant. Back to this plant, if they were sick, say from a headache, they'd take the plant leaf and put it around their head and tie it with reused tobacco thread. It worked later on—headache gone. If it was a leg ache, they'd tie a leaf around the leg with thread. Again, it worked—leg ache gone. Now speaking about sickness, La'friska's baby brother, Joseph, who was four

## Thoughts

younger than her, didn't have to resort to using this plant leaf; not like they did. For Joseph naturally got over things. For example, when they went to the field in the mornings to work, Joseph half of the time didn't have to go because their father sometimes would need Joseph to help him connect some type of farm equipment plow onto the tractor. The other half of the time, if Joseph did go to the field with them, later their father would yell out calling for Joseph to come and help him. Of course Joseph loved that he got to get out of the field. When Joseph did finish helping their father, Joseph wouldn't come back to the field to work. Instead, he was free to roam around and play, while the rest of them had to work. Oh yes, Joseph was very smart, 'cause if their father didn't need Joseph's help, Joseph devised his own tactics; he was brilliant. For example, if Joseph did go to the field in the morning, after being there for a while he got a headache, and their mother sent him back to the house. That afternoon in the field, Joseph would get sick again; this time he'd have a different ache: his legs, stomach, etc. Back to the house he went while they stayed in the field working. Later as they worked, they'd see Joseph running around playing. Yes, he was clever and knew how to get out of working hard when La'friska and her two older sisters were living at home. It wasn't till later, when they'd left home, Bonnie and Betsy, that Joseph had to work more, for La'friska and he were the only two kids left at home with their parents. Even then Joseph tried to get over on her, and he did, for example the two of them had to hoe the garden, Joseph wouldn't go right away, so she would hoe her half and leave his half. Well, when Joseph did come out, he'd try to claim her half, and they'd start a fight. In those days, Joseph was selfish all about himself. Speaking of fighting, La friska remembered how she and Joseph sometimes fought. It was Joseph's fault— again, his selfishness. Sometimes she got four beatings in a day, two in the morning, one from Joseph, and the other one from her mother. That evening, another two beating again one from Joseph and the other one from her mother. Joseph would start the fight and he'd beat her up. Joseph was fast; he watched Tarzan. Nobody had better call him Bomba the jungle boy; if they did, Joseph would come flying fast and beat you up. Back to the beatings, their mother would beat both of them because she wasn't around to see who'd started the fight therefore she would beat both of them and she'd say to La'friska, "You're older you should know better." At those times La'friska would be so mad; she didn't think she should have gotten the beating from her mother, because it wasn't her fault; it was Joseph's. Another example of them fighting, their parents and Joseph and her, they'd be gone somewhere and she and Joseph would get in the truck first. She would sit by the door. Well, Joseph wanted the door also, but she got there first. They'd start a fight; of course, he hit her first. Sometimes her face would be scratched up where he'd scratched her. There would come a beating again from their mother. La'friska remembered the last fight she and Joseph had. She was in the ninth grade. She was at the pump outside getting water to haul either to the house or to the livestock. While she was pumping, Joseph came and took her bucket off the pump and put his own bucket there and tried pushing her out of the way to fill his own bucket. Well, what a fight they had. La'friska was so mad, she recalled later walking along the path near the woods from her sister Marilynn's house; she was still so mad at Joseph that she thought, "Next time, I'll kill him." Well, I tell you God must have known it because to her knowledge she and Joseph never fought again. Speaking of beatings from her parents, her mother didn't believe in beating a child while you were so mad at them. She'd say, "The parents should cool off some if they were that mad at the child." Plus, she also believed a child should be told why they were being beaten or punished, and also she didn't think a child should be beaten the first time that they did something wrong, and that the parents should explain things to the child and talk to the child. If La'friska's mother did beat them, she beat them with the inside, which was the back of her hands, and she talked at the same time, saying things like, "Why did you do that, don't you know better, didn't I tell you not to do that don't do it again?" Her mother hands were wide and heavy, oh yes, she'd hit them on the top of their back or she'd put them between her armpit next to her side and she'd tear their butts up, or she'd hit them on their legs. Half of the time her mother beat them with the back of her hand. If they were going to get a really good beating, she'd beat them with switches. These switches came off the overgrown hedge trees on the side of the yard that was never pruned. These hedges grew into a big, tall tree. Her mother would get the switch, or sometimes more than one switch. She'd get three four or five switches, peel the leaves off, and then twist them together, and then she'd take them by the arm and commence to tear them up as they ran around her in a circle. Her mother would still be holding onto their arm as they ran around her in a circle. They'd be screaming and crying, but that didn't do them any good. When her mother finished with them, later they'd have welts on them. Welts are long, scraping, stratched, bruised marks. They had to put lard, which is grease, on their welt marks—talk about hurt! Those welts hurt, and if they were dumb enough to put rubbing alcohol on them, they found out the hard, painful way not to do it again. La'friska's father didn't beat them much; in fact, he rarely did. Of course, many times he threatened and promised to beat them, and when he did beat them, he made up for all the times he'd promised them. He's say, "Come here little nigger," and he'd be walking fast with a noticeable limp. At times like those when he'd be mad and walking fast, his limp would then be noticeable. This limp was from an accident. This accident will be explained

# Thoughts

shortly, but first back to her father finally beating them. Once again he'd be walking fast and saying, "Come here little nigger." He'd break off a handful of long switches, peel the leaves off, and tie the switches together. He'd take them by the hand swung them running around him in a circle and beat the holy hell out of them as they ran crying yelling and screaming for their life. As he beat them he made up for all the times he promised them he knew the date day time and incidents he was finally beating them for. For example he'd say, " remember last year 1960 on a Sunday evening four o'clock I told you to water the mules and you gave them that little bit of water it was hot you didn't give them enough water." Then he'd cite off another reason why he was beating them. Another example is when he'd say, "Remember two months ago on a Wednesday evening, June thirtieth, 1960, at six o'clock p.m., you was supposed to sloop the hogs and give them extra feed, but you didn't." By the time he'd finished with them, they were good and tired, and their legs were stinging and hurting. I say to you, talk about child abuse. In those days, parents didn't play and take no stuff; all parents in those days disciplined their children in that way, and the children didn't die from those beatings. Instead, the children towed the line, obeying the rules, and they turned out to be better human beings. About their beatings— when they'd done something wrong, her mother, over two-thirds of the time, if she hit or beat with a switch, she made them go get the switch and bring it back to her. Right now, the vividness of getting a switch to beat yourself is comical and very funny—nevertheless, it happened. Also in those days there were certain words they weren't allowed to say—for instance, butt. They could say "your tail," but they couldn't say "your butt." So you know they forgot about ever using curse words. They couldn't say the words lying or lies; instead, they used the word story or storying. For example, they couldn't say "you're lying." They had to say "you're storying." In the summertime, some days after working all day, her mother didn't cook supper her father had them go to the store and buy food for that night's supper. He'd tell them to tell the store owner lady, Mrs. Paulette, to charge it for him the store owner always did because they liked and respected her father for they all knew him for being a good and honest person. Her father's word was his bond, meaning he was trustworthy. Items they'd charge for supper bologna cheese sardines sodas and light bread which is now a day called white bread. La'friska and her sisters and brother loved this treat. With life on the farm as years went by La'friska's older sisters Bonnie and Betsy graduated high school and moved up north in New York living with their older sister Adlay and her family and also their older brother Junior and is wife Marisa. For four years, La'friska and Joseph were the last two children left living at home with their parents; that's when these two really had to begin to work, finally really knowing the meaning of hard work. Before, they didn't work as hard as the other Tashanti children because they were the babies in the family. After graduating from high school at eighteen years old, La'friska then too left home and came to New Jersey. For over eighteen years La'friska had worked and lived on the farm now she'd finally left that life behind the hard work so when she did returned home on visits and especially on vacations farm work didn't seemed so hard and hectic. Yes her parents still farmed but the work had gotten much easier, the best part no cotton to pick. Most farmers had stopped planting cotton (good God, halleluiah). What a blessed miracle after all those years of hard work and humid heat in those fields. It was at long last finally over. For years, that is, before La'friska had graduated high school, she'd hear her father saying "next year I'm a stop farming," but he didn't come the next year, and for years he'd farm, so returning home on visits was fun. She'd only be there for a short while and she didn't mind the working helping out for she no longer had to do farm work for a living. She began appreciating the beauty of living in the country to awaken to the sounds of the chicken crowing and cackling, hearing the sounds of the birds chirping. For upon rising out of bed in the mornings however early that might be to the sounds of the leaves rustling in the trees from the breezes of the wind blowing. Breezes that one can feel as the wind blows; breezes that are so refreshing and tranquil from air so fresh pure and clean. A oneness with mother nature's elements whether it's the early morning dew on the grass, or grasses growing , trees, plants, flowers, animals and etc era things in general blossoming coming to life. In La'friska's estimation the conclusion is a serenity of peacefulness and total freedom. Describing this panoramic scenery above, one can imagine the essence of its existence. Yes, La'friska loved coming home to see her parents and family. Her brother Joseph was now in college, and her two sisters, Victoria and Marilynn and their family, lived down home in the vicinity. Even though La'friska's visits home were enjoyable, being with and seeing her family, her complete happiness was awfully sad underneath it all. No one knew because she kept it hidden inside of herself for years. What she wanted was Dacosta Tiawan Gahenne! For now, you see, La'friska Tashanti was very much in love. To conclude this chapter on farm life, we must start by clarifying an earlier statement that La'friska's father sometimes walked with a limp. He walked with a limp because in 1951 when La'friska was a baby her father's leg was broken in a car accident. His tractor and wagon was hit in the back with him and her brothers in it, by a white man in a car. Doctor's said her father would never walk again. The doctors didn't know her father, he made a liar out of them because his determination made him walk again, plus her brother Joseph was created and her father raised ten children. Hats off too you dad! Cheers.

# Chapter Two
# Dacosta

In their earlier school years La'friska and Dacosta attended the same grammar school neither spoke a word to the other they ran in different crowds however La'friska knew of Dacosta because a classmate who is also a best friend name Yolonda Vanceburg is Dacosta's cousin. Through the years La'friska saw Dacosta around school plus Yolonda talked of him. Years later, La'friska was attending a different school while Dacosta was still attending their previous school. One day, she was visiting Yolonda's bus; she was at Dacosta's school while they were talking Dacosta came up and got into their conversation. The next week at his school, the same thing happened again. She and Yolonda were engaged in conversation when he came up. This time, Dacosta directed his attention only to La'friska. He stared lovingly at her with a smile on his face. Finally, he interrupted La'friska and Yolonda's conversation. Dacosta then said to La'friska, "When can I come see you?" La'friska looked briefly at him but she didn't bother to answer his question because she thought he was only teasing her. Instead, she continued her conversation with Yolonda. Days later at school Yolonda said to La'friska, "Dacosta and I talked about you, and he said you are getting to be something fine." To this, La'friska didn't think of it, however, one day at school she had slightly started thinking about Dacosta because he gave Yolonda a note to give to her. The note read, "I want to see you; I have something to tell you." She didn't know what to think of the note, and she couldn't imagine what he had to tell her. That very same evening, upon arriving at Dacosta's school, La'friska took Yolonda along with her because she was some what nervous. They went looking in search of Dacosta. She and Yolonda saw his cousins and friends, but he wasn't with them. While standing around looking, La'friska and Dacosta spotted each other. At the same time, they both walked toward one another. When they met, they both smiled and stared lovingly at each other. He then, with his hand, gently and lovingly reached out and straightened her sweater around her shoulders. Meanwhile, Yolonda and her cousins stared on, watching. He didn't tell her what that something was he had to tell her. Why, La'friska didn't know, and she didn't bother to ask him. She figured it was because too many people were around, and besides his cousins and friends were watching, and at that time she had to run and catch her bus home. That same evening, shortly upon getting home from school, Dacosta phoned La'friska. She was surprised to hear his voice, and she had no idea he knew her phone number. Dacosta told her he was at his cousin Conrad's house. After the silence in their conversation, he said, "Would you answer a question for me?"

She said, "That depends."

He said, "On what?"

La'friska said, "On what it is."

He said, "Do you love me?" La'friska was stunned by his question, but she gave a fast reply.

She said, "I don't know; I haven't thought about it."

Dacosta said, "Think about it, because I love you." La'friska was now silent. She didn't think or say anything.

Dacosta said, "I'll call for your answer." After he hung up, she was still surprised and stunned, but happily pleased to hear Dacosta say he loved her. Before he'd phoned, she was on the phone talking to a classmate, saying she didn't have a boyfriend. Now she called that same girl back and told her that a boy had just phoned and said he loved her. That next day at school, she told Yolonda that Dacosta had phoned, and said he loved her and he wanted to know if she loved him. Yolonda didn't say too much. She asked La'friska how she felt about him. La'friska replied, "I don't know yet. I hadn't never thought about him."

Yolonda said, "Now you know what that something is he had to tell you." Later that day in class, La'friska and the classmate whom she told a boy had phoned and said he loved her. They got together and had a brief discussion about Dacosta. The classmate's name was Tonya. She wanted to know what his name was, where he lived, what school he attended, and what grade he was in, and how did he look. While they were conversing, another of their classmates, Susan, who was Tonya's best friend, heard them, and she came over and got in on the conversation too. Both girls were fascinated and envious of her, and also they were happy and pleased for her. A week later, Dacosta phoned her when he said, "Do you love me?" She without hesitating or thinking, she said, "Yes." Just before his phone call, she didn't know how or what she felt for him, but when he said do you love me the way he said it, and the sound of his voice so smooth and sweet over the phone, overcame her. In that instant something happened to her; she was mesmerized by his words, his voice, and him; she said yes and knew it was true—from that moment and day on, she loved him. As the days weeks and months went by, her love for him grew more and more. She fell deeply and madly in love with him. She loved him with all her heart, body, and mind. Yes, La'friska Tashanti, age fifteen, a freshman in high school, she, in the month of September, fell in love with Dacosta Tiawan Gahenne. Now she was happy and content; she loved going to school each and every day because of her love for him and his love for her. She knew she'd see him some days, then other days she wouldn't see him at all because they attended different schools. By the time she arrived at his school, her bus would be getting ready to leave for home, however, once a week she did manage to catch an early bus to his school and go over and talk to him. At those times she was excited, happy, and nervous. She wrote him long, powerful love letters twice a week, confirming her love for him; she gave the letters to Yolonda to give to him. In her letters, she truly expressed her feelings, not holding back anything. She let him know much she wanted to make love with him, that if he wanted her body he had it, she was his for the taking. She had a necklace with a key to it. The engraving on it read, "He who holds the key to the door of my heart can open it." Well, she gave that key to him and said, "Baby, you can turn it in my lock any time."

 He smiled and said "I will." Whenever he would phone her, if he didn't volunteer to say he loved her, she would ask him "Do you love me?" He'd say, "Yes," and she'd say "Tell me." Dacosta would say, "I love you." Hearing him say that he loved her, a delightful feeling would come over her, making her feel good all over. She'd say, "I love you too; very much in fact, much too much for my own sanity, because my love for you is driving me crazy." Sometimes before she'd let him hang up he'd have to kiss her over the phone. At those times she'd be in seventh heaven, and she'd think to herself, if I can't get it in person, it's good anyhow. Many times she included a bar of candy along with the letter, saying keep sweet. Afterwards he'd say "I got your candy and thank you it was good." Once he asked, "How many children are we going to have?"

 She said, "A whole house full, and I want them to look like you, of course including me too." He asked, "How many is a whole house full?"

She replied, "Oh, um, eight or ten, give or take throw in some twins or triplets. He yelled with laughter and said, "Girl, you are crazy."

She said, "Yes, crazy about you." He never once wrote her back, but he would many times phone, especially in the beginning when their love was brand new; however, as time went on, his phoning ceased a lot. His cousins and friends became quite friendly with her; they would phone each other back and forth many times. His friends would phone her and pretended they were him imitating his voice, telling her what was on the letters to him; they knew because he let them read the letters. Many times when he did phone, she at first would doubt if it was him or not until after they'd talked for a while and she really recognized it was him. She would ask, "Did you get my letter?" and he'd say "yes." She would say, "What was on it?" He would tell her what was on it. Three months later at Christmas time she had 'cause to question his love for her 'cause she founded out from Yolonda that he brought another girl in his classroom a Christmas gift and he didn't buy her anything. She didn't mention to him that she knew about the girl's gift, nor did she hint that she wanted one she kept this knowledge to herself and her feelings but she was deeply hurt. As the weeks and months went by La'friska's love for Dacosta blossomed her into a very attractive young lady. Other boys noticed her and two of them said they loved her but she didn't bother with them or paid them any attention she was only interested in Dacosta. She hated when night time came because she would wake up in the middle of the night thinking of Dacosta wanting to see and be with him. She'd be awaked for hours thinking and fantasizing of being in his arms kissing and making love with him. She thought of many different ways to love him to feel his naked body against hers and to know the joyous thrill of his penis within her body how she needed and longed for him until her body would be burning on fire throbbing with passion and desire. She was a virgin but she would have gladly given up her virginity to him, he wouldn't have had to ask. All he would have had to do was want it. Dacosta never asked her if he could come courting her at home and he didn't they had their courtship over the phone in her letters and on the school yard. All those months during their steady court ship he never came to her house she never asked him to and besides she didn't know if or not her parents would have let her take company to her, she was partly satisfied being in love with him and having him say he loved her. One day months later she got one of the letters to him returned back to her. Another girl in his classroom her name is Lynn somehow got the letter and from the faded looks of the paper when La'friska received it back she knew the girl read it and then the girl gave the letter to another girl Myra to give back to her. Also that girl who gave the letter to her probably read it to. La'friska knew from the guilty expression on her face she read

# Thoughts

the letter too. Now La'friska was wondering about his love for her, not only did he buy another girl a Christmas gift now a different girl had someone else return one of her letters back. She was again hurt by this latest happening but still she loved and went on loving him, her wondering was tossed aside at times like when Dacosta's brother Peter or cousin Hutton when passing by would say to her "Dacosta said he love you." With those words spoken she would be alright however as the school season end drew near again she was hurt this time she was crushed and bewildered by his actions. It was Dacosta's school biggest and most important school function of the year which was social affair dance night she thought and was lead to believe by Yolonda and his cousins and friends that she was his guest for the affair. Yolonda also told her "Dacosta said to ask you if you'd be his guest for the dance?" Of course La'friska said yes and was delighted preparing herself for the big night. She made arrangements with a girl name Brenda to ride with her and Brenda's mother that night. The night of the dance arrived and La'friska was doing her work chores and she asked her mother if she could go to the dance. Her mother said no she explained to her mother that she was invited and had already set up arrangements to get to and from the school dance. Still her mother wouldn't let her go. That night La'friska cried herself to sleep, what little sleep she did get. She wondered what she'd tell Dacosta and what he was doing at the dance. The following Monday back at school she didn't have to wonder for long because she found out that it was a good thing she couldn't come to the dance that night because Dacosta had invited another girl as his guest. The girl was La'friska's classmate; also, the girl was an old friend of hers, plus she was the sister of the girl that had returned her letter to Dacosta back to her. This girl's name was Renato Grinds. Renato was very cute, with a brown complexion and a nice shape. She was friendly but somewhat quiet. Renato in grammar school went steady with Dacosta's brother Peter. La'friska wasn't so much mad at Renato; it was Dacosta she was upset and mad with. All that week she was deeply hurt and felted so alone until one day Dacosta's brother Peter passing in the hall way said to her "Dacosta said to tell you he love you." Well after those words La'friska felted better but she was still hurt by Dacosta's actions. She thought and wondered many times how could he love her and yet do the things he did. To her it seemed when it was time for him to show his love and respect towards her he didn't instead he proved otherwise. The school year ended and summer vacation began. It was a nice summer but not a happy time for La'friska because she had to work hard and mostly because she didn't get to see or did she heard from Dacosta not one word. Of course she wrote him long powerful letters. Summer vacation ended and the school season opened. La'friska was glad and could hardly wait; she now had a favorite song called "See You in

September." She wanted to see and be with Dacosta they both would now be attending the same school. At school she saw him every day several times a day, but still she didn't get to be with him, or did she get to talk to him much, because he didn't court her around campus and he didn't come talk to her. In fact, the only times he talked to her was when she approached him and still then she had to take the initiative at conversation. Once Yolonda even said to La'friska, "One of these days I'm going to make Dacosta walk you around the school." Dacosta wouldn't talk to La'friska, but she saw him throughout that whole month constantly talking with a girl name Kim Fluntly who was in La'friska's classes. The previous year La'friska and Kim were classmates; during that time they got along and were fairly friendly. La'friska was told by Yolonda and Dacosta's cousins that the reason why Dacosta and Kim would be talking was because of his cousin Bart; that they'd be talking about him because Kim liked and was going with Bart. School was now on its way; everyone was organized and settled into a routine schedule. La'friska and Yolonda were still best friends and palling around together, even though they were in separate classes. Dacosta still didn't go out of his way to talk to La'friska, but she still sometimes saw him talking with Kim with his cousins and Kim's friends and his friends surrounding them. This kind of action went on a month or so. Dacosta didn't tell La'friska if or not he still loved her. La'friska knew she loved him and she thought he loved, her until one day she learned otherwise. It was on a Sunday evening in October La'friska was home in the living room with her cousins they were talking and listening to music when the phone rang and La'friska picked it up. To her surprise it was Dacosta and she was delighted to hear his voice. Dacosta on the other hand was absolutely thrilled at putting La'friska down and telling her off right in front of his cousins and friends. They were in the background listening and laughing, egging him on. Dacosta was really enjoying himself. He said to La'friska "Kim doesn't go with Bart she goes with me." La'friska was shocked and speechless; she couldn't talk. Instead, she grunted painfully. Dacosta, however, was still having fun enjoying the things he was saying to her. He went on to say, "I don't love you, girl; I never did. I only wanted your pussy." At that remark, Dacosta and his cousins and friends really hollered and laughed.

After the laughing subsided, Dacosta said, "Did you hear me?"

La'friska said, "Yes."

Then Dacosta really lowered the bomb. He finished off saying, "Girl, I'm too good for you." He and his cousins and friends laughed at her and he hung the phone up in her ears without even saying good bye. Now La'friska was shocked and in somewhat of a daze. She knew what had just happened and she believed it was true, because now everything made sense about Dacosta and Kim always talking. Plus,

## Thoughts

the fact that Dacosta never volunteered to talk to her. Even though La'friska was in a daze, she went back to her guests and pretended like nothing happened, but inside, her heart and mind were slowly but surely breaking into millions of pieces.

Now the shock was beginning to take effect on her, but for the time being with her cousins there, she fairly managed to keep herself under control and entertain them. Finally, they departed, and afterwards she went straight to her room and fell on the bed. At this time she didn't cry. In her mind she went back over the words that Dacosta said to her. His words kept ringing in her ears, "Kim doesn't go with Bart, she goes with me. I don't love you and I never did. Girl, I only wanted your pussy." What tore La'friska up even more was him saying, "Girl, I'm too good for you." Then he had the audacity to laugh at her and let his cousins and friends egg him on. Remembering all that, plus the facts of past actions, she knew he was right when he said "I never loved you," because all along his actions proved it. She realized how dumb and naïve she had been, believing Kim was with Bart. When all along, right in front of her eyes, she always saw Dacosta talking with Kim instead of Bart talking to Kim. La'friska now knew that Dacosta didn't love her, but in her point of view, him, Kim, his cousins, and friends didn't and shouldn't have lied to her about who Kim was with. La'friska was still lying on the bed unable to cry, but was miserable and hurting from the knowledge of not having Dacosta's love anymore, thinking that he never did love her and thinking of him and Kim, visualizing them together in the future. La'friska, for a just a moment, thought of stabbing herself with a knife, because she didn't want to live with the pain of not having Dacosta's love. That night, she didn't eat dinner. Besides not being hungry, she couldn't eat, drink, or swallowing a thing down her throat. At this point, she still didn't cry. Now she felt sick. She felt a hurtful feeling in the pit of her stomach. She stayed in her room. She went to bed early but was unable to sleep restfully. She dozed off on and off throughout the night. She laid there thinking of Dacosta and Kim. Finally the morning came and she went off to school. At school in the bathroom La'friska saw a friend of Kim's. She told the friend who's name was Brandi to tell Kim that she wanted to see her. When La'friska said that, Brandi swirled around fast with an amused look on her face and said, "Dacosta told you?" La'friska didn't bother to answer and instead walked out. She heard Brandi saying, "Okay, I'll tell her." At lunch time, La'friska saw Kim with her friends, walked over to her, and said "You didn't have to lie about going with Dacosta; that's all I ever have to say to you." That next Monday, Dacosta and Kim brought their relationship out in the open. They no longer hid their relationship. They walked around campus talking, strolling the halls, and lounging in their favorite hangout spot with their family and friends surrounding them. A few days later, as La'friska and

Yolonda were walking, Yolanda said "La'friska, I think Kim goes with Dacosta." She responded "I know." After that day La'friska never mentioned Dacosta's name to Yolanda and Yolonda never mentioned Dacosta's name to La'friska. La'friska and Yolonda were in different classes. While La'friska was going with Dacosta, she and Yolonda had been friends palling around, but now Dacosta was with Kim. Now La'friska and Yolonda went their separate ways. This mostly happened on La'friska's part because Yolonda and Kim were in the same class and were now becoming friends. Yolanda was also Dacosta's cousin, and whoever went steady with Dacosta at the time, that's who Yolonda hung out with. Also, more importantly, Yolonda and Dacosta, once they started to go steady, their families put a stop to it since they were cousins. Now La'friska opened her eyes and realized that all along Yolonda didn't seem too thrilled about her being with Dacosta. La'friska realized that she didn't need or want friends like Yolonda and Kim. She realized that they deserved each other and she was better off without them. So now La'friska made new acquaintances, especially with one girl in particular named Janell Floyd. Although they became friends. On La'friska's part she didn't become too friendly because she had seen what best friends were like. As the weeks and months passed by, La'friska still loved Dacosta just as much as ever and was hurting deeply. She kept the hurt to herself and didn't confide in anyone, not even to her mother. No one in the world knew what she was going through. It destroyed her and nearly killed her each and every time she saw Dacosta and Kim together. On the other hand, Dacosta and Kim were very happy and they acted as if La'friska was not around especially Dacosta. He never spoke to her or looked in her direction even in passing, whether it was on the schoolyards, hallways, or the buses. He acted as if she didn't exist. Once she was walking backwards and accidentally backed into something. With her head held backwards and looking over her shoulder she looked up into Dacosta's face. They both stood rooted to the spot their feet were in, neither saying anything to the other. Dacosta looked right through her as if she didn't exist. She then straightened up and moved out of his way. Dacosta just walked on by her. As the months went by, whether she was home or at school, she fantasized about Dacosta; being in his arms, kissing, walking, talking, and just being with him. She fantasized so much until she was failing in two of her classes. She hated when breaks and lunch came around, because she would see Dacosta and Kim together. On the days they didn't sit together it wasn't so hurtful for her, since she didn't have to see them together.

In the fall and autumn months Dacosta and Kim walked around the school campus. But when the winter months came they courted in the classrooms and the hallways, which was known as lover's lane. In the springtime they again walked

## Thoughts

around campus or lounged on the front lawn, sitting on the grass or standing under a tree. The school year ended with La'friska failing two classes, but that didn't hold her back from passing to the next grade, because she had enough points. During her summer vacation, she worked hard on the farm and over in the community helping gather crops and harvesting. With the money she made, she had to give some to her parents and then kept the rest to buy school clothes. September came and school began again. La'friska was now a junior. The first week of school she didn't see Dacosta around campus. When she finally saw him, he still didn't speak to her, or would he look at her. She saw him on campus for a few weeks, and then no more, because he was now attending another school in another city and living with his married sister and her family. When she heard that, she was hurt, because now she wouldn't get to see him at all. La'friska went on at school and then one day she heard that Dacosta and Kim had broken up and that Kim was now going with someone else. La'friska didn't know when they had broken up, or what had happened between them, but she was very glad they did break up. Now she didn't have to see them together. La'friska often saw Kim talking with the sister and brothers of the guy she was now going steady with. The guy she was seeing had finished school and was working in another city.

It was now two years since La'friska had fallen in love with Dacosta, and it was a year since Dacosta last spoke to and broke up with her. La'friska's junior year in high school was interesting. She had new classmates and made other friends. Never once did she confide in any one of them or tell anyone else how much she was hurting for him still. Dacosta was far out of sight but not out of mind, heart, and body. She still wanted him just as much as ever. Night and day she thought and fantasized about him. That year during class she forced herself not to fantasize about him as often. She became more attentive during class, and that was probably due to Dacosta not being at her school for her to see him and Kim together anymore. Not many people knew she went with Dacosta. She continued to keep the pain and hurt to herself. Still she was hurting so terribly bad that the pain was too much to bear at times. Then one day this pain and hurt started to make La'friska think of what she would do to someone if they tried to hurt her mother in any way. She knew that she would get even with them by hurting them back viciously. She started thinking and imaging all kinds of thoughts. Her mind was in turmoil with her thoughts in a vicious cycle of trying to erupt from so much pain and hurt. With all these imaginative thoughts, the one certain thing still on her mind was her undying need and love for Dacosta. A few weeks before school ended, La'friska got Dacosta's address from his brother Peter. She wrote Dacosta a letter saying she still loved and wanted him. He never wrote or called her back. She assumed he must have received her letter because it was never returned back to her.

The school year ended and summer began. Again she worked at home and in the community. Two weeks before school reopened she went to New Jersey with Brandi and her baby sister. Her parents let her because her sisters and brothers lived in New York and New Jersey so they knew there were people there to look after her. Plus Brandi's parents wanted La'friska to come with them in order to keep their daughter company on the train. La'friska loved New Jersey and once it was time to go her family sent her home with the latest shoes, clothes, and some money. Once home it was the same as if she hadn't left. La'friska was excited waiting for school to begin. School day finally arrived and she was up bright and early. She could hardly wait. The sun was shining was birds were chirping in the trees and she even saw a red bird fly by. There's an old saying to see a red bird means you will see your boyfriend on that day. In this particular instant she knew this was true since today was the first day of school. She was a senior and also hoping to see Dacosta at long last. It had been almost a year since she last laid eyes on him. To past time she forced herself to eat breakfast that day usually she wouldn't eat in the mornings. Finally everyone was at school united with people they hadn't seen during the summer months. They all were dressed nicely because the first day of school is a big event where everyone wears their nice clothes. There were three senior classes totaling 150 students. With only three senior classes they were pleased because they were in the same classroom with at least some of the people they associated with. The first day of school is only a half a day. On the way to the bus La'friska's eyes searched the crowds looking for Dacosta. She became frantic when she realized she hadn't seen him yet but she wasn't giving up yet. She had waited much too long to give up. But who was coming around the bus none other than Mr. Dacosta. La'friska's heartbeat sped up as Dacosta walked by. She knew he had to have seen her still he wouldn't say a word. Dacosta was more handsome than ever. She wasn't looking bad either. On the ride home and at home throughout the evening and all night she kept remembering how he still wouldn't look straight at her or speak to her. She wondered why he kept doing it because she hadn't done a thing to him. She still loved him as much as ever. When she saw him that day she knew that she hadn't stopped loving him not even an ounce. He still had that powerful affect on her. Whenever she'd see him, that same sensation would come over her; her heart would beat faster and a sensational feeling would come in around her heart going on down into a strange feeling in the bottom of her stomach. School resumed and everyone organize into daily schedules. Being a senior is where it is meaning you get the best you choose the subjects you want to take and you pick the teachers whom you want to teach you. La'friska chose subjects such as home economics, algebra, French, government, and oh yes, English IV was a must, and the last subject was study hall. She was a bright student but she could have been brighter if she'd have applied herself more; she did enough to pass by. She didn't toy much with the ideal of fantasizing about Dacosta Tiawan Gahenne because she had enough to do trying to keep up with English and besides that she had a mean teacher a Mrs. Du Ponte who didn't tolerate or took no stuff from anyone. La'friska knew so did the rest of the seniors that if they planned to graduate they had better pass English IV it is a must requirement. Around one and a half months after school started La'friska saw Dacosta sometimes walking and talking with a sub freshman girl name Patsy Johns. Patsy seemed to be a pleasant and cute girl. La'friska was once again hurt and upset seeing Dacosta walking and talking with another girl when she loved him so very much yet he wouldn't look at or speak to her. Later she was even more hurt and upset when she learned Dacosta was going with Patsy. No one in the world probably not even Dacosta knew how hurt she was and what she was going through inside she kept it to herself. She was so torn up by his actions on the outside she associated with others and hung around with a new crowd. She wouldn't get overly friendly because she had learned from the friendship with Yolonda, so she didn't ever plan to have another best friend. When she needed Yolonda's friendship to help her through the ordeal with Dacosta she wasn't there. Yolonda never even mentioned his name to her. She and Yolonda still said hi to each other and sometimes their crowds would meet up and get into conversation. La'friska couldn't have worked at her class schedule more perfectly than she did. You see all this time since the start of school she Dacosta Kim and some of Kim's buddies they were all in the very same study hall class. La'friska sat on the one side of the classroom and they sat on the other side. La'friska didn't speak to them and they didn't speak to her, however, when Dacosta was in study class many times he didn't come at all; he'd cut class, but when he was there he'd pull up a chair right beside Kim and sit there and talk with her and her friends. Yet he wouldn't speak to her or look at her. La'friska knew he couldn't help from seeing her; he had to, because they ran into each other quite often in the hallways around campus, the class, and the buses. Why, Dacosta was even sometimes the bus driver to carry them onto the high school after they dropped off the elementary school students. Yet still he refused to speak to her. Once she was sitting on a car bumper at school with her legs crossed with her dress high up on her legs and Dacosta walked by with his friends. La'friska saw him glance down, looking at her legs, and she heard him say, "That girl is going to blind someone." There and then she knew that she had been right all along, that he couldn't help but to have been seeing her, yet he tried to pretend he didn't. La'friska didn't know what happened between Dacosta and Pasty, but for a few months she didn't see them around campus and the hallways together. The senior year was also sometimes busy and hectic with all the preparations such as class year ring at Christmas time invitations around Easter time banquet dances and finally the social affair of the year prom night. La'friska didn't go to neither the junior or senior prom she didn't know if or not her parents would have let her and also she really didn't want to because she didn't have a boyfriend. She still loved Dacosta but he didn't want her. She knew by not going to at least her senior prom that she'd be missing out on one of the most important parts of high school, which was senior prom night. The junior prom wasn't as highly rated as the senior prom, therefore many people didn't go to their junior prom. By not going to her senior prom, she knew that she'd missed out on one of the most special events of high school and that never in her life would she have that opportunity again; that special night couldn't be remade up again. So she missed out because she didn't have Dacosta to share it with her. Now that prom was over, graduation festivals was underway everyone was getting nervous and excited plus growing sad because now they'd be going their separate ways starting new adventures whether going on to college, jobs up north or whatever. La'friska knew when school was soon over that she wouldn't see Dacosta at all' this hurt and saddened her so much. Knowing this she got desperate, so she wrote him a letter, mailing it to his house. The letter was short sweet and to the point, reading, "I realize and know school will soon be over within just a few short weeks. There is something I haven't told you in quite some time, and that something is I still love you very much; in fact, I've never once stopped loving you. I want to see and be with you to know how it feels to be kissed by you, in your arms and making love to you with you. So Dacosta, read this next line slowly and carefully. I will give you anything you want, meaning my body. If you are interested, think about it and let me know, and baby I will meet you anytime anywhere." La'friska then added her telephone number. It was on a Friday when she mailed that letter to his house, and by the next day, which was a Saturday, Dacosta phoned her around eight o'clock that night. When the phone rang, La'friska was the one who answered it. Dacosta said "Let me speak to La'friska."

She said "This is me".

He said, "This is me, Dacosta." La'friska's heart almost stopped beating. She was partly afraid, nervous, excited, and delighted. It was over two and a half years since she had last heard his voice over the phone, and now finally she was hearing it again. He said, "I got your letter."

Thoughts

She said, "I believe you did."
He said, "Did you mean it?"
She said, "I not only did mean it, I do mean it."
Dacosta said, "I'll see what I can do. I'll try and work something out."
La'friska said, "Okay, I'll be waiting." Wait she did; she saw him at school and not one word did he say to her. He was surrounded by his cousins and friends as usual, so after a week or so of waiting for him to confirm something, she approached him in the hall one day when he was by himself. She just walked straight in his passage way right up to him looked him in the eyes and said, "Well, what are you going to do about it?"

Dacosta smiled and said "I can't get a car." They both walked away in different directions. La'friska thought, "He can't get a car; what's wrong with his brother's car? Why can't he borrow it? I've seen him a time or two driving it to school, and he had other girls in it, passengers he picked up on his way to school. She didn't worry herself about those passengers because she didn't think they were involved with him. Besides, she knew a classmate, Brandi Fletcher who was also Kim's friend, who liked and was going with Dacosta. She didn't know how he felt about Brandi because she didn't see him talking with her much, but La'friska knew Brandi liked and was going with Dacosta because she would overhear Brandi talking about him to her friends. One time La'friska heard Brandi say "If Dacosta's got any money I sure hope he spends it on me tonight." With those words said, La'friska thought, so she's going to be at the dance with Dacosta tonight. It hurt La'friska to realize he would be with Brandi and not her. She also thought, "So now he's going with Kim's friend; he is really going through that crowd. First Yolonda, then Kim, and now Brandi. She wondered and often thought, "What does he see in them? Especially Kim. He acted like he really cared about her, and he treated her like a lady, and even then he still talked to her. Why can't he say something to me? Kim doesn't look as good as I do." At another time, La'friska heard Brandi say to her friends that she wanted to have two kids, and name the boy after Dacosta. Well, hearing that really broke what was left of La'friska's heart. At this point, it was just painful heartache and misery. She didn't want to imagine anyone else ever having Dacosta's children but La'friska herself. As the days for school closing drew near, she kept wishing and hoping Dacosta would get a car and take her away from school from everything and make love with her. She very much wanted to know how and what it felt like to be made love to. Now Dacosta would sometimes look at La'friska as they passed each other. She would think, "Now that it's only a few more days of school left, he can look at me; why couldn't he have done it before now?" One day, La'friska and Dacosta came upon each other as they were passing. She looked at him and burst out laughing. Dacosta smiled and said, "What's so funny?"

La'friska looked at him and said, "Your bald head." Dacosta touched his clean-shaven head and they both burst out laughing.

He replied "I do have it shaved off."

La'friska replied, "Yes you do, but you're just as handsome as ever." At last, the big event was near with rehearsals for graduation awards night and finally the day and night in question—graduation. That night La'friska was nervous because she was participating before a large, packed audience, excited because after twelve years of school she was finally graduating. On the other hand, at the same time she was scared sad and lonely because she didn't want to finish school leave friends, never seeing some classmates again. She could deal with the part of moving forward with her life. What she couldn't handle was never ever again seeing Dacosta Tiawan Gahenne. She knew that after finishing school she would be losing all contact with Dacosta, and that hurt her like hell. For she loved him that much and still wanted him, and now her hope was truly gone. That night after graduating she looked for Dacosta, searching the crowds for his face, but she never saw him, so she went home with her family. She stayed in her room reminiscing through memories of the past, grammar school buddies and friends, high school associates, falling in love with Dacosta, and finally this very night graduating from high school and now being alone in her room. She was hurting to be with the guy she had loved so much for over three years. She kept thinking, "All these years I've never kissed his lips or been held in his arms. How have I stood it all this time? I want to know how and what I would feel like to make love to him and with him." Her heart mind and body was hurting and crying. Her body was burning for ecstasy. That night passed, and so did many nights that added into weeks and months during which she worked on their farm. Finally, when the tobacco crop was harvested in August, it just so happened that her sister Bonnie was home visiting, so their parents decided that La'friska should come back to Jersey with her so La'friska wouldn't later have to come by herself. La'friska was given one hundred dollars, and she had to spend thirty dollars of that for a train ticket. On the train ride, La'friska had hours to think and make future plans, but she didn't because she was so choked up finally leaving her parents, her lifeline; now she was mainly on her own. Even though she'd be living with her married sister Betsy and her family, she would now have to work and support herself and even send money home helping her parents out. It was now time she gave back to her parents; which she did. She gave abundantly and unconditionally. Her parents finally built the new house. La'friska could remember for years as she was growing up her father saying, "Next year,

I'm gone to build a house." He never did, because they were poor and just didn't have the money. Each year, with paying off the farm debts, they had no leftover spending money. With all the Tashanti clan working except baby brother Joseph, who was away at college. Joseph worked at odd jobs at college to support himself; he didn't have spare money to send home. La'friska and her brothers and sisters sent money back home constantly, especially La'friska. They all helped their parents built their new home. La'friska brought all kinds of furnishings for her mother. Why, on one of her visits home, she established credit in her name for her mother, and after that credit establishment, any time her mother wanted to buy something, she had no problem getting it, for La'friska's credit payment was good. In fact, her mother would purchase something, and in a month or two, La'friska would pay it off. So with her good job and her father's reputation of honesty, her mother got whatever she purchased. La'friska found living in New Jersey very cold in the winter. She loved going to New York, even though it was overcrowded. Her favorite sight to see was at night—the New York skyline. She had to acquire the taste for many kinds of foods. In their family Christmas time is special and family gathering reunion time. Some of the Tashanti children come home if not all of them so at Christmas La'friska rode home with her brother Junior and his family. Their parents were always glad and very happy to see them. Her parents would have their favorite foods. Her parents wouldn't rest and sleep peacefully until they knew that their children had reached back to their destinations safely, whether they were coming down home south or returning back to their home up north. As a matter of fact when La'friska was living home growing up through the years, she remembers her father being quiet and then saying to her mother "Madlyn I reckon those children getting on up that road now." Home at Christmas La'friska wanted to see Dacosta but she didn't. Being in New Jersey all those months hadn't faded her love for him. Men wanted to date her but she wasn't interested. Once in a while she would go out with them but nothing serious. It was over a year since she had seen Dacosta. Old saying if Mohammed can't come to the mountain then the mountain come to Mohammed. That's what happened because she wanted to see Dacosta bad. So she went to see Yolonda for the day, she knew that somehow she'd get to see him and sure enough she did. It was a Saturday and in Yolonda's area they played soft ball. La'friska didn't mentioned Dacosta to Yolonda so Yolonda never had any inkling why she visited her. At the ball game Dacosta came over to her and smiled saying "How did you get here?"

    She replied, "With Yolonda and her family." She liked the game but her only objective was to see him. She knew no one else knew that. They all believed she was a guest visiting Yolonda. La'friska knew many of the younger people at the game because they had attended school together. At one point Dacosta said to her "where are we going to night?" She thought he was just teasing her because his cousins and buddies was around so she replied "I don't know about you but I know where I'm going." They all laughed because she had gotten the better of him. Underneath she was crying inside wanting him to pursue her but like always he didn't. It was a year later before she saw him again, it was July and Dacosta's brother Peter and his cousin Hans came to visit her down home. She and Peter had always gotten along they were classmates and Peter was always a perfect gentleman with her. She liked Peter as her brother in law because that's how deep her love was for his brother Dacosta. She had undying unconditional love for Dacosta. She hadn't seen Peter and Hans since graduation she was so glad to see them, they stayed a short while. La'friska took the bull by the horns. She told Peter to tell Dacosta to come see her. Peter said he would and he did. It was kind of late at night when Dacosta came. She was dress for bed her brother Joseph told her someone outside wanted to see her she stepped down of the porch well she got the best shock of her life for there in person stood the guy she very much needed to see none other than Dacosta himself. Seeing the expression on her face one of sheer delight and pure joy then realizing how she must be looking she was embarrassed. Dacosta meet up with her as she walked towards him. They both looked each other in the eyes and smiled saying, "Hi." It was cool now from the late night air plus it had rained early leaving behind a cool dampness even though it was a little cool she didn't feel the coolness because the guy she loved for so long and wanted to see was finally there and being near him seeing his handsome face and terrific body and smile was more than enough to keep her warm, contented and so very, very happy. His cousin Seth was there too. Dacosta said "Seth didn't tell me until late and then we had a hard time trying to find your house. I was just about to give up this time if this was the wrong house." She replied "I'm glad you didn't give up and that this is the right house after all." He said, "What's happening? What have you been doing?" She replied, "Now that you are here everything is happening. As for what I've been doing living in New Jersey and working." During their conversation a long lock of her hair fell down in her face right over her eye and as they continued to talk he reached out his hand and gently moved the hair from in front of the eye to the side. As he was doing it she kept talking and looking at him. He said "a lock of your wig hair fell down." She smiled and said "it's not a wig that's my own hair." He said, "I don't believe you," and then he reached out and pulled her hair hard. She screamed and said "I told you that's my own hair." He said "yeah I guess it is." She said "I like your car I heard you had one." He said who told you that? She said, "I get the news; and are you going to take me for a ride in it?"

# Thoughts

He said, "It's to late; can you go?"

She said, "Sure I can; I'm my own boss. Besides, I'm a big girl now."

He replied, "Yeah, and a fine looking one at that. If you're sure, okay, lets go."

She said, "Not so fast, Tarzan; see what I'm wearing?"

He said, "Yeah, I want to see what's underneath."

She said, "All you have to do is pick the right place and find out, because baby the time is definitely right."

He said, "Well then, hurry up woman and get dressed." La'friska dressed in a lavender knit pants and sweater set with brown and tan suede heel shoes. She told her family I'm going out I'll see you later. Her father replied "With who?" She said Dacosta Gahenne. She got into his car and away they went. His car was a brown and tan mustang. They drove up town to the local hang out. Seth got out and Dacosta gave him money to bring back a beer for him. La'friska said "what about me I drink to." Dacosta smiled and said "Oh, I didn't know that now do you?" She said "oh yes I do." Dacosta and Seth looked at each other and Seth said "Hey man, what do I do?" Dacosta replied, "Bring the lady a beer" and he looked at her saying, "Baby tell him what you want."

She said, "Hopping gator."

Dacosta stared right back and said, "Hopping gator."

She stared right back and said, "Yes, I do like sweet things."

Dacosta smiled and said, "So do I, so do I, baby" and he pulled her over into his arms. They stared at each other and she was the first one to speak. She said "you know I've never kiss your lips, you've never kissed me." Dacosta replied "I know." She replied "I'm willing and ready to learn right now." They were staring at each other about to kiss when who should come back but Seth bringing the beers. Seth realized what was happening and said "sorry man bad timing hah." Dacosta said "sure is" and as he took the beers from Seth he said "now beat it pal get lost." Dacosta handed her a beer and said "here baby," as she replied "thank you." As they drank their beer they listened to music on the car radio. The music was soft, sweet and melodic just perfect for a guy and gal who for the first time after waiting for years to come together was about to get it on. As La'friska sipped the beer Dacosta asked her "how's the hopping gator?" La'friska stared at him and whispered, "Sweet." Dacosta had his arms around her shoulders and he replied, "let me see," taking the beer out of her hand. La'friska stared at him thinking he was going to taste the beer when instead he didn't taste it all He placed the beer on the dashboard, turned to her and pulled her closer into his arms. She snuggled closer and closer to him, repeating, "Um." Dacosta gently pulled her chin up until they were staring each other in the eyes. He gently stroked her whole face touching her nose, eyes, lips and he whispered, "Baby you have some beautiful eyes." She just stared at him but couldn't speak because his hands were sending vibrations all over and through her body. When his fingers touched her lips she moaned passionately burying her head into his chest. Dacosta said "I believe you are ready right now to learn." She whispered, "I am." He said "well, baby I'm about to teach you right this minute." With those words spoken they stared each in the eyes and their heads slowly inched forward and forward ever so tenderly their lips met. When that happened she was electrified and was trembling and shaking. Her mind, heart and entire body exploded in sheer joy and passion. Never before in her life had she felt this good for Dacosta's lips on here were so soft and sweet. Kissing, they both moaned with passion holding each other tight and clinging together kissing and hugging as they held onto each other for dear life. As they kissed she saw stars and heard bells ringing. She was flying high up, up and away, floating on a cloud of exuberance. She thought that she had died and gone to heaven. She couldn't believe it as they kept kissing; she kept asking herself "am I dreaming, am I?" He said, "No baby you are not." That kiss lasted for ten minutes before either of them came up for air. She laid her head on his shoulder and whispered, "I love you, please keep holding me this way, close and tight." Dacosta said, "I will but honey I want more and I know you do too." La'friska said, "I do darling. I want so much to make love to you and you make love to me. I've waited so long please don't make me wait another second longer." Dacosta said, "I'll be more than a second, give me five minutes at the most because it will take that long for me to get a room, but hold on baby I will." He left her in the car and minutes later he returned with a room key. He drove around the side of the hotel to the room and said "we are here." They went to their room and locked the door. Dacosta sat on the edge of the bed and pulled her over to him. She stood towering over him kissing his head while he kept kissing her breasts burying his head in them. As he pulled up her sweater and unhooked her bra he touched her erect nipples stroking them and finally when his lips touched her nipples she screamed out moaning, "oh darling what are you doing to me it is driving me crazy." He began sucking her breasts and she just fell into him as he laid her on the bed. As he continued sucking her breasts and touching her whole body she clung to him moaning over and over, "Dacosta, oh Dacosta." He replied, "Yes baby, what is it?" She said "I love you," and he replied, "I believe you." They were so heated up with desire that they both pulled the other's clothes off at the same time and speed. With their clothes off they explored each other's bodies and when at last they couldn't stand it any longer Dacosta got on top of her. When his penis entered her she moaned and when it was all the way inside her body she screamed and moaned it was like a volcano erupting within her. The

# Thoughts

look in her exotic eyes told Dacosta more than words ever could. They began making love and moaning and groaning. La'friska kept repeating, "Oh Dacosta am I dreaming am I?" Dacosta said, "No honey you're not it is really happening between us." La'friska said, "if I am dreaming darling please don't ever wake me up because if you do I swear I'll kill you, this is too good." They made love non-stop for two hours. They talked, moaned, groaned and even laughed as they did so. Neither of them reached a total climax but just the same it was good and satisfying and exciting. Dacosta said, "You weren't a virgin." La'friska stared at him and replied, "In the sense you're speaking virginity-wise, no, but in every aspect I am, because you are the only guy I love. You are the only guy I have ever truly loved, and the one I've wanted and needed for years and years, but you didn't want me. It's taken five years and three months for me to find out how it feels to kiss your lips and make love with you." She asked Dacosta, "Why did it take you so long? Why did you make me wait all of these years?" He slowly replied, "I don't know." She said, "You didn't want me." He said, "Yes I did, but why I waited this long I don't know. But anyway, wasn't it worth it?"

She responded, "Hell no, nothing is worth that kind of pain and heartache and torture. Do you have any idea how much I wanted and hurt for you? In case you didn't and don't already know it, I love you and I always will, no matter what." La'friska paused, saying, "Oh God, how it hurt the days and nights I longed for you, crying my eyes out sometimes and crying myself to sleep. It was good, but it wasn't worth it." She stared and him and said, "I want your baby; may I have it?" He said "No Friska I'm not ready for that scene yet." She said "By the way I wrote you a letter last Christmas did you get it?" He said, "Yes I did" She said "Didn't you believe me?" He said, "now Friska you know I didn't believe that, as healthy as you are." With those words spoken, they both burst out laughing uncontrollably. After getting themselves under control, she said, "But what if I had been telling the truth? You would have just let me die without ever having kissed your sweet tender lips and let me missed out on feeling your body inside me and against mine?" He replied, "But you weren't and don't you try that anymore. Friska, do you hear me?" She said, "No, I don't hear you." He looked at her and smiled, saying, "You heard me alright, woman." When he took her home that night, she clung tightly onto him, saying, "Please don't leave me; I don't want you to go." He said "I'll see you next time you're home." La'friska went to sleep that night happy and content. For the first time in her life she knew how and what it felt like to be made love to by the one you truly love. She kept thinking and recalling everything that happened just hours ago. Sometimes she thought, did it really happen? Is it true? I can't believe it, 'cause I've waited so long, for years—over five years and three months, to be exact. This is how long it's taken me to know and feel what it feels like to kiss and make love with him. Back in New Jersey she stopped the little dating she was doing for now she couldn't stand the touch or thought of another man touching her. She changed inside and out. She fantasized a great deal about Dacosta and thought of him morning, noon, evenings and especially during the nights all alone in bed. During the months that followed she started writing Dacosta powerful long letters expressing her love want and need for him. He of course never wrote back. Finally vacation time came and she went home, he came to see her once during her stay and he showed up late at that. She was hurting wanting to see him so much that when he did showed up she was so glad to see him she couldn't be mad. They went for a ride stopped at the local hang out drinking and talking outside with his friends. Much later they went to the same motel that they used the first time, only this time they had a different room. She was already feeling good from just being with him plus the liquor she had drunken made her more ripe and ready for him so when he finally took her in his arms after months of waiting she just melted against him and when they kissed, his lips so soft and sweet droved her wild. She was floating and loved every bit of it. This time when they made love it wasn't as satisfying as it was the first time they did it, or did they do it as long, but just the same, she loved it. She knew the reason why she didn't totally climax was because he didn't foreplay with her as much as she liked and she was ashamed and reluctant to tell him out loud but instead she kept putting his hands where she wanted it. He would take the hint for awhile and then stop. She kept asking "Dacosta am I dreaming? Is this really happening?" He said "no baby you're not dreaming this is for real." She said "If it's not and I'm dreaming, please darling, don't ever wake me up." He said "right now honey I won't just keep dreaming or whatever else you're doing." She said I love you." He said "okay baby I hear you." Again when it was time to leave she didn't want to go she kept refusing to get dressed and he finally threatened to leave her and she took the keys away from him. She put them under her body and said "Now what cha –gone a do?" He smiled and asked "what cha- want me to do?" She pulling her finger in a signal said "come here." He came and she patted the bed, he sat down and they stared at each other and she whispered," I love you. I want your baby. Please give it to me." He stared back at her and said "baby no I' m still not ready for no kids." She said "but honey I want so much to have a baby for you." He said "sorry maybe later." He kissed her and she melted against him for getting everybody or everything else in this world, and that's how he got the keys away from her. She said "oh no" and he smiled and said" oh yes now woman get dress." She said "no" he said "if you don't do it I'll ——." She said "what's the matter you lost for words, you'll what?" Dacosta said "I'll spank your behind." She said "try it." Then she rolled over on the stomach, revealing all of her naked bottom. He said, "Friska, don't be so fresh does your daddy have any idea how fresh his little girl is?" She said "Gee I don't know I've never told him and besides there's no reason why he should know after all I 'am a woman now." Smiling she said "if you are so darn determine for me to get dress why don't you put my clothes on me yourself, otherwise darling I can't and won't ." He stared at her and said "maybe I will yeah! I will at that" and he pretended doing just that. She burst out crying he said "what's the matter?" She replied "I didn't get enough of your love and now your hands have gotten me heated up. My body is on fire for you." He just stared and said "woman where did you learn to talk like that and who taught you these things?" She said "you did." He said "no baby," and he back away from her still saying "no Friska." She said "Yes, yes you did my love for you is so real and strong that it comes to me automatically plus the fact you made me wait all these years and months that now we are here together it's over flowing." He said "oh God woman what am I going to do with you?" She replied "right now make love to me or better yet let me love you and later I'll tell you what else I want." He smiled nodded okay and gathered her in his arms. They began kissing and she true to her words and bodily needs made love to him. He moan "oh don't stop, do it baby I love you." She said "no you don't it's only your lust talking." She wished with all her heart that he did love her. After it was over he said "now what else do you want besides my baby?" She said "to be your wife, marry me." He said "that's even worst woman I'm not about to get married now or maybe never." When they parted good bye she was crying and hurting terribly. He said "see you next time." In the months that followed she concentrated on her job. In the meantime Christmas was almost here. She shopped carefully lingering over presents for her parents but mostly for Dacosta. She brought him a watch, cuff links, a tie set, a handkerchief and cologne. Christmas arrived and La'friska went home. She loved this time of the year best because it could be filed with so much joy. It could have been perfect if she could have spent all of her time with Dacosta. On Christmas morning, her brother Joseph told her I saw Dacosta last night and he said to tell you hello and that he is coming to see you. She was in seventh heaven hearing Dacosta's name could make her feel that good. That night after Christmas Dacosta and his buddy Nahum Mortimer came to see her naturally they were late again. He apologized saying he got tied up with something. He didn't explain any further what that something was. Anywhere she was glad to see and be with him after all those months of wanting and waiting. They went to the hang out on the way there Dacosta let Nahum drive while he opened his presents. Dacosta said, "But I don't have anything for you." She replied,

"Well that's okay." He was happy and pleased about his gifts and he gave her a thank you kiss. At the hang out Nahum separated from them. They remained outside talking and drinking. Then Dacosta lowered the volume he said he was going into the army. La'friska screamed out, "oh no" and she just stared at him. Dacosta said, "I've been drafted I tried to fight it but I can't. You know what they say if Uncle Sam wants you he'll get you. You can't run or hide from him." She began crying saying "I won't get to see you." She fell into his arms resting her head on his shoulder and cried softly. Dacosta brought her closer and held her tight in his arms saying "I'll be home on holidays, at Christmas and on furlough leaves." With those words spoken she immediately stopped crying pulled away from him and stared in his face and responded with the word, really. He said yes, really each time you're home on long holidays I'll be here too, so now woman shut up crying and dry your eyes because I don't like your crying besides let's make love. She smiled saying "yes, let's do so. I love you so and I've been waiting too long. I need your body next to mine. I want your penis inside of me. I refuse to wait more than five minutes." In five minutes sure enough they were registered in their hotel room. This was the third time they made love. It was good and exciting but neither of them climaxed. La'friska knew the reason she didn't climax was because she was cherishing it taking it slow and making up for the lost time. Plus Dacosta failed to give her enough foreplay. She wanted to tell him but she didn't want to hurt his feelings and it was too embarrassing. So she chalked her lack of climax up to first being so glad and excited at finally being with him and due to lack of foreplay she needed and wanted. La'friska also knew Dacosta held himself back from climaxing. When they departed she ran back to him flinging herself in his arms crying saying I almost forgot. You forgot what. She said "that you are going into the services." He said, "I told you I'll be home on holidays and whatnots." She said "still it's not exactly like you will be a civilian where as I can see you whenever I want too." He said, "True but baby what can I do. There is nothing I can do. You'll just have to go along with the program too." She stared at him saying, okay then but for now don't leave me just yet. Please don't leave me, hold me close and tight in your arms that will help so much on those long cold snowy days and nights." As he held her close she kept rambling on about rainy days and nights. Hot and cold weather or whatever. She kept saying Yes hold me tight. Dacosta said, "oh damn, I forgot to tell you woman I'll be in the arms for the next three years." La'friska mouth fell open as she stared at him as she said, "no not that long." As reality sunk in she moaned pitifully. He said, "Yes baby three years that won't be so long." She replied quickly, "bologna that's a lie." He laughed saying, "you wanted to curse didn't you?" She said, "True, but still three years is long." He said, "Okay so it is

I will begin this long time starting next week." She pleaded for him to write to her. He stated he couldn't promise because he didn't know exactly what's in store for me during basic training which is rough as hell from what he heard. If I don't write which I am sure you know I won't, then I'll phone you sometimes.

Back in New Jersey the weather was freezing cold with some rain, ice and snow. To her it seemed each winter got worse and worse. She didn't care for winter especially the ice and snow part. She liked the summertime even though it was hot. Her favorite seasons were spring and fall. In spring things are blooming nature's rebirth with things coming to life. The fall even though the leaves are shedding and Mother Nature is preparing for a long sleep. The weather isn't too hot or cold.

Months later Dacosta phoned her and when she heard his voice her heart skipped a beat and then a warmth overcame her. She cried out "Dacosta I love you. He responded, "I know." He told her that he'd been busy in the army and that he couldn't talk too long besides the fact that he didn't want to run up her phone bill since he had called her collect. When he told her that he would be down home in July she was ecstatic with joy. At last July was here and when La'friska saw Dacosta she smiled and flew into his arms saying, "You are really here in the flesh." Dacosta said, "Yes I am, say that you are really happy to see me woman." She replied, "Yes I am, now kiss me man." He kissed her briefly and she said, "can't you do better than that after all I haven't seen you for months." He said, "Later baby right now were at your parent's house and they might be watching." She responded with "I don't care if they do see us honey, I love you and right this second I don't give a damn who knows it or sees us together." He responded with you are really something else. They went to a different hangout staying outside in the car or standing around talking and drinking. She would always never finish her can of beer. Dacosta was always forever busy talking with some guy or even gal explaining to La'friska this is my buddy or my cousin so and so baby I'll be right back I have some business to transact. Much later after waiting for what seemed like forever she would just reply with "okay Dacosta I've had enough let's go so we can get some alone time together." Each time he made love to her they'd try something new. La'friska still wouldn't and couldn't believe she was finally with him after all the longing and wasting of months. She'd still say, "Dacosta is this happening? Am I dreaming? And if I am don't wake me up please don't wake me." Throughout their love making she confessed her undying love for him. All he'd say was "I know" and "I believe you." She'd say, "I love you, I love you very much." She asked him may I have you baby? He'd still respond with, "No, not yet anyway." She started begging him to marry her. His response would be, "I am not getting married to anyone; at least not for some time, and then that may be never.

## Mattie F. Gaskins

The first two years Dacosta was in the service he stayed in the United States being stationed in different stated. He was stationed in Texas, Missouri, Georgia, North and South Carolina. During that time she wrote Dacosta many long and powerful love letters expressing her undying everlasting love for him. She would tell him how much she wanted and needed to see and be with him and how much she longed for his touch. She also begged and pleaded for him to give her a chance and marry her and let her have his baby. She told him that she'd love and take care of the baby all by herself if he didn't want any parts of it. Dacosta didn't write her back but he'd sometimes phone her especially when he wanted some money. He'd say, "I need this amount of money and I need you to send it to me right away baby. La'friska would send him the money whatever amount he requested regardless of whether she had it to spare or not. Even if she didn't have it she went out and got it. She'd think to herself maybe he'll realize how much she really does love him and like me better. Whenever Dacosta phoned her it was always collect. She didn't care because she was so glad to hear his voice. Just the sound of his voice would make her feel good. Also during Dacosta's service stay in the states she always saw him just once on each visit home. For some reason or whatever he never saw her twice on the same visit. He would make dates and promises but he never kept them. She would be so hurt and love sick by his actions. After each love making session she always prayed and hoped she was pregnant but no such luck because Dacosta wouldn't climax completely and he wouldn't let her either. Once when Dacosta was being shipped out to another state and she found out about it she phoned him and asked if or not he wanted to see her. He said yes that he didn't mind. Well La'friska hopped the first plane and went to see him. Of course, he met her flight and they went straight to a deserted spot in the schoolyard and made love. It was hot and the mosquitoes were biting like fools but she didn't care or felt a thing but her love for him. His good loving was stinging her body, heart and tearing her mind up. Dacosta's love making at the start always drove her wild but somewhere during the course of it the feelings would die down. She'd be thinking, wishing and hoping she'd get pregnant this time. Plus she'd also be thinking I need more foreplay should I tell him that I need more. Then he'd soon stop making love to her saying, "he was too tired or too high off liquor." At those times she would keep trying to attempt and seduce him but still he'd say no and if she still didn't give up he'd yell at her saying, "alright Friska I done told you to leave me alone. Now stop it woman, I've had enough and I'm tired." She would be so hurt and disappointed by his words and actions that she'd leave him alone and softly cry. If he heard her crying he would tell her that's not going to do you any good so hush up. To keep her quiet and not have her bothering him, he'd hold her in his arms so

## Thoughts

that he could get some sleep. During Dacosta's third year he was shipped overseas to Europe to Germany. Before he left for Europe La'friska was home on vacation. It was the month of August. He would be in Germany for sixteen months during which time he couldn't come back home. When La'friska heard that she was immediately sick and miserable. She said to Dacosta, "Please take me with you." He said, "I can't, you can't go, there would be no place for you to stay because you're not my wife." She replied, "Well, make me your wife, marry me." Dacosta said, "No, no baby I've told you over and over I'm not ready for that scene and I may never be." She asked him, "Why, what do you have against marriage?" He said I have nothing against marriage it's just not for me. I like being free as a bird without responsibilities. She said, "Darling I promise you now and forever I will never be a burden, responsibility or anything else like that on you because I love you and will do anything for you." I will be an asset to have, helping you in any and every way possible I can and know how. Please try me out and just give me one little chance and I'll show you. Don't let me be without seeing and being without you for sixteen months because Dacosta I've had years and years of not seeing and being with you. It's in your hands; it's up to you now so please do something about it. I need to be with you no matter wherever that might be just as long as we are together. "Dacosta said, "the answer is still no, no, no and sixteen months isn't forever. By that time maybe we'll both have changed and decided otherwise." She said, "I'll never, not ever decide I don't love and want to be with you. I'll always no matter where you or I might be. I'll forever and ever want to be yours and have you as mine." Dacosta said now that's part of the problem you want me as yours. Baby I don't want to be anybody's and I'm not anybody's and I don't plan to be yours or anybody else's for a very, very long while. Now La'friska do you get that?" I've had just about all I can take of hearing about your love wants and needs for me just drop the subject, after all these long years you have done just fine without me sensing from the looks of things, and I do believe you will still some how continue to do without me because baby one way or another you are going to have to 'cause I'm not getting hooked or tangled up on you or anyone else" She was now hurting terribly and softly crying from his hurtful words. She thought now how can I go on being without him even though I've done it for year's but then I only managed to survive. I merely existed. Dacosta interrupted her thinking saying "woman what's up? You're not talking and you know that you never shut up unless it's times like this, time after I've told you where to get off. Look Friska I don't love you but I do like you. You are attractive looking and nice but I just don't love you. Why don't you find someone who'll love and want you? Someone who'll love and want you just as much as you say you want me." When they said good bye she held her head high managing to hold the tears and hurt inside. She kissed him softly and lovingly on the lips letting hers linger just a bit and she whispered," take care go with God's speed good luck always and forever good bye love." With those words spoken she started walking away. Dacosta caught up with her and pulled her back around to him, staring in her beautiful exotic brown eyes and said "I'll phone you." La'friska by now couldn't hold back the flow of tears streaming down her face. Through blurred eyes she nodded her head meaning yes. She couldn't speak from being so choked up. He said "Friska baby don't cry it won't do us any good" and he pulled her into his arms holding her ever so gently and tenderly close. He whispered into her ears "talk to me." She said "what do you want me to say?" He said "whatever you want to and feel." She said "it's the same ole song as usual and like you said you're tired of hearing it." He said I really didn't mean to hurt your feelings." Whispering in her ears he said "tell me again." She wouldn't say a thing. So he again whispered into her ear and kissing it he said "please woman tell me." Well that woman part did it. When he called her woman she knew he meant business. His voice sounding so soft and lovingly sweet. She finally looking into his eyes whispered "I still love you, but don't worry I'm not asking nothing of you and I won't put no pressure on you." He replied "okay baby but don't you stop loving me ''cause it feels good to know somebody loves me." She replied "I couldn't ever stop even if I tried to." Dacosta said "in any case go inside woman, be good and until we meet again good bye." They both kissed each other and walked away. He turned and said "La'friska," she stopped turned and looked at him, and he said "don't take any wooden nickels." And he smiled. She smiled back saying "I won't" and with that she threw him a kiss. It was less than a month later on a Saturday she was on the way to work overtime on her day off. She got the mail out of the mail box and among the junk mail was an air mail letter from Dacosta. She couldn't believe her eyes, she wondered what Dacosta had to say and so soon after they had last seen each other. She was excited and afraid to open the letter; she thought maybe he's telling me he got married or something like that. She could hardly wait to get to work because she didn't open the letter until then. She was alone in the lounge. As she opened the letter she was nervous, excited and terribly afraid. As she read it she began to relaxed and got happy for Dacosta said he had arrived safely in Europe and was doing fine, that things over there was different but that with the help of God he would make it through and hoped to return safely back to the states when his sixteen months were up. He asked La'friska if she was pregnant saying, "He hoped she was because he really for the first time wanted a baby." Well when she read that she thought, "there is no baby because I'm not pregnant, oh God how I wish I were. I want his baby so much and now

## Thoughts

that I'm not pregnant he tells me he wants me to have his baby after all. As she continued to read the three page letter she then realized and knew why he wrote in the first place and secondly he was buttering her up when he said "I hope you are pregnant because for the first time I do want a baby. He said that because as the letter read on he said "I know you don't want to hear this you say every time I need something I come running to you. Well baby I need it. I need three hundred dollars but if you don't want to give it to me then don't, but baby I do need it because we don't get paid over here until three months. Please don't let me down I'm counting on you. Send it in two checks all at the same time so it'll be easier to cash and send it by my birthday. I'm sure you know when that is." Dacosta also signed the letter with "I love you." La'friska knew he was lying and buttering her up for the kill to send him the money. She loved him so much until she cared and didn't care that he was using and taking advantage of her love. She sent him the money right away along with a two and a half page letter. She told him no she wasn't pregnant but still desperately wanted his baby. She told him the three hundred dollars was his Christmas present and in return she wanted an engagement ring for her Christmas present. A week later she got another letter from him with the check returned. He wrote saying the check was signed by her on the wrong space. His name was supposed to be where hers was. To redo it and send it back right away. She knew the check was sign correctly but he was right in thinking she had made a mistake on her part. There wasn't no mistake it was the way her bank operated with checks signing the payee's name where the receiver's name should go. So she knew if she sent another check the same thing would happen again. So she phoned Dacosta, oh yes she used her brains where he was concerned. She had a way of tracking him down. She got the over sea's telephone operator gave Dacosta's address and rank and file just like that she was put through to him, even he was surprised at her tack and skillful knowledge of locating and reaching him. She explained to him the checks wasn't made out wrong it was her banks way of doing business, she add would a money order do? He said yes it would otherwise that kind of check wouldn't do. He explained what a hassle of a time he had trying to cash it with no success. When they had straightened out the details of the check. She said "what do you think of my Christmas present I want from you?" He laughed cunningly and said "I'll give you a ring but it won't be the one you want." She was disappointed and sad by his remark regarding the ring but it was so good hearing his voice. She was so glad and happy. Before they hanged up she said "I love you." He said "okay." She mailed the money order off to him. A month later he sent another letter, it was a post card with a picture of a cable car traveling across the highest mountain in Germany, covered with white clean snow.

He also wrote a few sentences saying "Hi how are you? I' am fine and hanging in here working hard and it's cold over here." La'friska wrote him beautiful love letters. It was Christmas time she shopped for her parents. When she started on things for Dacosta she shopped long and lovingly choosing gifts for him. His gifts included electric razor, wallet and key ring chain set, camera, cologne heavy sweater and wool socks. She thought of the socks to keep his feet warm because he said it was cold. She mailed the gifts in a gigantic box loaded with other goodies such as a home made nut and fruit cake. She made a fruit cake and she also brought one. She included a Christmas stocking loaded with Christmas candies, chewing gum, bars of candy, and a letter expressing her love and want for him. Christmas time at home was just as nice as ever, she enjoyed seeing everyone. Her mother's cooking seemed to get bigger and better tasting every time. She ate her heart out, especially thinking of Dacosta. She stayed a couple of days because she needed to get back to work. Plus Dacosta promised to phone on New Year's Day, and true to his words he phoned. She asked "did you get my box?" He said "yes thank you it was very good everything was." She asked if anything was ruined or spoiled. He said no that everything was fine; that all the guys envied him and they helped ate the food. He asked "Friska where did you learn to cook like that? The fruit cake was good." She told him that her mother taught her some things and others she learned on her own from trial and error. The first week in February she mailed him another box this one for Valentine's Day. In the box was Valentine cards, brought chocolate chip cookies, oatmeal and raisin cookies a heavy wool mohair burgundy wine sweater and last but not least the main reason why she sent him a box was to give him, his Valentine gift a red and white shorts under ware set with red hearts and red prancing ponies monogrammed on it. She cracked up laughing at her prank idea gift. She included another pair of under ware white briefs with two red hearts monogrammed down the front fly opening. She didn't hear from him for a while, then one day she was upset over the death of her uncle Harito and she needed to see and be with him to have his support, she phoned him and just hearing his voice hundreds and hundreds of miles away in another land and time zone calmed her and made her felt better. It was March cold and windy La'friska was so lonely for him she wanted to make love to him desperately. Her body longed for him burning with desire, oh how she wanted to see and be with him. Many upon many of times she cried and longed for him, even during the day and nights were worst. She fantasized about him; all her pleasures were make-believed. He was a habit she couldn't break and one she didn't to break truth being told. For the man she loved was a distant lover far, far away in another land. She wrote him saying "I wish I could see and be with you, can't you please try and come home even for just a day or

## Thoughts

so." If you will I'll pay your fare round trip. Sweet heart I need and want to see you." Dacosta later wrote back saying "I do want to come home I'd be a fool not to take up on your offer, but baby I can't. The only way I can come home is if I sign my name to do another year of time over here and I won't do that not for you or even my own mother or no one else. You'll just have to hang in there till I get home. It won't be so hard you can make it besides a couple more months and I'll be home. He added, "Friska, it's not that I don't want to see you; it's just that I can't. Please understand. I'm sorry, but I have to end this letter 'cause I 'm working long and hard. The army over here is taking all my time up in the fields and whatnot, working the hell out of me." Dacosta added "P.S. please call my mother and tell her I'm alright." He said that he hadn't written his mother in a while 'cause he was busy. He ended the letter saying "Hang in there, you can do it. I'll phone at the end of the month when I get back from the border." After reading his letter she felt much better and content, thinking, "He has written me four times since he went over there; maybe things are changing. I hope and pray things are." This last letter of his was what kept her going through the next weeks. Finally Dacosta phoned; naturally, she was delighted to hear his voice. She said, "I got your letter. It was sweet, but still I want to see you. So Dacosta, listen to me. Hear me out before you interrupt. There's an ole saying that if Mohammed can't come to the mountain bring the mountain to Mohammed." La'friska said "Dacosta, do you realize what I'm saying?"

He said, "No, I don't. Woman, what are you talking about? After all, you are paying for this call, so if you want to talk in riddles and nonsense, then go right ahead."

She said, "In translation, if Mohammed can't come to the mountain, then bring the mountain to Mohammed means, Dacosta if you can't come to me then let me come to you, how about that, now what do you say?"

Dacosta said, " Holy cow woman, what will you think of next?" She laughed uncontrollably and he joined in. Finally she stopped, saying, "Let me get myself under control; after all, this is costing me, but darling, you're worth every penny of it. Now back to matters on hand again—Dacosta, may I come to you; do you mind?"

He said, "No I don't exactly mind, but I won't have much time to spend with you 'cause like I told you they keep us busy over here, and besides, it would cost you a fortune to come over here."

She replied, "Let me worry about that. What I need to know is do you mind if I come and do you want to see me?"

He said, "I told you I don't mind, and I don't mind seeing you either."

She said, "Okay, that's all I need to know and hear. I'll be seeing you come August."

He said, "Woman, I believe you and I know you'll do just that." Now that she had his permission, she planned her trip, checking out flight schedules and destinations. During the months ahead, she planned her strategy. She booked air and hotel reservations, bought a new wardrobe, and her most strategic plan was that she stopped taking the birth control pills, because she planned to become pregnant by Dacosta when in Germany. She studied through brochures and travel guides of Europe, learning as much as she could about the places she was to visit. As the days turned into weeks, now the weeks were slowly but surely moving. She still thought of Dacosta and fantasized tremendously about him. She fantasized about how it would be when she got to Germany seeing and being with him after all this time. Of kissing him and making love with him and once again knowing the joy of being in his arms. Her body was burning and itching with desire for him. She wrote him a month before she left, letting him know what day and time she'd arrive. He phoned four o'clock in the morning waking her out of a deep sleep but when she heard his voice she instantly became awoke happily delighted saying "Dacosta." He said "yes it's me, who else do you think it would be?" She said, "I don't know it could have been anybody and I'm glad it isn't 'cause it's so wonderful to hear your voice." I miss you and I can't wait to see you." He said "well it looks like that's what you'll be doing when you come over here." She said, "Oh Dacosta I can't contain myself. I brought a new wardrobe, booked air and hotel reservations." He said "I believe you every time I see you; you have on something new and different." She told him "thank you." She also told him she was studying travel guides and different brochures of Europe. La'friska asked Dacosta, "Do you think about me?"

He said, "I must have because I phoned you, didn't I?"

She replied, "Yes, you did."

Dacosta said to La'friska, "When you come over here, don't expect too much. I say that meaning it in more ways than one; besides, it's a different country, and if and when you get here, you'll see for yourself."

She responded, "Okay for that piece of advice, now back to you and me."

He questioned, "What about me and you?"

She said, "I'm glad you phoned just now when you did because even in my sleep I was longing to see you and ear your voice and to now actually be talking to you; oh baby, I just loved it."

He said, "Yeah, it's nice hearing your voice and speaking to someone back in the states who I know." The next four weeks passed slowly, and at last it was August. La'friska left for Germany on a 6:00 p.m. flight from Kennedy airport on a Sunday evening. The flight was smooth and interesting. She was excited and ex-

## Thoughts

tremely pleased, for at last she was heading to the man she loved. On the flight were many soldiers and some were with their wives. La'friska envied the wives, wishing and hoping she could be like them going along with their man no matter where they were going. She kept thinking maybe she could convince him this time after coming this far he had to realize how very much she truly loved him. Seven hours later her flight was coming in for landing and just before it landed she was looking out the window thinking hey over here looks like New York's airport. As soon as she departed off the plane into the terminal she changed her mind fast and quickly because the people looked strange and only spoke their native language. She tried to ask questions and directions but many times she couldn't understand them and she thought boy am I in for it. She didn't know what they were saying. As she pressed on she found people that spoke English as well as German. With her luggage in her hand a nice friendly black soldier took her under his guiding hands and escorted them onto the subway to the train station. After arriving to the train station he gave her directions where to purchase her ticket and what track to go to. She thanked him kindly and he wished her luck. He also envied Dacosta because she came all this way to come and see him. After he left her she tried to purchase her ticket and that's when her luck went downhill. The ticket agent wanted their foreign money and she only had American money. She had to drag two suitcases and find the bank inside the terminal. She had a hassle trying to get to the bank asking different people directions. Some of the people that spoke English didn't know where the bank was or she couldn't understand them but she persisted and finally got to the bank to change some money into foreign currency. She purchased the train ticket and then she couldn't for the life of her get onto the right train. She repeatedly asked directions and questions and tried and tried but no one could tell her what train to get on to reach her destination. Finally a black soldier directed her upstairs to the military station. The soldier was also kind enough to offer to hold her luggage until she returned but she declined his offer. Since she didn't fully trusted him along with her being in a strange country she didn't want to lose her luggage and have nothing. The men at the military station were friendly and courteous. They wrote directions on paper for her and explained them to her as well. She thanked them gratefully and finally caught her train. The train only traveled so far and then she had to change to another train just as the military man explained. She had to run to catch this train and luckily she made it. She was tired but now well on her way. The train was funny looking not at all like the trains she usually saw. This one had the seats in rows facing each other and with a luggage rack over the head. The train looked more like a subway than a train. As she relaxed she thought of the hard time she had trying to get this far. She had become almost desperate and wanted to phone Dacosta's camp to locate him and she thought even that wouldn't have helped much because he was at the border temporarily and wouldn't be back to his regular camp for another week. While sitting back with her feet up and relaxing the passengers and conductor watched her with admiration and wonder written all over their faces. La'friska just stared back but paid them no mind. She was anxious and thrilled to be on the way to the guy she loved and wanted. Her destination was the last stop on the line. After getting off, she took a taxi to the hotel. Registered and checked into her room. She unpacked her dress clothes and took a perfume bath. The hotel furnished beautiful bath oil. After bathing and dressing she asked the manager where the army base was and how to get there. After it was explained to her she knew she would get lost but she took a taxi and was on her way.

    Once on the base she went to headquarters and they put a call through to Dacosta. When La'friska heard Dacosta voice she was so happy and pleased even he could hardly believe he was really talking to her and that she actually arrived safe and sound. She asked, "When do I get to see you?" He replied, "Tomorrow will you be alright until them?" She responded, "Yes, just knowing I'll see you then is enough to keep me going." He said well okay I'll see you in the morning. She thanked the men for their kindness and left the base to go back to the hotel. She didn't get lost; she followed almost the same route the taxi took when he took her to the base. The only trouble she had was when she tried to buy a bar of soap to take back to the hotel because she knew the hotel gave little bars of soap and that wasn't enough for her. She asked the saleswoman how much the price was and the woman started talking in her native language which she couldn't understand so she walked out of the store. Back at the hotel she was good and hungry because she hadn't eaten all day not since she was on the plane. She asked the manager what time the dinner hours started. When she found out she had another hour to go until six o'clock, she became extremely hungry not knowing if she could last that long. Finally the hour was over and she went to dinner. At dinner she had somewhat of a problem because the waiter spoke in German. She asked him to translate that in English and he did even though his English sounded foreign too. Her dinner consisted of steak, potatoes, peas and mushrooms. She had strawberry ice cream for dessert. Afterwards she went to her room and stayed there for the night. To occupy her time she read a book that she brought along on the plane. It was the only book she had which consisted of a true romance story and she'd already read half of the stories. Earlier when she returned from the base, she had the manager put a radio in the room. She requested a television but learned she wouldn't be able to understand it because the programs were all in German. Learning

## Thoughts

she couldn't watch television was a huge mind-blower because she loved to watch TV. Her room was on the third floor and it was on the backside of the hotel. She had a large window with a wide ledge. In the room was a twin side bed, a long couch, chair, table and a long dresser. It was nice and clean. She especially liked the way the room smelled and had perfume bath oil even though the packet was small. She went to bed but was unable to sleep because she was excited about seeing Dacosta in a matter of hours. She had longed and waited for this for so long and now it looked like she was going to get that chance her wish was granted. Even though she tossed and turned during the night she did at times managed to get some sleep. Six o'clock that morning she was up. She took a leisurely perfume bath, combed and brushed her hair and fixed her face using barely little makeup. By now she was past hungry. She was absolutely famished. She dressed and went down to breakfast at 8:30 A.M. Her hotel accommodations called for a continental breakfast with a choice of either lunch or dinner. She didn't know what a continental breakfast was. She thought it was a lavish meal of maybe choices of ham, bacon, sausage, eggs, omelets served with toast, rolls or whatever breads. Instead she found out it was only coffee, tea, and breads such as rolls, toast, buns. Cheeses, jams, butter and jellies. Upon finishing breakfast she went back to her room. She changed into a beautiful white suit night gown with the matching robe. Spraying herself with expensive Chanel no. 22 perfume. Afterwards she sat down waiting for Dacosta. She listened to the radio. The music consisted of jazz, rock, soul and Latin some of everything. The station was located in Nuremburg Germany. She was beginning to get tired of waiting. She prayed and prayed that Dacosta wouldn't stand her up. Eventually she laid down waiting and praying until she fell asleep only to awake a short time earlier. It was almost ten o'clock in the morning. She was lying on the couch when suddenly there was a knock on the door. Well her heart jumped and she got excited and nervous. She yelled out, "yes, who is it?" The voice called out Dacosta and she became instantly happy. He asked, "Are you dressed because I have someone with me?" She responded, yes, at the same time she was opening the door. When La'friska saw Dacosta she smiled and he smiled as he walked through the door and behind him another guy followed. Dacosta introduced his friend named Barodd Davenport. Dacosta then said, "Barodd this is La'friska Tashanti from home down south but she now lives in New Jersey. She's now considered a Jerseyan. They all laughed and La'friska and Barodd exchanged glances and greetings. They sat talking about what was happening back in the states and down home in the south. Dacosta asked her if she hand any problems with getting into town. She responded, boy, did I ever, you can't begin to know the half of it. Dacosta said, "Tell us." She said well the flight over was smooth, sort of nice in some way but I believe the stewardess was prejudice with their service. Anyway I arrived at Frankfort and just as we were landing I looked out of the window and thought hey over here looks like New York but when I got into the terminal I quickly changed my mind since I couldn't understand their language as I was asking them questions. La'friska relayed the whole story of her ordeal and what she went through to finally get here. They laughed especially when she added it took from 7:30 A.M. to 12:30 P.M. to get to the hotel which was only 50 miles away. I was supposed to get here in an hour. So after checking in, bathing and changing clothes I got a taxi to the base and you know the rest, except after talking to you I walked back from the base. Dacosta asked, "You didn't get lost?" She said, "No. I followed the route the taxi driver took when he went to the base. I checked the route as he drove. I took a few wrong turns but I made out just fine and it all led me back here. Oh yeah, along the way back I had one problem. Dacosta asked, "What was that?" She told him how she wanted to buy a piece of soap and how when she asked the price, the clerk talked in German, which he knew she didn't understand,.so she just walked out with nothing. They all laughed. Both guys remarked how comical she was. Dacosta said to Barodd, "You haven't heard nothing yet man she can go this girl is full of surprises." Barodd asked her how did she like it so far. She replied it was nice and clean and the sights were beautiful as she watched during her train ride. The mountains in the sky were so beautiful looking and tall as if they were reaching the sky. The people here look at me with wonderment on their face trying to figure out who I am or if I am someone important. Others have admiration written in their eyes. Then some look at me in a hatred way, probably thinking get out of my country you are an American a black one at that. Barodd said to Dacosta, "She is something else, beautiful plus a sense of humor you are a lucky man." Dacosta smiled and said "yeah." Barodd said now I'll leave. I know you two must want to be alone," he turned to La'friska and said "it was nice meeting you take care and good bye," and he left leaving them finally at long last alone. La'friska wanted to run into Dacosta's arms and stay there forever, but she didn't 'cause she didn't want him to think she was to pushy rushing things. They talked about nothings in general. Dacosta turned on the radio and they listened to the not so good music and he told her from 12:30 P. M. to 1:30 P. M. that station played the latest music from back in the states. She wasn't interested in any of that all she wanted was to be in his arms and finally she said "Dacosta you haven't kissed me yet." He smiled and said "so it is" and he kissed her on the lips. She said "is that all can't you do better than that after all you haven't seen me for months?" He said "you haven't changed, still pushy and forward and fresh as ever." She said "neither have you just as selfish and inconsiderate as ever, as a fact

## Thoughts

more than ever." She was laying on the sofa bed he came over and stared into her exotic brown eyes and said "what do you want?" She said, "Darling," and she reached out her hand gently tracing his lips saying, "I want you." Dacosta was smiling sweetly and kissed her hand again and again saying "your hands are so soft and your nails are so long." She kept tracing his face now with her other hand. He took her other hand and pulled her to him. They stared into each other's face and slowly their lips meet into a long passionate kiss. She melted in his arms pressing herself closer and closer into him. She was floating on a cloud. She kept repeating through their kissing "oh darling am I dreaming?" He said "No baby you're not this is for real." The more they kissed the hungrier she became for him, she couldn't get enough. He tried to take her gown off as they continued to kiss and kiss but she was so heated and stirred up twisting and swirling against him until he had a hard time trying to get the gown off. She had his shirt unbuttoned and open out pressing her breast into his chest. He was still working at taking off the gown and kissing her on the cheeks. She buried her head in his throat kissing his neck, chest, lips and cheeks again and again. While kissing his cheeks Dacosta had his hands in her hair. He whispered into her ears "baby you are too much you have to help me with this gown thing or else I'm gonna tear the dam thing off." She said, "I don't care, tear it off; I need you."

He said, "But it's so beautiful, no, help me take it off please."

She said, "I'll try but baby I'm so weak for you I don't know if I have strength to."

He said, "Try; just think how soon I'll be stroking your body finally giving you the love you said your body desperately craved and long needed."

She said "okay" and undid the hook he was so long at trying to do and at the same time she was still kissing him and pressing into him. He pulled away from kissing her and she went right along with him continuing to kiss him. He said, "Baby you have to stop or I can't get my clothes off."

She said, "Okay, but don't you do it; let me please, darling. I have wanted to do this for so long; may I now?"

He nodded yes. She began with unbuttoning his sleeves cuffs, off with the shirt, unzipping the pants dropping them down. She was doing this as she kissed him. She stopped and pulled away. He sat on the edge of the sofa while she pulled his pants completely off. She was standing over him with her arms around his neck. He pulled her closer to him and began touching her breasts. At his touch she moaned with pleasure as he caressed and took turns sucking her breasts she melted into him and felled on him. Dacosta knew she couldn't take it any longer so he crawled on top and entered her virginal first with his finger and then his penis. She cried out "oh God; Dacosta I love you so much please keep on doing this to me, it's so good." He said "I won't stop oh baby you are so hot for me until it's driving me crazy too." They made love passionately and lovingly. She was slowing down because she wanted it to last forever. He said "what are you thinking woman?" She said "that this is where I want to be forever in your strong arms, Dacosta please hold me tighter and tighter." He did for ten or so minutes and then he said "Friska we'll have a lot of time." She said "later for later I need it now. I could die any minute from your loving." He now said "I know I'm going to stop now 'cause the last thing I need is a dead body on my hands besides what would I tell your parents?" She said "I don't even know and right now I don't care, all I want to care about is you and me, besides if I did die I'm sure you'd think of something." He laughed and said "let's get cleaned up and dress we'll go to the base. I'll show you where to cash your traveler's checks. On the base you get more for your American money than you do in the banks." She said "okay later but for now let's finish making love I didn't get enough." He said "you shouldn't have held back." She replied "I wanted to cherished it and take my time." He said, "No woman, no, we'll have time for later, and that's that." She shut up knowing he meant exactly no and nothing she could say or do would change his made up mind. They walked to the base. As they walked he pointed out places of interest, some places didn't like blacks in them or they weren't allowed. He explained some of the foods they served was good and at reasonable price. Walking besides him and talking was so good and naturally she wanted it to always stay that way. They passed a Chinese American German restaurant and she said "hey look Dacosta Chinese food over here." He laughed at her surprise and said "yes they have it over here, there rice, egg and shrimp is delicious." She said "I call it shrimp fried rice." On the base Dacosta introduced guys to her as they pass by. He told her "there aren't many blacks over here as you can see, only the one's in service stationed over here as for black women a few who follow their husband." She said "would you marry me and let me be one of them?" He stared at her not expecting that to come from her. She stared back defying him with her eyes. He said "I'm sure you know the answer to that without my having to tell you." She asked, "Can I do anything to change your mind?" He said "no you can't." In order for La'friska to cash a traveler's check American express at that, she had to make it out to Dacosta. On the walk back they stopped at the Chinese American restaurant but it was closed on Tuesday's. She wanted to by a camera to take pictures but he told her to wait and he'd pick out one for her later. He also added "the camera you gave me for Christmas somebody stole it." She said "no." He said "yes it's true." It was almost four o'clock P. M. Upon reaching the hotel he said

## Thoughts

"it's time for me to leave get back to the base. If I get there before the sergeant leave I can get a ride back to the border with him. If I miss him I'm going to have to take the bus and I must be there in case they call formation. If they call it and I'm not there well baby I'm in deep trouble A.W.O.L and that means away without official leave." She said "okay I understand." He said "you will be alright, won't you Friska?" She said "yeah I will be." He told her how to get in contact with him on the border in case she had to. He said "be careful and stay away from the banks, cash your checks on the base. Oh yeah baby I need some money, I spent what I had to get to you. She gave him all the foreign marks she had. He said "I'll see you tomorrow," kissed her sweetly and said "so long." She said "good bye" and threw him a kiss. Back in her room she thought of him and what the day had been like. She later had dinner downstairs and around ten o'clock P.M. she was in bed reading with rollers in her hair the phone rang. It was Dacosta calling from downstairs. He told her to come downstairs. She quickly took the rollers out and halfway combed her hair, put on a velvet blue robe and went downstairs. Dacosta was sitting out on the patio drinking a beer. They spotted each other and meet one another. He kissed her hello and said "I haven't left yet." He was dressed in his army clothes. She was fascinated she had never before seen him in person dressed in his army clothing. Sure she had seen pictures of him in his army clothes at his house but never in person. She said "you look nice and handsome in uniform. This is the first time I've seen you in person with them on except for the pictures at your house. She asked Dacosta, "How come you've never given me one of your pictures?"

He said, "I didn't know you wanted one; anyway, I sent them home to mother."

She said, "I'm not your mother; she and I have different loves for you. She can't love you in the ways that I can; besides, you probably didn't want me to have one of your ole pictures."

He laughed and said, "You are funny."

She said, "Ha, ha, ha, you mean to tell me all this time you was at the base, here I was crying my eyes out over you, missing you, and all this time you were almost under my nose; just what were you doing?"

He said, "Hanging around with the guys drinking."

She said, "As usual, that's just like you," and she burst out laughing.

He said "What's so funny?"

She said, "You are, with beer suds around your lips and in your mustache."

He said, "Oh, I had to do something while you were telling me off."

She said, "I'm sorry, I don't mean to come down on you so heavy; it's just I do care a great much for you."

He said, "I know, but try not to lay heavy raps on me." She wanted to know what a rap was, and he said, "You know, marriage and children; that stuff."

She said, "As for children, I'll settle for one who'll resemble both of us."

He laughed, saying, "No way woman."

La'friska said, "Last year when you came over here you wrote saying you wanted one, or were you just pretending, buttering me up to get what you wanted then?"

He said, "Did I do that?"

She said, "Yes, you did do exactly that, and you said precisely that."

He said, "Okay, okay, I did then and maybe at the time I meant it, but now I don't want a baby at all."

She told him, "Lets not argue; I didn't come this far for that."

He said, "La'friska, why did you come, and be truthful."

She said, "Dacosta, I have never lied to you, but at this present time, I won't tell you the answer to that question. I'll do it later; I promise."

He said, "Okay, you must be cooking up something mighty good."

She said, "Extremely superb."

At that time Barodd walked up and Dacosta said, "Are you ready?"

Barodd said, "Sorry man, but yeah, I am."

Dacosta said to her, "Well baby, it's that time again. This is for real or we'll both, Barodd and me, that is, we'll be in trouble if we don't start making it back to border camp." He walked her to the elevator and they kissed. This time she cling to him. She didn't care who was watching. For the next three days she mostly stayed in her room waiting for him to come, but he didn't. She didn't want to chance missing him if and when he came. She only left the room for breakfast and dinners, except for the time she went to the base trying to cash another traveler's check, but because Dacosta wasn't with her, they wouldn't cash it. Plus, she had an identification badge of herself, and they still took their precious time. Finally with the check cashed she went back to the base bookstore and purchased five true store magazines. She was learning her way around and plus she was able to understand some of their language. She was asleep at 1:30 a.m. Saturday morning when the phone rung, she jumped from the loudness and instantly became wide awake. It was Dacosta phoning from downstairs. He wasn't allowed to come up that late in the night, so he asked her to come down and bring some money. Since she had a head full of rollers, she went downstairs with a towel on her head. When Dacosta saw her, he cracked up laughing and played with the towel. He was dressed in a black shirt and black pants and he was looking very handsome and half drunk. He told her he had been at the base hanging around with the fellas drinking and whatnot, and the time just slipped on by. Now he needed money to

# Thoughts

get back to the border camp. La'friska replied, "And so naturally you come running to good, kind-hearted ole Friska."

"I know, and besides, I know you love me," said Dacosta. "After all, you came way over here to see and be with me. Even after all the years I did you wrong, you still want me," he continued.

"Darling, don't rub it in, because one day, someday, you may be in for a surprise if you come running to me, no matter how much I love you and I want you. I just might make myself not be here for you only to teach you a good lesson," La'friska said.

"But right now I am here and so are you, so please give me the money so I can leave and get some sleep, and I'll come back in the morning," Dacosta replied.

"It's morning now," she said.

Dacosta said, "It's dark night morning; the light morning hasn't come yet."

"Big deal, so what," she said as she angrily shoved the money at him.

"Thank you and I'll see you in the morning," he replied. He kissed her and fingered the towel on her head. He tried to pull it off but she caught his hand and questioned, "You wouldn't dare?"

He smiled and said, "Okay, I will see you later." He walked her to the elevator and they kissed. The manager thought Dacosta was going upstairs with her as he called out and shook his head, meaning, no, Dacosta couldn't go upstairs. Dacosta stood laughing at her towel as the elevator door closed. Upstairs back in her room and in bed she couldn't sleep. She hadn't slept too soundly since she arrived in Germany, the past three days cooped up in that room with nothing to do or no one to talk too. She hadn't seen or heard from Dacosta until minutes ago, when he needed money to get back to camp. She became steaming mad at him when she thought about the three days she waited and waited for him to show, and now tonight when he was at the base he stayed with the guys instead of coming to her. When daylight arrived she ate breakfast in her room, as she waited for Dacosta to show up since he said he was coming. Afternoon came and he still hadn't come. She couldn't stand it any longer so she phoned his border camp and was told by headquarters that he caught the 12:30 P.M. bus. She was pleased thinking and hoping he was on his way coming to see her. She waited and waited and still he hadn't arrived at five o'clock p.m. She went to the base looking for him but was unsuccessful. The guard on gate duty wouldn't let her go onto the base, but he did phone trying to locate Dacosta with no such luck. She was heartsick. She walked back to the hotel and laid down to get some rest. Within twenty minutes Dacosta finally came and all he wanted to do was listen to the game on the radio. She had some room service brought to them along with cocktails. Later Dacosta was still listening to the game, but she wanted his affection and complete attention. She thought, even over here I can't get him away from the ball games. It's just like being in America, the guys are still fools over the games. Two hours after he showed up she thought, I've had enough I want his attention. So she began kissing on him but he was too enthralled in the game. She said, "Dacosta, I want your attention." He replied, "what is it, what do you want? Not now baby, I'm listening to the game; later." She said I've been waiting patiently long enough. He didn't bother to answer her. She sat on the sofa beside him running her finger though his mustache. He asked her, "do you like my mustache?" Yeah I do but I like you a whole lot more so let me show you, she remarked. She softly and sweetly kissed his lips letting them linger and started kissing him again. He replied, you showed me now let me hear the game. She said, I want to convince you too, don't you know all work and no play makes you a dull guy? Yeah, so at the moment I'll stay dull, remarked Dacosta. She left him alone and went to curl up in the bed reading a magazine. Her feelings were hurt. She wanted Dacosta to make love to her but instead he insulted and hurt her feelings. Later once the game was over the station played soft music. Dacosta finally made his way over to the bed and started playing with her feet. She was laid on her stomach with her feet in the air and he kept tickling them. She tried not to give into laughter but she couldn't help it and screamed out laughing. He tickled her feet even more and faster. She laughed and cried telling him to stop it, but he wouldn't so she cried real tears. Once he saw the tears and he saw them and said okay woman you're mine, now what do you want? She stared through teary eyes, reached out her arms to him and said you. He fell into her arms and they fell into each other long and tenderly. Finally she drew back her head with her hair falling over her face he touched her face moving the hair out of her face. They stared at each other and slowly their lips melted together kissing at first gently but their passion overcame them and they went at it greedily and roughly. They made love on and off touching and foreplaying on one another. She did oral stimulation over and over again on him. La'friska asked, "darling how do you feel?" He said good and relaxed as he played in her hair. She said I love you remember Tuesday night when you asked why did I come over here? Dacosta replied yeah as I recall you said that you were cooking up something extremely superb, as he laughed. She laughed too saying, "No you were the one to say I must be cooking up something good." I only added to the pot saying it was extremely superb." Okay tell me now and please don't lie, Dacosta said. She stared in his eyes and said Dacosta I have never lied to you, simply because I don't want to or do I need too. Baby for what its worth I do love you much too much and I don't ever plan to tell you nothing but the complete truth. Please always believe that. The reason I came

# Thoughts

to Germany is….I'll start with number two. I like to travel especially by airplane. I've always wanted to visit a strange and foreign land. That's why I work so I can enjoy it and Dacosta I wish, hope and pray with every fiber in me that you'll someday soon let me enjoy and share your life with you. Now reason number one is you. You are the reason I came to Germany. Forget about how much I love to travel. You are the main important reason why I am here. I wanted to see and be with you. You don't know how many nights I've cried myself to sleep longing and needing to feel and taste your love. Sweetheart so many times even throughout the day I longed for nobody but y-o-u. It is so hard for you to believe I'm so much in love with you. Please answer me, La'friska cried. He replied, "No, I guess not. You have been telling me this for years and you've show me in so many ways but La'friska, you want too much and I can't give it to you."

La'friska said, "You mean you won't give it to me, sweetheart. You can if you'll only do it. You don't have to want to; just do it for my sake please," she cried. He bolted upright in bed, eyes glaring at her and said, "I knew it; you didn't fool me for not one second. Let's go to sleep woman. Right now I am tired and pluckered out." She laid down resting her head on his shoulder and whispered, "Dacosta." Yes, he replied. She said I can't go to sleep unless you hold me in your arms. He asked, where do you think you are now?" She said close but not close enough and I refuse to budge. He said, "woman and closed his arms around her." She snuggled close whispering in his ear, umm now that feels more like it. Dacosta says, La'friska, woman if you don't go to sleep I'm gonna spank the shit out of you.

"If you're fool enough, then by all means, try," she replied. They stared at each other as neither said a word. She rolled out of his arms onto the other side of the bed. She was close to tears but she didn't cry. She just laid there hurting. She kept thinking I'm with him and he is still hurting me terribly. During the night they were both restless. The bed wasn't comfortable at all and that's why La'friska mostly didn't sleep on it. She slept mostly on the sofa bed which was a little better. In their tossing and turning they wound up in each other's arms again and stayed that way throughout the remainder of the night. Dacosta awoke early morning saying, "I've had it with this bed; its so uncomfortable and hard, and besides, it's hot in here." Later, Dacosta woke up and said, "La'friska I don't want a baby because I'm not ready for that." She said, "You don't have to be ready. Just let me have it. I'll take care of our baby and love it enough for the both of us. You don't have to share any responsibilities. I'll do it all."

He replied, "No, and that's what I mean; no. I don't want no baby, period, maybe even never. I will play with my nieces and nephews and other people's children, but I don't want none of my own, so Friska, get that idea of having my baby out of your head, because I'm not giving you one."

"So is that why you won't make love to me fully, making sure there won't be any baby?" she she asked.

"You are a fast thinking and absolutely correct," he replied.

She cried out, "Oh God Dacosta, what have I ever done to you to make you treat me this way? Sometimes you act like you care and then it's again it the other way around."

Dacosta replied, "You love me too much, and I don't want or need that from you or anyone. You want me to marry you, and I won't do it. I like and want my freedom. I may never get married, and if I do I'll let you know. My old man didn't get married until he was thirty-five."

La'friska said, "The way you said that, 'If I get married I'll let you know,' it sounds like I won't be the one you marry."

Dacosta said, "Listen, I haven't found that someone or anyone yet that I want to marry." La'friska was hurting deeply. She stayed over on the other bed and cried softly with tears rolling down her face slowly. Dacosta didn't even notice; he just kept right on talking, saying, "If that's another reason you came over here, to get married then you are totally wrong. I told you not to expect too much; besides, I didn't want you to come, but you came anyway. I told you I was busy working hard. Why my sister La Tonya wanted to come and I told her I was too busy I had no time to spend with her—." He finally shut up and laid there staring out the window while she was still crying. Much later he got up dressed and said, "I have to get back to the base and wash my clothes."

She said, "Alright," and just laid there.

He asked, "When are you going to eat breakfast?"

She said, "It's probably over by now, so I'll wait until lunch."

He said, "Maybe I'll see you later this afternoon." He was finished dressed and heading for the door. She got up and walked to the door behind him. He kissed her lips and said, "See you later."

She said, "Okay." She went back to bed and laid there hurting from his cruel words and thinking, it looks like I'll never have his baby or marry him. She also thought, I wanted to help him wash his laundry. I don't care if I do see his funky dirty underwear. All I care about is being beside him. For lunch she went downstairs. She went to the hotel manager, explaining she wanted a softdrink. She had been trying for almost a week to get a soda, but each time she tried to explain it to the waiter, he didn't seem to understand what she wanted. She kept saying soda, soft drink, and the waiter would say sparkling water, beer, wine. So now when she said soft drink, soda, the manager called the switch board operator over and the three of them stood there trying to figure things out. She thought, "I want a soda and I'm going to get me one, 'cause I'm not leaving until I make them understand." She tried again, saying, "Something cold to drink, you, know soda soft drink like lemonade, orange or grape soda, Pepsi cola."

The manager said, "Oh Coca-Cola." Well La'friska could have hit herself when all this time all she had to say was Coca-Cola. She told the manager, "Right, Coca-Cola." For lunch, she had two small cokes with her meal because the first one she drank in three gulps and they were small bottles, too. Four o'clock that afternoon she went for a long walk through the park. The sites were beautiful, especially the flowers, in all different colors and categories. As she was touring the park, a white man on a bench kept trying to call her over, making motions with his head and hand, but she kept on the other side, paying him no attention. Later, as she was leaving, she met a white guy from California. His name was Croghan; he had been in Europe on tour with his grandparents for two months now; he explained he had also taken forty rolls of films. Croghan was nice, friendly, attractive-looking, and very talkative. They walked out of the park together and walked opposite the street to the hotel patio. He was deep in a conversation about religion. La'friska thought, this guy has soul; he is very hip and together. They ordered cocktails and sat conversing about the world and life in general. Croghan said tthat after leaving Europe he was stopping in South Carolina, and he asked if he could stop by and say hello. She said, "Okay, sure." To prove neither of them meant it, he didn't ask for her address, and she didn't give it to him. They were just being polite and making conversation. When she departed inside the hotel, she and Croghan found out they both stayed there, but she didn't tell him which floor, and he didn't ask, and besides, she wouldn't have given him the correct room even if he had asked. Shortly after returning to her room from the patio outing with Croghan , there was a knock on the door. She thought it was the maid checking to see if she was in because at night the maid would enter her room when she was in the room and refreshing it tidying things up and La'friska especially loved the part where the maid would have her bedroom slippers on the floor at the bed with a white towel spread on the floor and her slippers on them. The maid didn't speak English but she was friendly always smiling and she did her job well. Anyhow, La'friska thought it was the maid knocking. It wasn't; it was Croghan with a glass of something red in his hand, and he said, "Something cool to quench your thirst," as he handed her the glass. La'friska took it and thanked him. At that, Croghan walked on down the hall wherever he was going. La'friska made sure her door was doubly locked. She thought someone gave him my room number 'cause I know I didn't, but then she remembered I'm black it wouldn't be hard locating her floor and room number. Anyway, Croghan was a perfect gentlemen with her. Still, she wasn't the type to completely trust others, especially in a strange land. So she put the glass in the bathroom on the shelf and thought, it looks so pretty and red—very colorful—and then she poured the drink down the drain. She never saw or heard from Croghan again. Dacosta didn't come to see her that evening or the next two days. During that time she went shopping. She didn't shop that Monday because it was a European holiday, and the stores were closed, but after that day she went shopping each day. She really knew her way around by now. If she went in a store to buy something, she'd say to the clerk, "You speak English," and if they said little bit then she'd say okay then you can help me and she'd tell them what she wanted and keep explaining until they understood. If they spoke in their language's German or French she'd walk out of the store thinking, "No, you can't help me." On Tuesday she watched a parade festival outside the hotel's window ledge. She was getting lonely and depressed. She thought, what's the use and I might as well go back home for good. On this day she had lunch at the Chinese European restaurant. She explained to the chef and waitress that she wanted pepper steak. As she sat waiting for lunch, these two men, one black and the other white, were eating their meal and they asked her to join them. The white one said, "She's prejudiced, she won't do it." La'friska walked over to their table, sat down and said "that's a lie. I'm not prejudiced but when provoked I can be and I am." The white guy said "she's got spunk. I like that and you are beautiful." The black guy agreed saying "yeah on both counts she is." La'friska stared at them and said, "thank you both on your compliments on my looks." As she waited for her lunch they talked. The black guys name was Drew and he was a mess sargeant at the base. The white man's name was Paul and he owned the laundry mat on the base plus he had a chain of laundrymat's. Paul had five adult children. He spoke seven different languages which included German, French, English, Spanish, Italian and Russian. He also made sure that all of his children learned several languages. Paul was 48 years old and had served twenty years of that in the army being transferred and stationed all over the world. La'friska's lunch had arrived and she was enjoying it even though the chef had the two orders mixed together. Her order of pepper steak in big chunks over shrimp egg fried rice it was truly delicious. The two men asked how long had she been in Germany. She told them she had been here a week. They questioned what she was doing alone. She said, "she was vacationing and visiting her boyfriend." When they found out that her boyfriend was in the army on the same base, Drew wanted to know his name but she wouldn't tell Drew. He kept asking but she still wouldn't tell them. Finally Drew said he was going back

## Thoughts

to the base and he would call formation to find out who he was. They laughed and she said, "would you really do that." Yes, Drew responded. She asked him but why because it either way its none of your business and it won't do you any good whatsoever. Drew said I can always try it and find out and see. Drew and Paul were fascinated that she had come that far to see her boyfriend whomever he was. During their conversation La'friska mentioned she believed that she was paying too much money per day for her hotel room. They told her to check out the hotel document on the door of her room or to check out the brochure guide. Paul insisted upon picking up the price tag for their meal plus he ordered and paid for a takeout dish for her to eat later back at the hotel. Paul and Drew chauferred her back to the hotel. Paul's car was a beautiful. It was black, custom built with a computer, telephone, television, stereo and bar model. La'friska was impressed by his car. She'd never seen or ridden in such a beautiful or expensive car. She was fascinated mostly by the locks on the door because Paul controlled them with the master switch located on his driver side. Twice she made the mistake of trying to open the door as she got in and out of the car. Paul and Drew accompanied La'friska to her room to check out the hotel's brochure guide and rate sheet to find out if or not the hotel manager was over charging her more than he should. After carefully reading and studying the information they said no you are not being over charged this is a luxurious hotel and here you have a luxury room that's why the cost is so high, and Drew commented that's the price you pay when living in luxury. Paul added take advantage of it the swimming pools, steam room, sauna's, sun deck's night life partying enjoy it La'friska Tashanti because you are paying for it whether you enjoy it or not. Drew put in "he's right La'friska." She said "yes I know starting right now, I'm going downstairs outside and lounge around enjoying this lovely hot sun." She accompanied them down stairs thanking them for their help and kindness they had shown her. Paul said he had more business to attend, so he'd push off. Drew said I'm on vacation so Miss Tashanti if you don't mind may I sit and talk more with you maybe then I'll find out the name of your boyfriend whom you came all this way to see. La'friska said "correction came to see and be with and yes you can sit out here for a while with me, but I still won't tell you who my boyfriend is." They sat out back on the patio surrounded by other people. Drew told her his wife and three children had recently left Europe for back home setting up living arrangements and in two months he would retire from the army and go home to his family. He showed her snap shots of his family. He also told her ,"you are here in Europe your boyfriend is busy working and me I'm on vacation all this week let me show you more of this country. Cities like Paris, Rome and France it's all around this area." She said "no thank you because I don't want to go with you. I' m sorry I don't mean to be rude or cruel but I don't want or need to be with anyone other than the guy I came to see and be with even though he is busy I'll settle for what I can get from him, but thank you Drew for the offering I appreciate it but still no thanks." Drew said "okay I understand and you are a very straight and forward person." She said "I try to be in that way one can eliminate unnecessary problems, complications or whatever arises." During their conversation Drew took of his dark shades and asked her to put them in her bag so he wouldn't loose them or crack them up. They sat outside talking for a total of three hours and she said "I've been out here long enough and anyway I have pressing matters else where to see about, so thank you kindly for your help and time. It was nice meeting you good luck and good bye." Drew said "same here but can I call to see if or not you might change your mind? " She said I can't stop you from calling but either way it won't do you any good. Upstairs in her room five minutes later there was a knock on the door. She yelled out yes and Drew said "it's me again ." She said yeah what do you want?" Drew said "you have my shades in your bag." She said "okay just a moment and she got the shades opened the door a crack and said "here you are." He said "thank you." She said "you are welcome and good bye," and she closed the door in his face. She could tell Drew didn't want to go but she didn't care. She made real sure the door was locked and bolted. She gingerly bathed and dressed in a beautiful black low-cut jump suit, sprayed herself with lots of perfume, and walked to the base. Barodd was the guard on duty at the gate. He remembered her and said he hadn't seen Dacosta lately, he phoned around trying to locate Dacosta but couldn't find him. La'friska waited around for an hour talking with the guys, they were talkative and friendly asking questions about what was going on back in America. She answered their questions as best as she could. One guy in particular a black guy she didn't bother to know his name because she didn't care for his attitude and remarks. He was arrogant and constantly used profanity he was twice enlisted in the army but now he was banded from the base but he stayed at the gate bull jiving with the guys. He kept stressing how much his clothes especially suits and under ware he had. His wife was white and German with money. This guy also kept needling La'friska as to why she would come all the way from America to see a guy who really didn't care much about being with her even after journeying all that far. When he said that it really struck La'friska. She was deeply hurt and embarrassed, but she didn't let on; instead, she retaliated saying, "In the first place, you are not me, and in the second place, I didn't ask for your opinion or do I need or want it, and besides, what I do or don't do is none of your dam business." The other guys cheered her on and told the guy to lay off her and mind his own business, and he wasn't supposed to be on the base grounds period. These guys from their attitudes and admiring glances liked and respected her. One commented saying, "I wish some girl would come to see me." La'friska asked Barodd for a piece of paper. She then wrote a note saying I'm leaving tomorrow for home just wanted to let you know. She gave the note to Barodd asking him to deliver it to Dacosta. She caught a taxi back to the hotel 'cause it was after nine o'clock p.m. at night. She was hurt by that one guy words because she knew it was true. Dacosta didn't care about her or being with her even after she came all that far. Hearing someone else confirm it was hitting home to close to her heart. She wondered if the whole base knew it and if they were all talking about it behind her back. She recalled earlier that evening another guy mentioned Dacosta must be crazy to keep you waiting like this giving you this kind of cold treatment what a fool he is. I sure as hell wish I was in his shoes. Upon arriving back at the hotel she had the switchboard operator made arrangements for her returning departure back to America. She was confirmed for the next day flight time 2:45 p.m. Later lying in bed restless she leafed through pages, really not interested in the contents because her mind and heart were aching and hurting from Dacosta's inconsideration and lack of caring for her. Ten-thirty in the evening. Dacosta phoned saying he had gotten the note and asked why she was leaving so soon. She said she was tired of being alone and she could have more fun back home instead of staying here and getting the treatment he was giving her. He said I told you before you came I was busy and he told her to wait until later besides she had two weeks left to go. He said sit still and I'll be there tomorrow night okay. When she heard him say those words she was instantly happy and truly delighted. She said okay. Now she couldn't sleep at all 'cause she was to happy and excited thinking I'll see him tomorrow night. She plan the next day event's When morning came she prepared herself making sure she looked her best at all times downstairs whether breakfast, lunch or dinner time. She reminded herself that she had to keep her image and appearances in tact for she was the only black in the hotel that she knew of. Plus the occupants at the hotel looked and watched her so scrutinizingly. La'friska classified the Europeans into three categories especially the women. Some of them were envious and jealous. Others were admiring her youth, attractiveness and sophistication wondering and trying to figure out who she was. Last the others looked at her with such hatred in their faces as if though they wanted her out of their country because she didn't belong plus she was an American invading their country to make matters worse she was black at that. After having a late breakfast she went to the bank cashed travelers checks and went shopping. She brought souvenirs and trinkets for special person's in the family like parents, favorite nieces and nephews. One item in particular struck her fancy a carved wooden gray long tree whistle with two birds on top red and white. She toyed with the whistle blowing it repeatedly checking out its sound it had a sweet loudness melody. She thought of her favorite niece Falaria deciding to give it to her, knowing she'd get a kick out of it. Taking time out for lunch she ate at the Chinese restaurant and while eating she meet a black guy from the base his name was Kirk. He joined her and they talked about where home was and what was happening back in the states. He asked her how she liked Germany and the country of Europe itself. She said she liked it , it was clean and beautiful, that she just loved the scenery and all the beautiful flowers in the assorted colors, sizes and categories. Kirk told La'friska he knew of her because the guys at the base was talking about the chick from America with the great body and exotic brown eyes who traveled all this far to see her man, and he added looking at you now I can see for myself. She asked Kirk to recommend a good brand wine and liquor explaining she promised to bring her brother Junior a bottle of each. Kirk said "I'll do even better than that I'll walk you to the store if you don't mind and personally pick them out." She said, "Alright then I'll be much obliged." Kirk picked out the bottles a red German wine and a Zurich scotch. Kirk brought a white German wine for himself and asked her if she h ad tasted any Zurich or German wine since being there. She said no she hadn't tried the wines, but she did have other drinks. Kirk insisted she try the wine he had brought and she agreed saying okay my hotel is right ahead we can sit out front on the lawn terrace and drink it, and they did. The wine tasted okay to her but she wasn't crazy about white wines especially very sweet ones. Kirk asked "do you mind if I sit and talk with you nothing more, I'm not giving you a line because I know you came to see your boyfriend and just by looking at you and talking with you this past hour I can see you are a nice respectable person and in love with someone else." She replied, "Alright, there's no harm in talking or being friendly and yes I'm very much in love with Dacosta. Also no I don't want or need guys handing me lines because it's not going to do them no good." She and Kirk sat outside for three hours conversing. They talked about their families down home back in the states, their schools and life in general. Kirk told her about his girlfriend Lysander back in the state of Virginia. He said that he loved Lysander a lot and they had been going steady for over three years but he didn't know if or not they'd get married especially any time soon, he wasn't ready for that scene yet. He said they wrote each other a lot and he miss being with her, and that Lysander letters said the exact same things and she was sitting at home waiting for his return. Kirk said "I wish she could afford the money to come over here like you did to see your Dacosta and when I write her again I'm going to mention how you came over here to see your man. What a nice person you are, plus beautiful, and that your boyfriend is the envy of the guys, especially the black

## Thoughts

ones on the base." Kirk said he saw Dacosta around the base but he really didn't personally know much of him." They were in different regiments. Kirk confirmed Dacosta's busyness saying the troops in Dacosta's group worked harder than any other unit. When Kirk confirmed that she felt better remembering Dacosta's words, the army is working the hell out of me. La'friska said "thank you very much for confirming how much Dacosta works because he's told me that several times. I didn't know or really believed him." Kirk said "it's true you can believe that, but in your case I don't and wouldn't care how busy he is or not for that matter. Myself if it was me I make time. He should every free moment he has spend it with you." La'friska said "I believe he doesn't want to be with me to much. I know he doesn't love me, but I do love him very much and I want him so I'll settle for what I can get." Kirk said, "He has to be a complete fool; how can he not love and want you."

She said "I really don't know, but I'm going to keep on until I do have his love and respect; he is supposed to come tonight. I think I'll go in now and start preparing myself."

Kirk said, "Okay, I best be getting on back to the base. I wish you luck tonight and always with Dacosta." and Kirk departed. La'friska had an early dinner and back in her room and she gingerly pampered herself bathing and dressing in a peach colored sleeveless low cut dress. She waited and waited for Dacosta to come, and finally she undressed, changing into a sleeping gown, crying and thinking, he has done it again. Why in heavens name does he keep doing this to me? She was miserable and hurting until she became terribly restless, going from bed to sofa chair bed to setting chairs and stool finally she made a pallet on the floor and laid there staring at the ceiling listening to music on the radio. Some of the songs were familiar, like Marvin Gaye's distant lover. After days of listening to the station in Nuremburg, she was acquainted with some of its musical sounds and lyrics. Later there was a knock on the door she yelled out yes a voice said it's me Dacosta. She took her time unlocking and opening the door. Dacosta came in dressed in black pants and white shirt he was extremely handsome. Her heart was beating just from the nearness of him and seeing his handsome face and gorgeous body was breath taking but because she was so mad at him she didn't let the sight and nearness of him get next to her mind. He sat on top of the table staring and smiling at her and said "what's the matter with you woman?" She replied " what the hell do you think is the matter with me?" I'm sick and tired of waiting here for you to show your ass up and when you do it's late in the night after you've done hanged around bull jiving and pussy footing with whoever you be with and where ever it is you be." He said "so what I'm here now, you know I didn't have to come." She said "yeah I know you didn't have to come and if you are going to take that attitude you about as well take your ass on back where ever you came from." He said "don't get smart with me woman or I'll leave right now." She said "go ahead take your dam ass on get going." Now he was startled and surprised by her out spokeness, he laughed and said "hey the little woman is mad and means business" and he added woman you had better watch your mouth. I don't like no one cursing at me especially women and you baby are no exception." She shot back "you dam right I mean business. Yeah I'm mad darn right mad. I'm tired of your inconsideration to my feelings. As for watching my mouth I'll say any dam fucking thing I want to and baby," pointing her finger in his face she continued saying "there is not a dam thing you can do or say to stop me." Dacosta was still staring at her his eyes and face expressed disbelief, as though he couldn't believe what he was hearing and seeing. He said "boy woman you can be mean and nasty when you want to." She said "correction mean and nasty when the occasion suits my purpose." He said "oh is that what you call it." He glanced over to the table saying I see you went shopping. She said "yes I did, you see Dacosta sweetie I have nothing else to do with my time and money, " note she was smiling as she said time and money. He smiled back and said "I can sure use some of it, give it to me ." She said "no thanks you.ve already gotten enough." She looked at the presents on the table and said "oh by the way I got you something." She gave him the present. He was surprised and kept smiling as he opened it. He took out the bird whistle laughed and blew it a few times, smiled and said "hey I like this." Well she was thunder struck here she was trying to get even with him for making her wait and wait on him enduring his cold treatments and here the gag back fired in her face. She was feeling low and rotten like two cents, for the whistle she had just given to him was the one she'd brought for her niece Falaria. She had wrapped the whistle earlier while waiting for him to come and when he didn't naturally she thought I'll fix him. I'll show him just how much I care by giving him this small cheap present when he does show up, that'll fix him. Now instead the joke was on her 'cause he really loved that whistle. She could tell by the expression on his face and his actions the way he held and kept blowing it. He said "hey Friska are you here with it," stop dreaming woman baby you seem out in space." She said "I'm here but I don't understand you, and I can't believe it , here I give you a cheap gag gift and you seem to absolutely love it." He said "I do" he was still smiling and blowing it. She said but Dacosta I've given you several expensive gifts before and you weren't to overly thrilled about them, but here now you seem to be nuts over this cheap one." He ask "how much did you pay for it?" She said "I don't know I brought it with some more items I purchased but, it couldn't have been much." He said "Friska about your going back you about as well stay you've paid all this money and besides

# Thoughts

you are here now." She replied " that's a nice switch I didn't know you wanted me to remain. Do you want me to stay Dacosta?" He said "if you know how to behave yourself yeah, but if you can't then I'll have to turn you over my knees and show you , maybe then that'll teach you." She said "you'd better start spanking," then she felled over his knees. He was still sitting on the edge of the table. Dacosta laughed and hit her once slightly hard. She jumped up and said," you wouldn't." He said "try me again and see especially after you've cursed and blessed me out." She was standing in front of him and she wrapped her arms gently and tenderly around his neck saying, "I'm sorry but you deserved every last word of it and I don't take any of it back." They stared at each other and gently kissed. He pulled her over to the sofa bed and they kissed and kissed. She was already heated from their earlier fight but now she was getting hotter and hotter blazing on desire. She said, "Dacosta there is something I must tell you." He said "what?" She was ashamed but slowly and softly whispered I have my period." He looked at her and half way blushed. She returned his look and held her head down from the shameness. He said, "okay but can't we still make love?" She was surprised and asked do you want to?" I mean it will be messy besides I never made love with my period on." He said, "yeah it will be messy but , I want to and we can use a towel or sheet then it won't be so bad." She sprang back saying, "how do you know. Tell me just who have you been screwing with her period on?" He said, "I'm not going to answer that now Friska, right now I want you." Well just having him say I want you was enough satisfaction for her. She got the sheet and spread it on over the sofa. Dacosta laid on it and pulled her on top of him. They kissed and carried on with their foreplay. He laid there while she unbuttoned his shirt, opened it back and ran her hand over his chest gently touching the hairs kissing them and coming back up to his sweet lips, they were so delicious. She couldn't seem to get enough of them, she kissed them, bit them, suck them licking and tasting. She forced his mouth opened and went inside and captured his tongue sucking and kissing it. She finished undressing him and then herself. She was the aggressor wild and wanton. Dacosta pulled her back on top of him and entered his penis inside of her. She moaned crying out darling and they began to move together making sweet , oh so delicious love. She went wild doing freaky wonderful way far out things to his body, kissing, licking, sucking and caressing. Dacosta held onto her buttock's tightly as she rode him like a wild stallion. She was something else crazy wild and fiercely ferocious making such sweet beautiful love to him, so full and complete that when she climaxed it was tremendously explosive like thunder and a lion roaring, lightning flashing striking across the sky, a rocket ship rocketing up to the moon, a volcano erupting, bursting into flames, an avalanche breaking up in pieces falling to the ground. Yes her climax was all those things, more and then some it was that powerful. Afterwards she called out Dacosta's name again and again, "Dacosta, Dacosta, oh Dacosta I love you." She went limp on top of him crying loudly. He held her tenderly and close saying, "come on baby take it easy I know it was that good ,but why are you crying did I hurt you?" She kept crying, but shook her head meaning no. He said "talk to me." She cling tightly to him, stopped crying and said, "no darling you didn't hurt me physically, but yeah you hurt me in another way. It was so good and wonderful that it hurt, but it was a good hurt." They stayed locked in each other's arms for a while longer until they remembered her period, but before they remembered it, she whispered into his ears I love you and if I had known fighting with you would produce such a violent and wonderful release I would have done it a long time ago." Dacosta said, "now you know." She said 'yes' and kissed him tenderly. Later alone in bed she recalled the night remembering the violent argument she and Dacosta had and it leaded to them making passionate love. She now had a love hang over, just remembering the way they had made love and afterwards how he held her close and lovingly. Also the way he touched her face turning it ever so gently to look into her eyes. She now trembled from the sweetness of recalling those things. She also recalled memories of the incident when later they were bathing and dressing. She was in the bathroom using wads of cotton as sanitary napkins, because for the past two days she had been trying to buy a box of sanitary napkins but every store she went in the clerk didn't know or understood what she was talking about. She kept saying sanitary napkin, Kotex for your period, but still they didn't understood and she couldn't seem to make them. She thought I have to use something, so I about as well use the cotton. Maybe this is what they use for sanitary pads besides its shape and looks like one. Now while using the cotton Dacosta was in the bedroom, she went a little ashamed, but she said, "Dacosta what do women over here use for sanitary napkins?" He jerked his head up blushing and said, "I don't know I never had that problem before." They looked at each other and burst out laughing outrageously. Now later remembering this she cracked up laughing rolling over the bed, and she thought he can be so sweet and charming at times. Oh God, father in Heaven, I do love him so very much in all fairness much to much for my own good. Please let me have his baby and better yet I want to be his wife. To stand by his side through thin and thickness always wherever he goes forever and ever. Still feeling and cherishing her love hang over, before she went to sleep, drifting off she thought tomorrow I'm going shopping for my Dacosta. I have to get him something nice to compensate for the whistle I gave him. Thinking of the whistle led her to recall her and Dacosta

## Thoughts

at the door kissing good night and he turned the whistle over examining it , smiled and blew it into her face.

She whispered, "You must want to get thrown out of here or better yet get arrested for disturbing the peace. You know the old folks resting and in bed this time of night." Even after locking the door she heard him going down the hall blowing the whistle. She felled a sleep with sweet memories of Dacosta and she awoke the same way only more so with a stronger love hang over. After having breakfast she proceeded shopping. For hours she went from store to store trying to find the right gift for him. She thought of getting him a shirt but changed her mind, thinking if I buy him a shirt he might think that I think he doesn't have any clothes. I can't get him pants because I don't know his size. If I get cologne he may think that I think he stinks. Yes, she worked herself into a turmoil. Finally she stopped at the jewelry shop which the first store she entered the first day she came to town. For an hour she stayed in the store checking out watches, cuff links, tie clips etc. Suddenly a thought hit home, she thought Dacosta is never on time even if he isn't standing me up. He needs to tell time and what better present to give him than a watch, maybe then he'll be on time. She now only checked out watches trying to figure out which one he would like. She had a hassle of a hard time and finally decided on a foreign wide gold watch trimmed in black and gold with three time zones and names of popular cities like New York, Chicago, Miami, San Francisco, France, Italy, Germany and Switzerland engraved on it. She asked the sales lady, May I bring it back if he doesn't like it?" The sales lady said," yes you may." La'friska said "what if he really doesn't like it at all, do I get my money back?" The lady said, "yes again you do and we aim to please every customer." La'friska paid $395.00 for the watch plus at the last minute she told the sales lady, I won't exchange it so please engrave it with his name on the inside of the band Dacosta Gahenne love forever L. T." The sales lady was just as delighted with La'friska's purchase as La'friska herself was. La'friska was pleased with herself on finding the perfect gift. It was Thursday and after having a leisurely dinner La'friska entered the bar and lounged there drinking exotic Pina Coladas. The next morning after having breakfast she was in her room preparing eventually to go shopping again, but she wasn't in a hurry, slowly taking her time. Suddenly there was a knock on the door; she said "yes who is it?" The voice said "Dacosta." She let him in and said "what a nice surprise and so early in the morning." He said "yeah, well I took the day off." She was so delighted and said "perfect timing I was preparing to go out shortly." He said "where?" She said "to the bank and then browsing around shopping to my fancy." He said "it must be nice having nothing to do and money to blow." She said "sometimes it is then again it's not so hot, to me it depends on the situation and the individual I want to spend it on and in my case it's you sweet heart," and she kissed him saying "good morning." He said "okay later but right now we going to shake the sheets." She said "what's shake the sheets mean?" He said "woman I thought you were smart, it means make out screw the F word." She blushed saying "I've never heard that phrase before. I know others like let's get it on, give me some, or give me a piece and oh yeah the cat's name remember pussy. When a guy say to a girl give me some pussy." Dacosta laughed real loud saying "yeah." Then he looked seriously at her and said "woman back in the States who are you giving my pussy to, 'cause you are my woman?" She said "since when you decided I'm your woman? You could have fooled me by your actions." He said "the way you did it to me the other night, you were very wild." She said "Dacosta you have some nerve asking questions like who I'm screwing, when for years all I want is you." He said "I don't be with you or around, you could tell me anything. I don't know that." She said "you should realize and know by now how much I love you. My God man after all these years chasing endlessly after you. How am I ever going to convince you?" That in itself should tell you the facts, besides Dacosta for your information and unconcern even if or not I had sex with someone else it's your dam fault. I get horny and need love." He said "my fault how the Hell is that?" She said "Dacosta are you trying to start a fight like the other night because sweet heart I don't want to fight. I want to love and be with you." He said "no I didn't come here to fight. I took the day off to spend time with you." She walked over to him sitting on the desk and she put her arms around his neck and looked into his eyes said," thank you very much and I love you," and she kissed him sweet and tenderly. He pulled her closer into him as she stood between his legs. They kissed affectionately for a long while until she said, "oh no my period remember," and she was embarrassed hiding her face in his chest. He held her tenderly saying "yeah." She eventually raised her face staring into his and said "I went shopping yesterday just for you." He smiled saying, "oh yeah, what did you get me?" She reached behind him and handed him the gift. He continued holding his arms around her as he opened the flip top lid on the box. When he saw it his face lit up and he flashed a big beautiful smile saying, "woman how much did you spend?" She said, "Darling it's the thought that counts." He replied, "Thank you, it's nice and looks expensive." "You're never on time; now maybe you can be." she replied. I thought this was the perfect gift for you, she stated. He laughed saying, "Am I that bad?" She replied, "Yes, you are." Later they walked to the base and they chattered constantly, La'friska thought this feels so good and right. I want to be by his side forever. Dacosta turned to her and said, "La'friska I need some money for my stereo equipment set. Please give me $800.00 dollars. I need it bad. I can get it over here way cheaper than back in the states. She said give you $800.00 and what do I get out of the deal? He replied, "Baby you have me what more do you want?" She said you know what I want but you not willing to accept the offer. I want to be your wife and have your baby. Your only baby, yours and mine. Dacosta replied, "Woman that is too much for me to give just yet." They got off of the money topic and talked about other topics. She asked, "How is your bird whistle?"

"It's in my room," he replied and burst out laughing. She didn't know what was going on and stared at him. He asked, "It's was so funny how last night after the lights were out and every one was in bed I quietly went and opened the door and loudly blew my whistle. Well you should have seen the guys jumping out of bed and grabbing their clothes to put on. They thought the sergeant was calling assembly. She burst how laughing and said, "yeah go on what happened?" Dacosta said, "I turned the lights on and all eyes focused on me with the whistle in my mouth. I blew it again several times and that did it. The guys realized it had been me pretending assembly and they came after me like a coyote chasing a wolf. They both burst out laughing. La'friska said Dacosta sometimes you say the funniest things. One of these days you are really going to crack me up completely. He laughed and said, "Friska, you're not so bad yourself, always saying funny things." On the base while waiting on line to cash the traveler's checks, Dacosta asked her to give him the money for the stereo. She didn't tell him yes or no. She just kept him in suspense knowing that full well in her mind and heart she'd give him anything he desired. On the base and during the way back they met several of Dacosta's army acquaintances. He introduced her to them. When they passed by the Chinese restaurant on the opposite side of the street, they saw a small child about three years old was outside alone and he yelled out waving his hand.

At this time they were in the middle of conversation but when the child said "hi" and waved his hands, Dacosta yelled "hi" and lowered his voice saying "you little jap." Meanwhile he continued on talking to La'friska. She burst out laughing at him and his remarks, "You little Jap." She asked, "How do you know he's a Jap?, Dacosta said I don't know but he looks like one. They both laughed. She said, "Ooh that's not nice he is only a baby and he was so sweet." She said, "Dacosta, I told you, you would make a wonderful father." He replied, "Yeah well maybe someday but not anytime soon." She watched Dacosta lovingly and thought that was so sweet and very touching the way you said hi to the little boy. If only you'd let me have your baby. I would be the happiest person alive and better yet if I had you along with your child I would certainly be the happiest person in the world. They walked and talked along the streets stopping now and there checking out and buying whatever items caught her fancy. Hours later returning back to the hotel she realized how much she brought. Perfumes for herself and her mother. Cigars for her father and other souvenirs for other members of the family. Dacosta said, "You didn't buy me anything today." She said, "I did yesterday remember the watch on your arm." He replied, "oh yeah, but today I need a stereo set. I've been asking all day now woman now let's have it. I need an answer. La'friska said again, "Dacosta, what's in it for me? What do I get?" He answered, "La'friska I know what you want but I'm telling you again that I'm not ready for that scene so there has to be another way." If you won't give me the money then loan it to me, he asked. I'll pay you back. I'll take out an allotment in your name. I promise I'll have them mail it to you each month until it's paid off. Please I need it. I know I say this to your every time but this time is a bargain. I'll be missing out on a good thing if I don't jump on this deal now. I can't let this one slip pass me. Won't you help me like you always do?" She stared at him thinking I should continue keeping you in suspense making up for those hurtful, awful years you kept me waiting. She said, "Dacosta you made me wait five years and three months to first kiss you. Now why should I hurry in a matter of hours rush to give you more money. I gave you the watch to make up for the cheap whistle plus mainly because I love you. You are my love." She told him if you don't really want the watch, I'll give it to my father. Oh but wait I can't, your name is engraved on it. Dacosta said, "No other man is getting my watch, including your father. Besides I know you love me enough to give me this money." She replied, "God help me I do." Dacosta reached out and grabbed her tightly in his arms. She held on for dear life thinking this is where I belong and need to be forever. Dacosta said, "woman what am I gonna do with you? Your love is too strong and too much until I don't know what to do. You see I've never had a love so strong for me as the one you have for me and I do know how lucky I am to have someone like you, but Friska woman I'm not good for you simply because I don't love you any girl for that matter. You need a man who'll give you the baby you so badly desire. Someone you'll love you in return. I like you a lot though."

She said, "But I don't want anyone but you. I love only you. Do you have any idea how it feels to want one particular person and you can't get them. There are others who want you but you don't want to be bothered with them."

"Is it that bad," he asked.

She replied, "Yes it definitely it is." They stood holding each other. She was so overcome with love for him that she began to tremble. He noticed and asked her what the matter was. She answered, "My body's desiring your loving touch and I want to love you and yes you can have the money."

## Thoughts

Dacosta said, "Thanks babe and I do like you a lot." Upon saying those words he pulled her to the bed. She lay on the bed and reached out her arms to him. He went into them and there they lay kissing, touching and gently caressing each other. Time is moving by, La'friska said to Dacosta. I love being over here with you, she said. He replied, "I know you do." She said, "You're making me feel so good that I want to cry." He said, "Don't I'm here with you now and this is no dream." She stared into his eyes and said Dacosta I love you. He didn't verbally reply instead he kissed her until she whimpered with desire. He made sweet affectionate love to her. She was floating on the clouds of joy full with ecstasy. Afterwards, they remained cuddled in each other's arms. He asked her, how'd she like it over here? She replied, "I love it here. This country is so clean and beautiful, but I must admit some of the people lack a lot to acquire in their attitudes. I classified the Europeans attitudes the same way I told you and Barodd about my second day here. Plus I told this guy Kirk the same thing the other day but I'll tell you about Kirk later." He interrupted her saying, "Kirk who, no later tell me now." She said, "Okay, Kirk is a black guy on the base, as a matter of fact he says that he knows of you." I met him Tuesday when I had lunch at the Chinese restaurant. We ate our meals together and talked." She gave Dacosta all of the details of her conversation and walk back to the hotel with Kirk. He was the perfect gentleman and even wished me luck with you, my Dacosta, she said. She said, "besides, Dacosta don't you trust me?" He said, "Yeah I do, but you have to be careful over here. These guys don't see many black women and even the ones they see or married or spoken for. In your case you are beautiful, came from America and are vacationing." She replied, "All of the guys except one that I have talked to one over here have been perfect gentleman. They haven't gotten fresh or said anything out of the way. The only guy that used vulgar language words around me was this black guy. I don't know his name. He was at the guard shack on the base Tuesday night when I went looking for you. Anyway, this guy was thrown out of the army and is banned from being on the base. He's married to a white German girl with money." Dacosta cut in adding, "Yeah I know of this guy. They call him Pyrites or something like it." That guy doesn't work and he doesn't have too. His wife takes care of him because she has money. They tried to throw him out of Germany but so far they haven't been successful. He asked, "La'friska, what did this guy say to you?" She explained how the guy kept using obscenities in his conversation with the guys and bragging about his clothes and underwear. She said as for what he said to me, he asked me why would I come all the way from America to see a guy that really didn't care about being with me?" As La'friska repeated those words she looked sad and Dacosta picked up on it. She added, "I didn't like the way he looked at me." Dacosta asked her what kind of look? She said, "As if he was interested in me."

Dacosta said, "That does it La'friska, stay off the base unless I'm with you. Do you hear me, woman?" She replied, "Yes I hear you but why are you acting upset?" Dacosta was now smoking a cigarette saying, "I don't want you anywhere near this guy because he is woman chaser and he had no damn business saying that to you." What's between us is none of his concern, Dacosta replied. She said what others may or may not say about us doesn't matter to me. I don't concern myself with their views or opinions but I know Pyrites words and some of them were true, you do treat me that way. He explained, "You make it sound like I don't care about you at all and that I treat you so terribly. That I don't come to see you at all. Well what do you call this woman, I am here now," he said.

She said, "Yes you are here now but sometimes you could be here more if you wanted to instead of hanging around with the guys." He replied, "I do need time for myself. I told you many times I'm not ready for a heavy scene. I'm not in love with anyone." She became saddened by his words. He said I don't mean to hurt you feeling but let's chill for now. She replied, "Okay no heavy scene or rap." She made out the travelers checks for him as she was preparing them Dacosta picked up her pack of checks and ask how much money did she bring over here? She replied, "A couple of thousand." He asked, "how much and stop stalling and tell me the truth." She responded, "why should I, it's personal." He stated, "These are words from a woman who claims undying love for years." She stared at him and answered, "Four thousand dollars, now are you happy?"

He answered, "Yes." He said, "That's a lot of money," and he tore off two one-hundred-dollar checks, saying, "Please, didn't I take the day off for you."

She said, "Dacosta don't press your luck by taking advantage of my love for you." She started saying one of these days, as he kissed her lips shutting her up saying thank you again. Dacosta told her that he would like to stay there with her and cuddle with, her, "But now with these checks I need to get back to the base cashing them and then off to Nuremberg to see about the stereo. I'll see you later tonight." Dacosta left and she stayed in her room sorting through her purchases and thinking I must be a fool to give him a thousand dollars. Why fool myself. He can get anything I have and what's more, he knows it. She went downstairs to dinner and lounged outside on the patio for a while, but other loving couples reminded her of missing Dacosta, therefore she returned to the room. She waited all night for Dacosta to return but he didn't, and she really didn't expect him to because for now he'd gotten what he wanted—the money and sex. He phoned after 12:00 a.m. saying he was just getting back to the base 'cause he missed the other bus and had

## Thoughts

to wait. That it was now late and she and he knew the hotel manager wouldn't let him up. So he'd see her tomorrow, which as he put is later today. She said, "I haven't much choice in the matter but kiss me good night so I can go to sleep." He said "Okay," and kissed the phone, saying, "Girl, that was sweet."

She said, "Yeah, right," and she thought he's lying and bull jiving. Hours later as she was relaxing having breakfast out on the patio, a meal of potatoes, bacon, and eggs, she could never get her eggs completely well done, therefore she learned to eat eggs somewhat soft. She also had assorted buns and pastries with jams and jellies. She thought, "This is the life what living is all about. I wish Dacosta was here with me; it could be a honeymoon. Plus us touring Europe together." Back in her room she was getting bored, she tried listening to the radio but the music wasn't that good, she was tired of reading. So finally she opened the window and sat leaning out the ledge watching the sights of people passing by on foot or in cars. Hours later there was a knock on the door. She thought it was in her dream for she was napping. Realizing the knock was real, she yelled out "Yes."

Dacosta said, "Woman, let me in." She got up and let him in he stared at her in her undies and said, "I hope you don't open the door dressed like this for everyone." She realized how she was dress and said, "I was napping. I thought the knock was in my dream."

He said "No shopping today."

She said, "No, maybe that's why I became bored." He said "get dressed and you can treat me to dinner."

She said, "Let's have room service."

He said, "Okay, let's." She phoned down their dinner orders along with a bottle of German red wine. She dressed in a green gown and peignoir set, combed her hair, but stayed bare footed. He laughed saying "Friska, no shoes."

She said, "No, I want to feel free; or better yet, bare feet and pregnant," and she rolled her eyes at him and laughed when he stared at her. She said "Don't worry, I'm not getting mushy." He said, "Thank you." Eventually their dinner came, the waiter set up their table to her liking, and Dacosta tipped him a few dollars. The waiter left saying "bon jour and good nam." As they dined on steak with peas, mushrooms gravy and potatoes, rolls with butter and drank the wine, they talked and listened to the radio music. Dacosta asked "can you understand the language any better?" She said "yes, for instant I know good nam means good evening or good morning it depends on the time of day." He said "that's good, true." She continued beta is German meaning thank you. Vos es los in German means what's happening. She said I know that one vos es los for years 'cause my eleventh grade History teacher Mr. Plessis taught us that one. You remember Mr. Plessis? Dacosta said, "Yeah, I was in his homeroom class for three weeks before I went back to the white school. Remember I told you about cutting the white boy." She said, "Yes, I remember; there is no way I'll ever forget those years in high school." She thought to herself, I'll never forget what you and those girls did to me and put me through, especially you and Kim Fluntly. Even now I have night mares about you and Kim together. "Anyhow, back to the language, it's interesting, and I like to hear them speak it." She raised her wine glass to Dacosta's and said "bon jour." He smiled and said "bon jour and vos es los." They both smiled and resumed their conversing. She said "back to the language, I know most people speak German or French. I also know the words auf weidersehen means hope we meet again." Dacosta said "that's good, why even I didn't know that one and I've been here for months." He then tried pronouncing auf wei and he paused. She said "watch my lips wei der se hen." He said "okay I got it, auf weidersehen." She said "yes you have it, au revoir which means good bye in this case you're not leaving. You just got here and besides if I have to tie you up to keep you here I will." Dacosta smiled and laughed saying "wild woman plus kinky." She said, "Tell me about the stereo set; did you buy it?" He said "yeah I was going to tell you when I first got here but when I walked through the door and saw you naked I got side track and then we went onto other topics." He continued saying "I spent the whole thousand. I got a good quality brand and I'm having it shipped home to the States. So when I leave here in a couple of months I won't have to worry about shipping arrangements. I talked turkey to the man plus I told him I'm in the army and I showed him my dog tags and identification card so he gave me a break." La'friska said "the set sounds like a good deal with a bargain." Dacosta was fumbling with the silverware and asked "How do you know which one to use; there are so many."

She laughed and said, "I know what you mean; in fact, too many. I don't exactly know myself. I just make it look good. Besides I don't eat all the different courses, like the soup, there's a soup spoon, salad fork, appetizer fork, main course which is meat and vegetables, there is the knife and fork for that and then the desert spoon or fork." She added, "They eat so extravagant and dainty. Me, I only need a knife, spoon and fork, those three I know how to use." He said "you're funny you say funny stuff." She said "I just speak the truth I don't try or set out to be funny, it's naturally me." He said "I know but still you're funny sometimes." She asked "Dacosta did I tell you I meet your mess sergeant?" He said "no you didn't when?" She said "the other day earlier in the week Tuesday, I think. I had lunch at the Chinese restaurant and he was there with a white man name Paul who just happens to own the laundry mat on the base. She told Dacosta the encounter with Drew and Paul. She didn't hide anything, for she didn't need to lie. For her love

# Thoughts

need and want for him was that true, strong and real. She asked "did your mess sergeant find out who you are, 'cause he said that he was going back to the base and call formation." Dacosta laugh and said I don't know and we didn't have no unusual assembly. He add you're sure getting around meeting people, here I thought you were here waiting patiently for me, now I find out otherwise." She said "I can't stay cooped up in this room all the time. I need air plus food to eat." He said "what's wrong with downstairs food besides you're paying for these meals whether you eat them or not." She said "I want to try other foods." Dacosta said "I keep telling you to be careful over here these guys don't see many black women." She said "I'm careful Dacosta but there isn't too much harm in making conversation, is there?" Besides I'm not as trusting with people as you might think plus remember I now live in the New York, New Jersey fast track area. She added I told you about Drew's family recently departure back home, he has a wife." La'friska also added, "I shouldn't tell you this, but Drew invited to show me the area Paris and Rome. Of course I said no because I only want to be with you." Dacosta stared at her and said "What a good offer; some people would have jumped on it." La'friska stared back at him with sadness in her eyes and asked, "Will you ever believe I only need and want you?"

    Dacosta said, "Come here woman, I want my dessert now." He kissed her long and hard, she whimpered, moaning and groaning against him saying" oh I like it more, give me more, much more." They made love and spent the next few hours lying in bed listening to the radio music coming out of Nurnberg. Each in there own mind's world as they lay spent from their desire. They eventually drifted off to sleep in each other's arms. La'friska awoke many times and stared at him lovingly, longing to arouse him with a kiss, but she thought no I won't, because he'll be yelling at me for messing with him. She drifted back off to sleep with a smile on her face from the feel of his arms around her. Later she awoke with him touching her breast. She opened her eyes and looked into his brown eyes. Her breasts were aching to be sucked, and she pulled his head down to them and she whispered into his ears, "Please sweetheart, suck me." He saw the need and desire in her eyes and body and he reciprocated giving her the release her body so very desperately needed and craved. She whimpered over and over "Oh I love you Dacosta please don't you ever stop, I need you." He suckled her breasts so long and hard as she moaned and groan moving her virginal against his penis that she had an orgasm without him even entering her vagina. The sucking of her breasts was that powerful and good. She cried wet tears falling onto his head and shoulders as he held her tightly until her tears subsided. He said "Woman, are you trying to kill me? That was a lot of hard work; you have two of them. I couldn't suck both the same time."

She touched his lips, shushing him so she could kiss him. She held his face between her hands and she kissed and kissed it all over, devouring his lips and tongue. She said, "While you were sleeping, I wanted to do that so badly. She reached out and stroked his hard erected penis. He moaned and said, "Do it baby don't stop, more, harder," and she obliged. He rolled her over on top of him and he entered her body. She went limped on him and he cried out no baby please don't stop, move. She said "I won't stop I just want to feel you inside of me, you feel so good." And she tightened her virginal muscles around his penis. He moaned because it was that good. She said "I promise you not one drop of your love will be wasted because darling I want it all and then she rode his body like a wild unbroken stallion. He stroked her hips, smacked and hit them as she rode him galloping all over the wide open plateau. Afterwards he said "keep this up and who knows I might start loving you after all. She said "it's your lust you're feeling. I wish, hope and pray you'll love me .You once said you did, remember." Thinking of this she said, "Come to think of it, the day in question, you've made my life either a living hell or a joyous event since that day years ago." The day was now Sunday and they spent the day in her room listening to the radio, sleeping late and making love. That evening Dacosta returned to the base saying "I'll see you Tuesday night until then I'll be busy practicing for a parade, the parade is Tuesday afternoon. Through the next days, La'friska sometimes remained in her room, went shopping or sightseeing. She loved how clean and beautiful the landscapes were. The streets were so clean that you could eat off them, in her opinion. Also she thought the flowers are so bright, colorful and well maintained, that if some tourist abused them they'd probably be in big trouble. Tuesday night came and Dacosta was now with her. When she saw him she felled into his arms saying "it's been the longest two days. I'm glad to see you." He said "You act like you miss me. What will you do when you return to the States if this is how you act now?" She became sad looking from his words but then she said, "Right now you are here with me, so until that time, I refuse to think otherwise." He said, "What have you been doing?" She said, "Nothing specific, just relaxing reading listening to music, shopping, and sightseeing." He asked, "What else did you buy?" She pointed to the items on the table. He said "Friska, don't buy too much, because you have to declare it by making out a list of what you brought, and when you go through customs, they might want to know where you got it and also to see the receipt. They may want to know how you can afford them; plus, a trip over here is expensive." She asked, "How was the parade?" He said, "I just participated under orders of course, but otherwise things were cool." He stayed over two hours and they didn't make love; she wanted to, but Dacosta seemed tired, so she left well enough alone. He left back for the base; at least that's

## Thoughts

what he told her. Late Friday night, Dacosta phoned and said, "I'll see you tomorrow night." When he did, La'friska was restless and upset with him, because as usual he was late. When she saw him, she said, "Well, well, look who's here, the prodigal son himself finally returns." Dacosta smiled and laughed, saying, "Yeah it's me in person, I'm at your beck and call, please have mercy on poor exhausted Dacosta," and he flashed a big smile at her.

She stared and said "Very melodramatic , but if you think for a fleeting second that's going to get you over, baby, you are sadly mistaken." He said, "A guy can try, can't I?" He grabbed her and said, "Woman, what have you been doing all this time by yourself, I do hope?" As he talked holding onto her, she was staring in his face with a devilish smile on her face. When he noticed her devilish smiling, he said "You had better been by yourself, or else." She finished for him saying, "Or else what, go tell me what you going to do." He said, "Tan your back side." She said, "Oh, is that all, I'm so disappointed; I thought it was more the way you came on so strong." She said, "Honest, Dacosta, sometimes you give me hope that you care for me; then again, I don't know. You've got me living in confusion. Just a minute ago you acted like you'd ring my neck or something." He said, "Yeah, that too. Now what man you meet since I last saw you?" She kidded with him saying, "Gee, I don't and can't remember all their names; there was Tom, Dick, Harry, and etcetera." She laughed, seeing his puzzled stare. He said, "Come here, woman," and he roughly pulled her over, saying, "If you don't stop lying to me, I'm going to smack you one on the lips." She smiled, saying, "Alright, a kiss, I could go for that," and she wrapped her arms tightly around him saying, "kiss me," and he obliged. Later, they walked to the base and cashed checks so she'd have money to change into foreign marks to pay when she checked out of the hotel on Monday. Dacosta said, "Are you looking forward to going back home?"

She said "No, you should know I don't want to leave you. I always want to be where you are. I don't and wouldn't care if it was Alaska or the seven seas just as long as we were there together. Just say the word and I'll stay."

Dacosta said, "I can't, and besides, what about your job, apartment, and whatnot. How will you get along?"

She said "I'll think of something, but I'll survive."

He said, "No you can't do that; I won't let you. You can't stay. In a few months I'll be back in the States and we'll take it from there and see what happens." They spent Saturday night through Sunday afternoon together. During that time, even though La'friska was where she wanted to be, with Dacosta, she was still sad because she knew that within a matter of hours she'd be leaving the country and the guy behind who she truly loved, wanted, and so desperately needed. Dacosta noticed how quite and sad looking she was. He said "Don't do that to yourself; nothing lasts forever." At those moments she would throw herself into his arms and cling ever so gently and tightly holding on to him. He'd say, "What am I suppose to do with you, woman?" She'd answer "just keep on holding me in your arms. Many times tears rolled out of her eyes but she didn't let him see it because she knew he didn't like her crying. Dacosta told her that he was going to get one of his buddies name Jamie Mendon to accompany them to the airport in Frankfurt because Jamie knew the way pretty well plus Jamie could help with carrying the luggage. Dacosta said "I also thought about us spending the night in Frankfurt but then where would Jamie sleep, certainly not in the room with us. Also Seth is stationed there; I thought maybe I'd stop there to and see him." She said "I didn't know Seth was even in the army."

Dacosta said, "Yeah he is, I thought that you knew."

She said "No I didn't, how could I have, I only saw him sometimes when I was with you. As for where Jamie would sleep I don't care let's go to Frankfurt, I think that's a wonderful idea." Dacosta said "No that would be rude let's just leave matters as they stand. Now come here woman and make love to me 'cause this is it for quite a while." La'friska moaned and felled into his out stretched arms. They held each other tightly kissing and exploring one another's body. She cried out "Dacosta please don't ever stop, if you do I think I'll kill you." He said "if you do then woman I won't ever be around to make love to you and also you'd be in jail for killing me." They both laughed and she said "in that case I think we'd better keep on doing what we're doing." As they made love La'friska was very wild and floating through the heavens. Dacosta was feeling the needs too; he was horny and tender and loving with her. He made sweet love to her, but still he wouldn't let himself ejaculate, because he knew how much she wanted his child. La'friska, on the other hand, was still wild but taking it slowly, cherishing it, trying to store up enough for the long separation when she wouldn't be getting any, so she was storing up for future purposes. All too soon from her standpoint Dacosta said, "Woman you should have enough to last you for a while; I'm tired now."

She said, "But I'm not finished yet; I want more."

He said, "I didn't tell you to hold yourself back; you shouldn't have done that, now woman stop being greedy." La'friska knew from his attitude it was no use in trying to seduce him back into bed—that he'd only yell at her and hurt her feelings as usual. She thought this is it for this time; she was heartbroken and so very sad that she hardly slept. Throughout the night she was very restless tossing and turning. Early morning she got up and finished packing her luggage. Thinking this is it. I'm really going to be on my way. After bathing and dressing she went down-

## Thoughts

stairs alone because Dacosta had left earlier. She returned to her room and throughout the remaining hours she stayed there, feeling alone sad miserable and hurting for the guy she loved and was about to leave behind. The hours passed by and Dacosta and Jamie arrived. Jamie was friendly, talkative and handsome looking. While La'friska was putting the final touches on things, Dacosta and Jamie drank the left over bottle of wine. Finally she was all prepared and Dacosta said to her "are you ready?" She looked at him sadly and nodded her head meaning yes. As she looked around to see if or not she had forgotten anything Dacosta and Jamie had her luggage ready to walk out the door. La'friska looked back one more last time knowing this was it good bye. As she walked out the door closing it behind her, she was sad and hurting. Downstairs, Dacosta took the money from her and paid the hotel manager. The hotel bill was twelve hundred American dollars, but was paid in foreign marks. They took a taxi to the train station. Dacosta purchased the train tickets and La'friska gave him all the left over foreign money she had saying "here from here on out it won't do me any good." Dacosta took it and said "thank you I sure need this." They had to wait fifteen minutes for the train and at last they boarded it, and were on their way. Jamie sat on the opposite side of their isle. They talked until later they changed for their next train. This time Jamie had to sit in another car because their car was filled up. She and Dacosta were now alone in a car compartment all by themselves. She was glad because she wanted to be alone with him. She said "are you going to miss me?" He replied "I got along without you before you came, didn't I?" She was hurt by his choice of words and she said "I guess so, but still you didn't have to be so heartless. She asked, "Will you think about me at all?" He said, "Sure, I'll think about you some, but I won't think about you too much. I won't let myself get strung out on you."

She said, "You haven't kissed me yet."

He said, "We haven't been by ourselves either." He then briefly kissed her lips. She clung, kissing him back, but he pulled away, saying, "We're in public."

She said, "I don't care if we are, my mother could be watching and I wouldn't care." They sat talking looking out the windows watching the country side. The mountains looked like they were touching the sky they were so tall. Later Jamie came up and said, "This is the last stop." Dacosta said "Friska why didn't you tell me?" La'friska looked out the windows saying "I wasn't sure, I thought it looked familiar." Dacosta said "this is the route you came you should know." La'friska stared at him getting hot herself and replied "how am I suppose too know everything. I only came this route once and it wasn't backward at that, besides I don't live over here. I'm going home remember."They took the subway to the airport. There they checked her and her luggage in. They had a long wait of two hours so they decided to have dinner in the restaurant. La'friska had a cold ham platter and Dacosta had a jumbo steak with French fries with the works. When both La'friska and Jamie saw Dacosta's plate they both agreed that they wished they would have known his plate would look like that because then they would have ordered the same thing. Dacosta laughed at them as he enjoyed his food. Jamie had a turkey sandwich with vegetables and fruit. Afterwards, they toured the terminal sightseeing. Later they sat down waiting the remainder of the wait out. During this time she wanted to tell Dacosta how much she'd miss him and more but Jamie was around. She didn't want Dacosta to start yelling at her and getting loud on her especially in public. So she kept her feelings and thoughts to herself. Although at one point as they talked Dacosta commented, "I know you are hinting about marriage and a baby and La'friska the answer is still no. I've told you this so many times so I don't know why you keep harping on it?" She was terribly hurt by his words and she knew that Jamie heard him. So for the remainder of the wait she kept away from the topics of children and marriage.

Finally her flight time was announced and they walked her to customs in the corridor. As they were walking Dacosta said to her, "well you can say that you did something that no one in your family has done. You came all the way over here." La'friska took that as a compliment. When they got to the corridor that was as far as Dacosta and Jamie was allowed. La'friska thanked Jamie for coming and helping with her luggage. She told him it was a pleasure to meet him and shook his hand saying God Bless and goodbye. She and Dacosta turned to each other kissed and said goodbye. She had to hold back the tears as they kissed. They both stared at each other, smiled, and said goodbye. When La'friska walked away she didn't look back. She wanted too but she wouldn't. It was a long corridor and she walked gracefully, full of pride and poise. She felt and hoped Dacosta and Jamie were watching her. Seated on the plane she sat by the window. It was almost an hour before her plane took off. She wondered if Dacosta and Jamie had left the terminal. She also thought of racing off the plane and going back to Dacosta. As the plane finally took off she thought of telling the pilot to turn around and take her back. During the flight she kept her head turned towards the window staring out into space. Plus she was crying and didn't want anyone to notice. All throughout the seven hour flight she cried. She even paid to see the movie playing during the flight but couldn't concentrate because she was crying. She cried herself to sleep. Her flight arrived in the morning hours. When she went through customs she realized what Dacosta meant about buying gifts. The customs agent went all through her luggage, cleaned and dirty. He made her mad asking her, "Where did you go? Who do you know over there? How long did you stay? Why did you go?" She an-

# Thoughts

swered his questions in no uncertain terms letting him know by her attitude that it wasn't any of his damned business. She felt that he was really overstepping his boundaries when he asked her why she went. She felt it wasn't any of his business who she saw and why she went. When the customs agent spotted her watch he immediately asked, "Did you buy that over there?"

She replied, "Yes, I did." The agent asked her did she have a receipt. She got mad and said no I don't and I have no idea that I had to keep a receipt just to please you. The agent became thunderstruck and told her she could go now. She took a taxi all the way from Kennedy airport in New York to New Jersey. Once home she walked and moved around in a daze. She was so lovesick that her heart hurt for Dacosta. During the remainder of the week she stayed home and she mailed the gifts and trinkets to the members of her family. The following week she returned to work. With Christmas on the way she learned Dacosta was back in the states but still in the army stationed in North Carolina. She cried and deeply hurt when she heard that from his brother. She thought he couldn't even phone me and let me know. He knows how much I love him. He hasn't paid even one cent of the thousand dollars I loaned him. I should have known he was lying when he pretended he'd take out an allotment in my name to repay the money back. She thought, "what a fool I was, naïve and blinded by love and dumb that I couldn't see him again lying to me just to get what he wanted." Christmas time arrived and La'friska went home. She was glad to be with her family. Dacosta came and took her out once. She was angry at him but when she saw him her anger quickly diminished. She said, "my heavens Dacosta, you could have let me know that you were out of the service instead I had to find out from others." He told her that he wasn't completely out yet but he would be in one month and a half. "Besides Friska, who told you anyway," he asked. She replied, "it doesn't matter who told me. What's important is that you didn't bother to tell me. After all the love and concern for your health and safety. You know I'm interested in your welfare. After all I do love and care for you very much." To answer your question regarding who told me just know that I have ways of finding out things, especially about you as she gave him a venomous.

They went to hang out and stayed outside in the car with Dacosta talking to mostly everybody as they passed by especially his cousins. Later they went to a motel. Of course La'friska was high off of love for Dacosta especially after months of not seeing or making love to him. Tonight when they made love was no different from the others. Naturally she couldn't believe they were really absorbed in making love. She had waited so long and needed it so much. She enjoyed their love making but not as much as she wanted too and could have if only Dacosta had given her more foreplay and they made love longer. But of course, he didn't and therefore she didn't climax. But she still loved and treasured every ounce and second of it. Kissing his lips that were so soft in fact too soft and so sweet and delicious that she always went out of her head floating through space and time circling the clouds. Nothing else mattered but her love for him. Even though she realized and truly knew that he didn't love her. She would just settle for what little he did give to her.

La'friska didn't give Dacosta a Christmas gift because he never gave her one. Besides, she had already given him more than enough to be exact, a thousand dollars. She now knew that the money was lost to her because he never had any intentions to repay her back. As a fact she said to him why did you lie to me about taking out an allotment in my name to pay me back. He was startled and blushed from being ashamed but he quickly recovered saying, "oh come on Friska, you know I was half way lying and conning you. Besides you gave that to me because you do love me. I know that and so do you. Anyways I didn't have it then and I still don't have it now. Chalk it up to how much you really do love me." She said, "thanks a lot for rubbing it in of course. I'm positive you know that's what you're exactly doing." She told him, "for future purposes I'll remember your bragging remarks and conniving tricks." When he took her home the next day before departing she said, "What will you do after you're out of the service?" He told her that he wanted to stay in the states and take it easy after the past three years of service life. Telling her that he needed a big long break. She said, "why don't you come and live with me. Please—I want you too much; so much." He told her no, but that sounds good. She said think about it and always know anytime day or night I'll forever be anywhere you want me to be. Just say a word and I'll come running fast as I can.

Months later before vacationing she wrote Dacosta and told him she'd be home soon. By now he had been out of the service for a few months. La'friska arrived home on a Saturday morning. She was glad to see and be with her parents and family. When she went to pick up Dacosta she was absolutely delighted. Dacosta seemed pleased to see her as well. She knew she looked her best and even Dacosta complimented her. She wore a mid-length Indian style black dress embroidered in red and white with black high heel shoes. They had a beautiful time together. He was so attentive and loving starting from the moment she picked him up until she dropped him back off at home. There was sweetness and variety in their lovemaking. Throughout the night, she constantly awoke to kiss his lips and treasuring her time being with him. Once he awakened and started making love to her but then he stopped saying he'd had enough and was exhausted and sleepy. She tried to coax him but that only made him angry as it always did. He yelled at her saying harsh words as, "leave me alone now woman I'm tired and sleepy; I've had enough so don't be greedy, maybe later." She left him alone and laid there thinking, I've held back because I was treasuring it and greedy because I was making up for past time and also storing reserve up for future remembrance when I can't get any from you." When morning came they left and drove around sightseeing and then went to the park. She was quiet and sad because she knew it was almost time to depart from him. When they said goodbye she was sick with heartache from already missing and longing for him. She knew this was the only time she'd see him on this visit, because she never saw him twice during one of her visits. Even though he'd make dates with her but he never showed.

During the months she still worked at her job. Men wanted to date her but she wasn't interested. She knew her life was lonely, terribly miserable and she hurt for only Dacosta. Jesus only knows how much she wanted and loved him. Again it was Christmas season again. La'friska was excited to see Dacosta. Christmas was better than ever. Saturday evening she and her niece Falaria went to the store and then went on to Dacosta's house. Something was pulling her towards his house. She was scared he wouldn't be there and she was also anxious and nervous. He was there in the yard with his buddies. She sat there waiting for him to come over and when he didn't she blew the horn. He looked up and then came over. She said, "you act like you don't want to see me." He replied, "I didn't know that was you. I thought you were someone for my sister." She told him now that I see you I'm fine and dandy. He said, "watch it you have company" as he pointed to Falaria. Then he asked who is she? They went inside the house and visited with his sister Vicky. Later they left La'friska and Falaria in one car while Dacosta followed in his car. She dropped Falaria off at her house and went into her house.

While she was dressing Dacosta was in the kitchen talking with her family she almost had to drag him away. They finally left and he said "I told you not to get fancy, now I have to go home and change. They went back to his house for him to change his clothes. Later they left and went to the local hangout, staying outside there for a while and then they returned back to his sister Vicky's house. They had the house to themselves. It was cold but she hardly felt it, in her mind and heart she had Dacosta to keep her warm. For she was right where she wanted to be with him at his house. He stuffed his stomach eating and when he was done he came and sat by her, taking her in his arms and kissing her for the first time that evening and in months. She responded wild and ready, she was so over ripe for him. He took her into his arms. And they stood kissing hungrily. He beat her undressing and jumped into the bed under the covers. Seconds later she joined him and she screamed because the sheet and covers was icy cold. She instantly jumped into his arms. He held her instantly melting the coldness with instead an electrifying warmth. His soft sweet lips sent her floating through space and time. She was his for the taking or anything else he wanted to do with her. As they made love she kept saying, "Darling, am I dreaming? Is this really happening?" He said "It's really happening; you're not dreaming."

She said, "I'm really in your arms and your bed?"

He said, "Yes, you really are."

She said, "Oh, how I've wanted this for years, darling; dreams do come true." Later, while they were still making love, his sister and her family came home. Dacosta said, "Be quiet," and she did. He made sure his door was locked and they lay quietly in each other's arms, kissing and caressing. She fell asleep thinking this is where I want to be forever right here in his arms in his bed. I've wanted and fantasized this for so long and now it's finally happened. During the night she awoke to the sound of the rain outside against his window. She kissed his face and lips. Later he awoke her by his outstretched arms across her stomach. She instantly became awoke saying "Umm, that feels so good," whispering in his ear, "Don't stop; I love you." Dacosta awoke and got up; she laid there pretending that she was still sleeping. He came and quietly shook her and saying, "Get up and get dressed quietly." She was afraid to get out the bed for fear it would squeak and they would know she was there. Later, Dacosta gave her a change purse out of his car. He said, "This is your Christmas present, I don't have anything else to give you." She thought some other girl probably left it in your car. Throughout the holidays including New Year's Day, she had a strong love hangover. She moved around in a dreamy daze. She kept remembering being with Dacosta in his arms at his home. It was the best Christmas of her life from simply being with him. She felt that love hang over deeply for a week. Describing her hang over the first day hang over was fresh and new, she kept thinking and remembering yesterday at this time I was with Dacosta and we were doing this and that, reliving the whole thing. On the second day, a little of the daze lessened along with a bit of the hang over. The third day and so on through the sixth day, the feelings eased off more, then again at other times it was strong and felt so good. The seventh day hang over is by far the worst than the first day hang over because she kept thinking last week this very same time Dacosta and I were together. She went through every detail reliving that experience and it hurt more than hell. Why, hell couldn't be any worse, she thought. The feelings were good caused she remembered what it felt like and in the same breath it was murder and hell all rolled into one, because she wanted to be with him and feel it, but she knew that she wasn't and wouldn't be with him, that made it hurt worst. During the next two years La'friska constantly tried every-

# Thoughts

thing thinkable to get Dacosta but still nothing worked. As a fact things got worst. The harder she tried to get him the more she couldn't because he just wouldn't let her. She tried all kinds of different ploys and strategies to reason with him and convince him still nothing helped. Dacosta stopped phoning her except when he wanted something which was namely money. She would refuse then phone him back saying okay I'll get it for you. She'd think maybe he'll like me more if I give it to him. He'll see how much that he means to me. She tried and begged him to come live with her, that she'd help him get a job. Dacosta always refused saying "I've had enough of traveling plus I don't believe you. I know you mean it now but then one day you might get mad and throw me out, then I'd have no place to stay with no money or job." She'd say "I'd never do that I love you and want you to much." He'd still refused and each time she'd later ask him whether it was over the phone or in a letter that she wrote, he'd still say "no I've had enough of traveling for now." Yet later she'd learned that he drove his uncle or some cousin back to Ohio or elsewhere, but yet when she asked and begged him to come see her. He wouldn't but instead he'd run all over other states. When she'd tell him this he'd come up with some off the wall explanation saying I had to drive my uncle back home or he was tired and is old.

Once she thought Dacosta was finally on his way to visit her for the Labor Day Weekend. She wired him the money and waited through the next day in the afternoon to see if he was on his way. She phoned his home all morning but no one was there. She became happy thinking, "He's on his way." But when he didn't show up that morning, she started phoning his house again. Finally, at 2:20 p.m., she phoned his house again, and this time who answered the phone, no one but Dacosta himself. Well, she was shocked, thinking, "Oh no, I don't want him to answer the phone. I want him to be on his way to me."

He said, "I'm sorry I can't make it. I was all prepared but the money didn't get here in time." She told him that he could have called her to let her know. Here I am sitting and waiting for you. I didn't know what had happened. I constantly called your house this morning to see if you'd left out and when I kept not getting an answer I thought you were on your way and now you tell me you are not coming. He replied with, "The holidays are half over so it doesn't make sense to come now." She was so hurt and sick that she bust out crying. He said, "Now Friska, don't do anything foolish. You aren't, are you?" She hung the phone up in his ear. She was so mad and hurt by his actions. She cried all throughout the night. She refused to phone or contact him in any way during the next few months, and he didn't bother with contacting her either. She often thought I hung up the phone up on him; he could have contacted me to see if or not I was alright.

The following Christmas she phoned his house and told his sister to tell him she was home, she wanted to see him and for him to come and take her out. On Christmas night at 9:30 p.m. he came to see her. She was mad with him since she was home for three days and hadn't seen him yet. He was just getting to her and late at that. She thought, he must not respect me to come this time of night because to me no guy who respects and likes a girl comes to see her this late at night. Yes, she was mad, but when she saw his handsome face, her madness evaporated. Her heart skipped a couple of beats and thumped loudly beating faster and faster in her chest. They both smiled shyly and brightly. She had to contain herself from rushing into his arms, and besides, her father was there talking to him. They sat talking and eating cake and coffee. Dacosta said, "You gained some pounds." She told him yes she did, but so did he as well. She asked him, "What are you doing eating everything in sight?"

He said, "Yeah I eat the entire pot not leaving any for anyone else." They both bust out laughing hysterically.

Later they went out riding by all of the hangouts to see who was out and what was happening. It was now 10:35 p.m. as they drove through the quiet dark streets. Dacosta made conversation asking her what was happening in New Jersey. She answered all of his questions. As they talked, a devilish thought popped into her mind. She asked him, "When was the last time you got some?"

He looked at her and blushed, smiling, and said, "You don't think I'm going to tell you do you? Woman why you wanna ask a thing like that," he asked.

She said, "I wanna know; tell me."

He told her it was last month. La'friska quickly and loudly yelled out, "Just who in the hell you been screwing?" Well here I am all along wanting you, crying my eyes out hurting, and you're out screwing someone else. She asked him, "Just who in the hell is she?"

Dacosta looked at her and stared, "I'm still not going to tell you. It was just somebody I know. It didn't mean nut'ting."

She said, "No, don't tell me her name. I don't want to know'; its better if I don't know." She asked him did he love, whomever she was.

He told her, "No; I don't love anybody, and I keep telling you this."

She said, "That means you still don't love me, either."

He replied, "Look, I like you a lot, but I don't love you." Dacosta questioned, "Just what about you, who have you been screwing? I know there has to be someone."

She told him, "there could be someone and there is if I wanted him, but I don't. He's nobody you have to worry about. I love you and there is no one else in this whole wide world or could and will there be anyone who could ever take your

# Thoughts

place." She told him she was a one man woman. Then she slid closer to him saying let me show you. She kissed his cheeks working around to his lips. He asked her, "What cha trying to do to me woman, your blocking my driving." She replied, "I'm sorry for getting in the way but not for kissing you and she rested her head on his shoulder. He put his free arm around her drawing and holding her closer. She whispered in his ears, "That feels so good."

He whispered back, "Umm yeah you're right it does feel good," and he took one eye off of the road and kissed her lips." She nearly went wild for his soft sweet lips that always affected her this way making her float. She kissed him back so passionately and fiercely that even his responded hungrily and lovingly. She whimpered, "Oh darling this feels so good, don't ever stop. I do love you so much." He said, "I know, and I like you a lot." Then something happened to Dacosta as he went wild kissing and holding her tightly talking out of his head, asking things about the could-be guy. During a long explosive kiss he asked her was the other guy better than him. She whispered, "It's you I need and want; no one else will make me explode like this. I love being with you." By now they had parked outside of one of their hangouts. Dacosta said, "I want to do you now, but will have to wait until later because we're here outside of Ghents. So my woman, get your body under control," he told her.

She said, "I can't get like that."

He asked her, "What will it take?"

She said, "A kiss and a gentle hug." Dacosta smiled and told her to "come here woman." She went into his arms laying her head on his shoulder. He told her they would just stop for a while and wish him Christmas cheers. He told her, "I promise we will get it on later and it'll be just as good or maybe even better." La'friska got herself calmed down and under control by fixing her hair and smoothing her clothes. She was wearing a brown and tan Gaucho pants set with tall brown leather boots, a brown wool tan cap and a brown leather bag. Ghent's place is the name of a spot owned by a friend and former classmate of Dacosta. Ghent was glad to see them and even gave them drinks on the house celebrating the Christmas spirit. There were two other guys there at Ghent's place. After finishing their house drinks Dacosta brought a bottle of red wine and they began to drink it. When they first arrived, Ghent was already loaded on booze and weed. During the time they stayed Ghent got even more loaded and finally ripped up. This time Ghent was so high that he didn't hide how he thought and felt about La'friska. Right in Dacosta's face Ghent said, "man Dacosta you got some woman," as he stared at La'friska saying, "I wish she was mine." What I wouldn't do with her he told Dacosta as he stared at La'friska and screamed out, "oh Lord." Dacosta and La'friska bust out laughing hysterically since they knew how ripped up Ghent was. Ghent kept pouring them wine and lighting up weed and passing it to them. He especially kept passing the weed to La'friska. Sometimes she'd take few drags and give it to Dacosta. She knew that wasn't her habit. She didn't need drugs or alcohol of any kind to entice her. Dacosta was a natural enough high for her. Just kissing him drew her into a sea of the abyss. Dacosta would do away with it, he was also high. La'friska was feeling more than good herself by getting a buzz. Still she was aware enough to know what she was doing, where she was and what was going on. As a matter of fact the few drinks and pulls from the weed made her think clearer than ever. Ghent kept talking and staring at her saying to Dacosta, "yeah man you got a seven million dollar woman here." Dacosta laughed and he and La'friska stared at one another.

Later, a classmate and friend of La'friska's named Janelle Floyd came in with another couple. They were both surprised but happy to see one another. They hugged and talked. Meanwhile Ghent stopped staring as much at La'friska. Janelle was surprised to see La'friska with Dacosta. Dacosta sat in between them looking so handsome and La'friska wanted to kiss him and almost eat a piece of him. She hadn't kissed him since outside in the lot before they came into Ghents. She was anxious and longing too kiss him. She and Dacosta smiled at each other and touched hands. Later Dacosta's brother Peter walked in. He was surprised and glad to see La'friska and Dacosta together. Peter told La'friska he didn't know she was home and they hardly saw each other anymore since they graduated. La'friska liked Peter. Too her he was her brother in law because she loved his brother Dacosta that much forever and ever. They all talked a while about how they were doing and getting along. Later Janelle and the couple she was with left and Peter followed behind shortly thereafter. Now La'friska and Dacosta and one other guy remained at Ghents. While La'friska and Dacosta were talking and staring lovingly at each other Ghent started up again. He stared at her hinting how beautiful and well curved she was. She paid his remarks no mind. However, Ghent continued on. Finally Ghent said to Dacosta, "Can I talk to your woman for a minute?" Dacosta stared at La'friska as she stared back at him. Dacosta told him, "If she wants too." Ghent said, "Let's go into the back; I have something to ask you." She got up and went into the back with Ghent. Dacosta yelled out, "Watch yourself La'friska." She walked to the curtain door and stood there. Ghent said, "Come on in."

She replied, "No, it's dark in here; give me some light." She didn't move until he put the light on. Then and only then did she go in. She was feeling high and somewhat woozy from all the drinking and smoking, but she wasn't that far gone. When she got to Ghent, he quickly grabbed her and said, "I'm a pimp, girl, and I

# Thoughts

want to suck your pussy so bad." La'friska was shocked and as lightening struck, Ghent's face flashed before her eyes. She thought she had met up with the devil himself in hell or wherever he was. Just as quickly as Ghent had grabbed her and said those awful words, she quickly pulled away from him at the same time she said, "No, I don't want you to. I only want him, Dacosta," as she walked out and went back to Dacosta. Ghent came back out and made some kind of remark to Dacosta saying, "Two million." La'friska really didn't know what he was talking about, but she thought after he got me back there and I refused him, now I went down from seven million to two million. I guess he found out that he can't have me. La'friska's head had lightened up and she was still shocked and upset by Ghents words and actions. She was really feeling funny and weird but she didn't let on how she felt. Ghent was continuing and pouring drinks and lighting weed but now she refused them. Even Dacosta said he had enough to drink saying, "No man I don't want nut-ting." La'friska cracked up laughing and so did they. Ghent was so torn and ripped up now he was preaching to them. Ghent said to Dacosta, "Man that woman loves you, can't you see that? Just look at her. Those eyes are telling the story. She would do anything for you." As Ghent said those things, La'friska and Dacosta stared, smiling at each other. She said to Dacosta, "He's telling the truth." She thought to herself, "He knows and he's really telling the God's honest truth describing exactly how I really and truly feel about Dacosta." She also thought, "If Ghent can see and observe this so clearly and plainly in such a brief time, then why hasn't Dacosta believed me and why won't he, especially after all those years and time." Also she thought, "It's taken someone else to get him to see what I've been trying to tell him and convince him of all these years." Yes La'friska thought and almost believed that she had a guiding star that night helping her to convince the man she truly love that she most surely and definitely loved him. Ghent kept on saying, "Dacosta, you got it made. I mean, man, you are good looking. Me, I'm ugly just barely passable, but you got it made, you, man." She and Dacosta cracked up laughing uncontrollably. Ghent went on preaching, even getting down on his knees again and again back up, saying, "Man, with a woman like that, oh Lord what I wouldn't do," and he then went down on his knees again and back up. Dacosta and La'friska were still hysterical. She said to Dacosta "he's crazy." As Ghent preached on saying, "I know you want his children, don't you?" Dacosta turned to her and said, "Tell the truth; go on," and he was flashing his devilish smile as he said it. La'friska openly admitted, "Yes, I want his baby," and she turned to Dacosta and stared straight into his eyes, saying, "Very much." Dacosta just smiled. Her confession really drove Ghent to preaching and threw him to the floor on his knees saying, "Oh! Lord God, man, what's wrong with you?" Dacosta, why don't you give this woman a baby, your baby, 'cause she only want yours." Ghent now looked briefly at Dacosta, and as Ghent was shaking his own head, he also was muttering what a fool, and Ghent turned to her and stared, saying, "I hope the hell I would do in his place."

La'friska said, "Sorry, but no you don't and won't in my book qualify." Ghent screamed out, "Oh Lord, she has set me straight." Dacosta cracked up laughing hysterically because Ghent was kneeling on the floor praying saying, "Oh God, help us all." Well La'friska and Dacosta stared at Ghent and burst out laughing uncontrollably. They laughed so much and so loudly that she fell onto Dacosta's shoulder and he gathered and held her in his arms. She said, "Dacosta take me out of here." He said "Are you ready to go?" She said, "Yes, let's go." He said, "Okay and as they walked out, Ghent was yelling, don't leave now; not so soon," but they didn't pay him any attention; instead, they kept on going to the car. Dacosta opened the door on the driver's side, and before La'friska got in, she kissed him. He responded to that kiss and she knew he was pleased. After Dacosta got in and before he started the car, he asked, "Why do you want to leave so soon; weren't you enjoying yourself?"

She said, "Yes; I want to be alone with you. I've been waiting more than long enough, and now I'm tired of waiting, and besides, I've also had enough of Ghent." Dacosta smiled saying, "Okay let's go get it on."

She said, "Yes, I can hardly wait," and she kissed him sweetly, resting her head on his shoulder, sitting close next to him. As Dacosta pulled off of the parking lot, he said to her, "La'friska, what did Ghent say to you?" She stared at him, not brave enough to say the words that Ghent had said to her, so she fell back onto his shoulder, clinging to him, and she started crying and said, "Oh Dacosta, how could you let Ghent do that to me? You must not care for me." Dacosta was alarmed and he held her closer, saying, "Wait a minute baby, what did he do to you?" La'friska slowly said "He said he was a pimp. Dacosta, I thought that I had met up with the devil himself. I still can't believe it; did that really happen?' Now she really cling tighter onto him. His hold on her also tightened and he said, "Look, Friska, I had to let you find out for yourself what goes on in this world, and I told you to watch yourself." La'friska was still whimpering, saying, "But how could you?" Dacosta I love you and you know it, yet you let him do that." Dacosta said, "What did he do to you? Are you telling me everything?" Hearing him say what did he do to you are you telling me everything and remembering Ghent word's "I'm a pimp girl, I wanna suck your pussy so bad." Well, she was feeling strange and weirdly upset from Ghent's words, plus mixed with the true love and desire she felt and was right now was feeling for Dacosta and needing him, she cried even more and louder, clinging to him. She wanted to tell Dacosta all of what Ghent said to her, but the words just wouldn't come out, and she also thought, how can I tell him that Ghent wanted to suck my body. Dacosta still held her tight and lovingly while she continued clinging to him. He said, "Ghent really was loaded. I've never seen him so ripped up before. He was also trying to get us loaded, especially you, that's why he kept pouring drinks and giving us reefers, but Ghent should have known better; I wasn't gonna let him do that, and Friska I know you have a strong mind." She said "'Cause I keep trying to get you." He smiled and kissed her with one eye still on the road. She felted such a powerful rush of love for him coming from his words and actions. She felted so mellow and good to know he felt that way also. She could tell from his response that he was so sweet and loving; that she felt and knew the night had a lot to offer with much , much more yet to come, because she was where she most desperately wanted and needed to be with the only man she loved. She thought maybe tonights the night. It seems and feels like I have a guiding star helping me along; maybe he'll marry me and let me have his baby. We could have a beautiful life together. I would love him every second of each and every day, twenty-four hours every day for as long as I should live, and even if I was dead, my love would linger on because that's how powerfully strong it is, ever lasting dow wow good. It was now 1:00 a.m. on Monday as they drove through the dark, cold deserted streets. La'friska was still sitting close to Dacosta with her head resting on his shoulder. Dacosta was driving with one hand and the other arm was around her. She was so overwhelmed with such powerful love and lust for Dacosta that this particular night she knew he felt some of the same for her. She could tell by his voice and actions. Of course she also knew the liquor and reefers affected his feelings too. As they drove along the highway she couldn't wait that long to kiss him and touch him, so she began kissing him passionately, squirming in his arm; naturally he responded back kissing and touching her just as lustafied, holding her tight and lovingly. La'friska's mind, heart, and body was on fire for him, and so was he for her. She kept squirming and now whimpering saying, "Darling I love you." He said "I know." She said "Well, do something about it. Anything; I don't care."

He said "I can't do to much right now honey, I'm driving."

She said, "Oh I want you so badly right now, baby I don't know if I can wait that long. I just can't." He said, "Just hang on please, we'll soon be at my cousin's place."

She said, "No I don't want to go there, I want to be completely alone with you in a room of our own. Please; I've waited so long and now I refuse to have it otherwise."

He said, "Okay, if you don't want to go there, then we'll have to keep on driving on to the big city."

She said, "Alright, I'll make myself wait that long." As they headed for the city she still laid in his arm with her head comfortably resting on his shoulder while he held her close and gently loving. She refrained from kissing and touching him but she did constantly touch his open shirt, stroking the top, his neck, and chest. Finally they stopped at their favorite motel, but there was no vacancy. She was sad and disappointed. He said, "Baby, I told you it would be hard to get a room this late at night, and especially this night Christmas." She said, "Let's try please." He looked at her and saw the love, disappointment, and determination on her face, and he said, "Okay, we'll go on to the city, and if we can't get anything there, then baby that's it, but first there's a few places I want to check out." She was relieved that he was going to keep on trying, but she was worried and fearful that if they didn't find something in the city that he'd give up, and she so desperately wanted a room of their own so she could freely give her love to him. Moaning and screaming with pure joy to her heart mind and body delight, they stopped at another motel. This time, this motel wasn't in occupancy;it was being renovated. They drove on and she raised up just as they shortly passed by another motel, and she said, "There was a light on in the office of that motel; a man was sitting inside."

He said, "Are you sure?"

She said, "Yeah, I 'm sure. Please let's go back and check it out."

He said, "Okay" and he turned around and went back to the motel. Before he got out of the car, she said, "Let me give you a kiss for good luck." He turned to her and smiled, and she kissed him lovingly. La'friska rested her head on the back of the seat, locking the doors just in case an intruder appeared. Dacosta stayed in the motel office eight minutes or so and came back with a key. She was so very happy. He said, "We have cabin number 29, but first let's go get some food; I'm hungry. Across the street was an all night store, and he asked what she wanted. She said, "Nothin; the way I'm feeling right now, I may never eat again, and besides I don't want food—I want to eat you."

Dacosta said, "Soon baby, and you can eat all you want. After Dacosta got his sandwich and beer, he ate it as they drove around the motel searching for their cabin number. La'friska was high off her love for him. She so desperately needed to feel his love and body joined with hers in love making. Plus the alcohol and the reefers had her feeling good and kind of woozy, but not for a second did the alcohol and dope affected her mind's capability. As a true fact, it made her, especially the reefers, think clearly and see better, as if though she was psychic. All that night she somehow was psychic, knowing and finding out whatever they wanted to know. Such as earlier raising her head up at the right time and convincing Dacosta to return and check out this motel, and giving him a kiss for good luck. Now as

Thoughts

they drove around searching for their cabin munber, Dacosta asked, "Where is it?" La'friska looked around briefly and with the psychic powers she was experiencing she felt and knew she would find it, and she did. Looking to her right she saw cabin 29 and, pointing, she said, "There it is," and sure enough it was. When Dacosta tried the key in the door, it wouldn't open. He tried again and again, but the door still wouldn't open. They didn't know what was wrong. Dacosta said, "The guy said number 29."

She said, "And this is 29, but we can't get in; why won't the door open?"

He said, "The key fit, but it won't open."

She said, "Maybe it's the wrong key, or the guy told you the wrong number or something."

He said, "Let's check the key out in the light." And together they walked under the overhead light and wow, what a relief and pure pleasure it was looking at the key in the light, because the number on the key was 28, not 29. They both at the same time said, "It's the wrong key." And they smiled. Dacosta said, "Unless the guy told me the wrong cabin number meaning another number instead. She said, "If so, why don't we try number 28 and see what happens." Dacosta smiled and said, "Yeah why don't we; okay baby let's do it." Then he said "But where in the hell is number 28?" La'friska was feeling a love jones so desperately strong for him that she could hardly tolerate it any longer. She knew that they had to hurry and find cabin 28 and she also knew that they would because she was feeling psychic and to boot she was desperately overconsumed with love vibrations. La'friska's eyes briefly scanned the area, and at the same time she thought, "Now where is number 28," and in that very same instant her eyes focused and rested on the cabin across from them, because from the light beaming on that cabin, the number was 28. She said, "There it is," pointing her finger in the direction. Dacosta said, "Hey, you're right on the ball with it."

She said, "I sure am because darling, I've wait long enough, too long in fact, and now my love just won't let me wait not one more minute long." As he opened the door she said, "Finally, we're here at last, all alone; we made it baby."

Dacosta said, "Yeah I know, for a while back there I didn't think we'd get a room." While Dacosta was in the bathroom she locked their cabin door all the way because she knew he always half-locked, the door and she didn't want someone breaking in on them or interfering in any way, because all her love was for only Dacosta. She hadn't been with him for months, and now the time was right at last; she was going to get what she had been wanting and needing, fantasizing and waiting on for so long to long. Dacosta was now undressed and in bed. She got into bed and felled into his arms, snuggling closer and closer until she was stuck like glue to him. She whispered, "Hold me, Dacosta; just hold me." He held her close, so lovingly sweet. She uttered, "Umm," and said, "It feels so good being in your arms at long last. I've waited all night and months long for this and now that I have it, I want you to just hold me for a little while longer before we make love. I want and need to feel your arms around me, to comfort me from the pain and hurt." She clung to him remembering all night the endurance she went through waiting for this final time. Remembering, she instantly thought of Ghent the things he had said to her and instantly she felt weird and disgust for Ghent. Suddenly she began whimpering and said "Dacosta how could you let Ghent do that? You know I love only you." Dacosta became alarmed and said "Just what did he do? La'friska, did he touched you?" She continued to lay in his arms and cling to him not knowing how to or wanting to say the words Ghent had used. She finally said, "He—grabbed me—and he—," As she said the next words, she clung to Dacosta with all her might and she finished the words saying, "He—said—he—wanted to suck my pussy." She began whimpering, saying, "I can't believe that happened; did it? Dacosta, am I crazy?" He said, "No, you're not ," and he held her lovingly while she continued whimpering. He squeezed her and tightened his arms around her. Feeling this and cherishing being finally where she desperately needed to be, well, she stopped whimpering also, 'cause her body was so close to his, it started tingling, and her head on his chest felted so good and naturally wonderful. She drew back and looked into his face and as they stared at each other she whispered, "I love you very much."

Dacosta said, "I know and I like you a lot."

She said, "I want you now. I'm ready. Oh darling, I'm so ready for you, and with those words spoken, she leaned forward into him and began kissing. He kissed her back and gathered her tightly but ever so gently to him. Their kissing became long and fierce. She whispered through their kissing, "Am I dreaming, Dacosta; am I darling?"

He mumbled, "No you're not, baby; this is for real." She kissed him fiercely, saying, "I hope so; oh God, I hope so." Dacosta's lips were so soft and sweet and his kisses always drove her wild, and tonight was no exception. It was for more powerfully potent. She could hardly believe it was happening that they were really together at last after wanting and waiting. She thought this must be a dream but then she told herself well if this is a dream I'm going to keep dreaming on and if it's a fantasy I'm going to act it out because this is so good I want it. I love and want him so much. Her heart mind and body was on fire itching burning with love and desire. She was in another world floating through space time and everything else. She also knew Dacosta was feeling some of the same way too, because his actions confirmed and proved it. This was truly a magical night. They both were wild and wanton, especially her. She was always wild before, but this night she was wilder than ever before. She was practically insane with her wantonness and desires. They made love with such fierceness and wantonness that by the time they were finished they had wiggled from out of the bed onto the floor. Even he commented on that, saying, "How did we get on the floor? Boy, we sure was going at it." La'friska of course enjoyed their lovemaking; it was one of their best times together, but still she didn't totally climax, because Dacosta stopped making love before she had finished, and naturally he wouldn't let himself climax either. He said he was tired and sleepy and that he'd had enough. Just before she fell asleep in his arms, she thought, I hope with all my living breath here is where I stay forever and ever. Lying beside you in your arms. I would be the world's most happiest person if only I could share your life with you standing along side you with whatever come may whether hell or high water good times or bad. During the remainder of the night she awoke twice. Once to kiss his lips and the second time she kissed and touched him until she roused him awake. They started making love for a short time and again he stopped repeating "Friska I've had enough and I'm sleepy; go back to sleep." La'friska replied "I can't go back to sleep unless you hold me in your arms." Dacosta with his eyes closed said "what do you want me to do?" She said "reach out and take me in your arms." He did and felled right to sleep. When morning came as they proceeded to get dressed and leave on their way home she was quite and sad 'cause she knew once again as always time was near for them to depart. Before Dacosta left he gave her the necklace she had admired in his car the night before. Now he took it and lovingly placed it around her neck saying "this is all I have to give you for a Christmas present." La'friska said "all I want and need for a present is you to be with you." He said, "You want too much and I can't and won't give you that; besides, you've had me all night." She said "last night—just one night isn't anywhere long enough." He said "well baby I tell you, you'll have to make that last until next time," and then was smiling saying "that isn't so long off just months away." She knew there was no use or sense saying anymore because it wouldn't have done any good. So once again like all ways they departed again him going his way and her back to the north. There she was in a daze for two weeks having a love hang over from him. She kept constantly reliving that magical enchanted night that they had spent together. She had hoped, wished, and prayed with all her might that she'd be pregnant. As time passed on by she was becoming more and more depressed and bored with life and her job. She wrote Dacosta letters but he never wrote her back, and also she phoned him; sometimes once in a blue moon he'd be at home, but mostly he was always out somewhere.

As the months went on by she realized that she couldn't go on this way longing, loving, and wanting Dacosta and never really having him, especially the way she wanted to have him to be his wife, bear his children and just share his life with him. Once again she wrote him begging and pleading, please let me share your life with you. Let's live together, that is, if you won't marry me. You don't have to love me back. I have enough love for both of us. Again, he didn't bother to reply back, until she was home on leave, which was months later. Then he said, "La'friska, I've told you over and over again I'm not getting married to you or anyone else, especially right now. I have my freedom and I'm gonna keep it that way." She said, "You can still have your freedom; I won't tie you down in any way. You can come and go as you please. All I ask of you is to give me some of your time and let me share my life with you. I'll work and make your life comfortable and full of love with peace, joy, sunshine, and everything."

Dacosta replied, "You say this now but later you'll think otherwise and want more. No, Friska; the answer is still no."

She said, "Think about it before you really decide."

He laughed and said, "Woman, don't you ever give up?"

She said, "No, never, 'cause I know what I want, and baby it's you; you're definitely it. I need and want only you; nobody else will ever do," and then she wrapped her arms around his neck, kissing his lips, cheeks, and face all over. Dacosta laughed and said, "What are you trying to do, mug me?" And he still continued laughing. She said "I love you and now you're laughing at me." Dacosta asked "why do you want to marry me so badly?" She said "because to me when you love someone you want to show them and do things to keep them happy. I want to be by your side through whatever trials and hardship tribulations, joy whatever come our way ectetra.in life. I want to share your burdens and sorrows to excel in your joys and happiness. To go to sleep next to you in your arms or what have you. To turn to you in the middle of the night for whatever reason needed and when the morning's come I want to start the new day off sharing it first with you. There is no other way to say it except Dacosta I know how I feel about you and that's I love you and I want very much to be with only you."

He said, "Maybe someday I'll wake up and realize what I have in you. I just then hope it won't be too late." As time passed on, weeks turned into months, until months added into years. Years into more years. Through all this time, La'friska's love and need never decreased, not one iota, for Dacosta. How she still loved and wanted him. She tried at every chance to show him and convince him how much she really did truly care for him, but it just wasn't any use, because nothing, not anything, did any good. The more she tried, the less she convinced him, and that

## Thoughts

only made him treated her worse. Now he didn't even phone except a few times when he was in a tight spot needing fast money for whatever his purpose was. Now she was more desperate than ever. She desperately wanted to marry him and have his baby, but as always, whenever they were together, Dacosta wouldn't let himself climax fully. She knew that she could have children 'cause her doctor said she could. She wasn't so sure about Dacosta if he could produce any or not, even though years before he once told her that one of his ex girlfriend to be exact her name is Patsy got rid of his baby by having an abortion. Dacosta still kept telling La'friska I don't want no kids, I'll play with my nieces and nephews. La'friska would watch him if they were around his nephews or she'd remember her own niece Falaria that Christmas the time he was so sweet and playful with her. She would think to herself you'd make a wonderful father, if only you'd just try it with me. Now she stopped asking him to marry her and also she didn't keep harping on how much she wanted and loved him because she realized and knew it wouldn't do any good; nothing did. It only made matters worst he'd eventually get upset and angry so she just stopped asking. Then one summer night when she was at his house outside sitting in the car waiting for him to dress and be on their way. Dacosta came out later, and upon sitting in the car talking, he said, "You wanna go to the city and get married tonight?" and just as quickly he changed his mind, saying, "It's too late; everything is closed." Well La'friska's heart dropped because she had almost come so close to getting what she wanted; to marry him. She tried to coax him into going to the city and checking things out; but still it was no use trying. She was now more upset than ever, because she had just come so near to getting him, and he was the one to bring the subject up. She thought, "He almost married me." Later, after they were in the motel room, she said, "Dacosta, I'm not going to let you get away that this easy. Now marry me tonight. I don't care about the city might be closed or you having a second change of mind. All I know is for years and years I've loved and wanted you and now I'm damn-to-hell sick and tired of living without you. You in one state and me in another. Just say the word I'll leave my job furniture and everything just so long as we're together. I don't care where we live it; could be in an old barn surrounded by poisonous snakes and tigers or whatever else for all I care." She sexily and lovingly wrapped her arms around his waist and looked him straight in his brown eyes, saying, "Darling, I don't care; I just want to be with you. Please let me. Just give me a trial period. A month or a couple, or however long, and then if you still want out, then I'll let you go no matter how much it'll hurt, but first I beg you give me that chance."

Dacosta said, "Baby, I can't. I don't want to give my freedom up; I want and need to be free."

She said, "You can still be free to go and come as you please, I'll just wait patiently until you return. I'll cook great gourmet meals for you, wash and keep your clothes clean, the house spic and span along with holding down a job. I'll work and help save so we can do whatever we desire. On top of all this I'll give you plenty of love and affection twenty four hours a day every single day as long as we both shall live. Also Dacosta, even if you don't marry me now or never, I'll always love you forever as long as I shall live, and baby this I sincerely know is true. So take the chance. You won't be sorry, because you have nothing to lose now or later. I'm a woman true to my words; besides, I've never lied to you and I don't plan to start now or ever in the future, come what may."

Dacosta replied, "No, baby, even though it sounds good, but no dice; I don't believe it."

She said "are you calling me a liar?" He said, "No I am not, and I don't mean to, but La'friska, you're asking too much from me. Even so you now say all this, later you might change your mind. You see, I don't want to give it not one small chance. I want to be totally free to do my own thing, with no responsibility, no one to get in my way or tie me down, and I'm not giving my name to no one. Right now I don't love anyone, but if I ever decide to marry I'll let you know."

La'friska was deeply hurt and saddened thinking about the way he said that: if I do decide to marry I'll let you know. In her mind she was thinking that the way he said that led her to believe if he should marry, she wouldm't be the one he'd marry. La'friska's life for almost fifteen years had really been truly miserable and full of pain and hurt from loving and wanting Dacosta so badly. God in heaven, how she desperately and truly loved and wanted that guy. She would have walked through the fires of hell or done anything in this whole wide world for him; given her life if necessary in order to spare his. She would have worked hard and honestly by the sweat of her eyebrows and hands in order to give him whatever he wanted and needed. All she wanted in return from him was to share his life, to see and be with him through whatever came their way in life. She knew that no matter whatever life dished out to her, with him by her side she could and would be able to deal with it and come through it no matter what the consequences.

Through those past fifteen years, she had tried everything imaginable, thinkable and unthinkable, to get him—to convince him how deeply and very much she truly wanted, needed, and loved him, but still nothing helped at all. Dacosta just didn't care about her; not really one little bit. Oh, granted if and whenever he wanted and needed something, namely money, he would then pretend and butter her up so he could get whatever he wanted, and he always succeeded, because she would each and every time to give him whatever he asked for. Many times she would neglect herself in order to send him what he required, and afterwards he didn't have the consideration or thankfulness to let her know he had gotten whatever she sent him. She always had to track him down to find out. Recalling once when Dacosta was in the army stationed overseas as he and La'friska talked on the phone he told her to phone his mother and tell her that he was well, doing fine, and received the package that she had sent him. La'friska phoned his mother and relayed the message. She also asked his mother if she or anyone else dropped Dacosta when he was a baby. His mother halfway laughed and replied, "Not that I know."

La'friska replied, "I just asked because he is so hard-headed." Also recalling several times when La'friska and Dacosta were together battling through disagreements, she would ask him, "Dacosta, why are you so hard-headed? Did your mother drop you on the floor or something when you were a baby?" He would smile and respond, "Yeah and stomped all over me," while he continued to smile his conniving smile. She would also bust out laughing with him. Through these years, she had come to realize and know Dacosta was selfish and very inconsiderate of her feelings. She didn't know or understand why he treated her this way, especially with her of all people. She loved him and he knew it, but still he treated her like he really didn't care a damn about her feelings. She knew he didn't treat other people that way. Not his friends, cousins, or other acquaintances, at least when she was around him and listening to him talking and being around others. That's how she knew he was considerate and kind to them. Sharing with them and caring about their concern. La'friska especially remembered how nicely he had treated the other girls he had gone with such as Patsy Klein, Brandi Fletcher and especially Kim Fluntly. He had treated Kim with such respect and from what La'friska had seen he still had treated her that very same way even after him and Kim had broken up. She would never get over how respectfully he had treated Kim.

Through these long past few years she would at one time or another recall what respect Dacosta had shown and treated Kim with. La'friska knew and believed that she would never in life get over the pain and miserable hurt from Dacosta and Kim. Yet still La'friska loved and wanted him with every fiber of her being. She never let pride stand in the way of her love and want for Dacosta. She was a firm believer in asking for what you want and to beg and plead if necessary and even then if you don't get it, don't give up. Keep trying on and on just don't give up so easily especially if it means so much to you. To La'friska to let pride stand in the way of love for the one you love is terribly sad, lonely, painful and miserable. It was almost unbearable and a very hurtful thing. It's all of those things and more, much more and then some rolled into one.

There's an old cliché', "to era is too human." Well La'friska's motto is, "to pride is loneliness." It means to ask for what you want and then to try to get it. If it's in your power and even if you don't get it at least then you'll have peace of mind knowing you did try asking and not letting pride stand in the way. Yes, she had no pride when it came to Dacosta. That guy was her everything. No man could or would ever take his place. No other would ever scratch the surface let alone dent it from where Dacosta stood. She knew and believed within her heart mind and body beyond no doubt that through those fifteen years she had done just about everything as much as she could to get Dacosta. Now she didn't know what else to be except turn to God more.

Through the years she'd prayed to God to have a life with Dacosta. Now she prayed even harder. The pain of loving and wanting him was unbearable. She was tired of being miserable and hurting but even God musta wasn't listening for whatever reason because her prayers weren't answered. La'friska had turned to God asking for his help. All her life she'd heard that God answers prayers. That woman Eve was made from Adams rib cage to keep him company. She wanted company and love too. After years of praying to God and her prayers weren't answered this was where her loss of faith in God begun. She was always thankful to God for her health and strength but she also needed love and a man to keep her company sharing life together.

The last time La'friska saw Dacosta was in the February 1978. She rode the bus home and Dacosta met her bus which arrived late in the night. They went directly to a motel and stayed until late morning. To make a long story short, nothing changed everything was still the same including the sex. In the morning, Dacosta took her home. Her parents weren't expecting her because they didn't know she was coming home. La'friska came to see and be with Dacosta. Even she was surprised when she phoned him and asked if he wanted to see her. So she left New York on the next express bus. When she arrived home her parents were surprised but very happy to see her. She and Dacosta stayed in the kitchen around the heater fire with her parents. Her mother was at the stove cooking. They sat around talking with her parents, especially her father who was a great talker. La'friska saw the look in her mother's eye. Her mother was wondering what was going on between her and Dacosta. The look she had was so serious. La'friska thought her mother either thought she was pregnant or they were getting married. Even though her mother never asked questions or said a word, that look which passed between her and her mother said it all. As a true fact growing up when they were in church sitting in separate areas. If her mother wanted La'friska to come to her. She'd give La'friska a look and she'd know to come to her. The look that passed between

## Thoughts

them this morning was different. Her mother was wondering what was going on between her and Dacosta. Her father and Dacosta didn't even pick up on those looks between her and her mother.

At this time her father was telling them a true story that she had never since forgotten because of its hilarity. Her father said one night this man had a dream that he got hurt. So to keep the dream from happening the next day the man stayed in bed, as he was laying there a snake fell out of the ceiling and the man jumped out of bed and broke his leg. The moral of the story is, if it's going to happen it'll happen anyway. When her father told this story she and Dacosta laughed so hard and so much. In La'friska's vivid imagination she could just see a snake falling out of a ceiling. In 1978 La'friska almost died from pnenmonia, upon recuperating she wrote Dacosta a letter explaining that she'd been very ill and he never answered back anything at all. Anyhow in 1978 was also the last final time her parents saw Dacosta. As a fact, it was also the last time La'friska saw Dacosta until twenty-two years later. Upon completion of this story in the final epilogue the reunion meeting of La'friska Tashanti and Mr. Dacosta Tiawan Gahenne.

# Chapter 3
# Life Beyond Dacosta's Realm

In 1979 La'friska's father leg was amputated. It was the very same leg that had been broken from the car and wagon accident by the white man in 1951 when La'friska was a baby. The hole in the wound opened up getting severely infected and her father wouldn't tell anyone, not even her mother, and he also wouldn't go to the doctor right away until it was much too late. By then the cancer had spread through. It was the weekend on a Saturday night. La'friska father requested that she took off from her job for a week and he'd pay her to come take care of him. Two days later upon getting cash from the bank she took a flight home. Of course she wouldn't let her father pay her. She was happy to take care of him even though seeing his leg cut off nearly destroyed her, but she was strong for her parent's sake. For there was nothing she wouldn't do for them. Whenever they wanted or needed something all they had to do was call on her and they did. She brought them everything and remembering their birthdays , Christmases, Mother's day, and Father's day. She was their money backbone. This was late spring of the year 1979. During the following months when La'friska would be down home she saw her parents go through life's changes. Her father now had a prosthetic leg and he walked with a walker. He even still drove his car with the help of an attachment connected to the pedals When La'friska would drive the car she had to learn to move around this attachment. Her father was older now and slenderer and in helping him sometimes she'd pick him up in her arms and move him wherever it was he needed to be. Several months later which was the next year the Spring 1980 her father died from the leg cancer. That's when she learned his leg was amputated to give him more time to live. La'friska was glad she had taken a week off again from her job when her father got sick again just before he died. During that week she spent with her parents, she heard when her father said to her mother, "Madlyn when I died and should you ever remarry promise me that you won't put some other man ahead of what I worked for my children." Her mother said, "of course not." La'friska was deeply touched that even practically on his death bed her father's concern was for his children. La'friska returned back North and five days later her father died in the hospital. Her father death hurt and crushed their family, for he was the head of the family and a very wonderful man. Life could never be the same again because their father was gone. Yes they still had their mother whom they loved very much, for she too was also the backbone of the family, keeping everyone and everything together. They all grieved very hard, especially their mother; it was devastating for her. La'friska never forgot her mother's sad sorrowful words, "No one to sit on the porch with." It hurt La'friska knowing how alone and sad her mother felt. Her sisters and brothers had families and jobs another life to return to, but her mother had nothing but to remain at home living in a house with constant reminders of the husband who died. Her parents had been married for over forty-eight years. Even La'friska had a job to return back to; plus she had a man friend, but she wasn't in love with the guy. They were friends and lovers and had known each for years; also the guy was married with children. La'friska didn't want him. He was a safety net, being married, even though he too lied, saying one day they'd be together. She never answered him otherwise because, she knew he was still married, and mainly she had been waiting on Dacosta, which was now over. There's a saying and belief that when God takes a life, he also creates a new one. La'friska believed this was true, because within the month her father died, she became pregnant by the married man, whose name was Roderick Antuan, and he was nine years older than her. Roderick came South for her father's funeral to comfort her, plus he had meet her parents before. Roderick always bragged, saying he made their baby that night of her father's funeral and burial, when they were in the motel. After her father's death for the next three months La'friska phoned her mother every day to talk with her and hear how she was doing. In the month of July, La'friska went down home South and told her mother that she was pregnant. Her mom took the pregnancy news very well; she didn't seem to be upset. La'friska 's visit was enjoyable, but still her father no longer alive at home made a difference; that life would never be the same with her father gone. Of course, she was so very glad and happy that her mom was alive; at least she and her sister and brothers

## Thoughts

still had one parent still alive. La'friska would never forget her mother's words on that visit, because those words probably kept her from miscarrying. La'friska was running through the field like she did when she was a kid, and when she approached the ditch, she heard her mother's voice yell out, "You'll be sorry," and so she didn't jump the ditch as she had done growing up. By not jumping, she probably saved her baby's life. Anyhow, nine months after her father's death, her daughter was born that very same year. Her mother adored her new grandbaby. The baby was beautiful and so very precious, because she was like another life to take the place of her father, she could tell even her mother thought so. One day at home back up North while talking on the phone, La'friska heard from a good friend who was a classmate named Lysander Valon that Dacosta had gotten married to a girl who already had a baby; that they had a big wedding at his home. When La'friska learned his wife's name was Cayuta Bowen, she instantly knew what she looked like, because La'friska remembered her from school being in a lower grade. Cayuta was a cute girl, short in height, with a brown skin complexion, short hair, and an average figure. When Lysander told La'friska that Dacosta had gotten married, she didn't let on to Lysander how upset she was. .La'friska was so very hurt knowing Dacosta had finally gotten married. He never told her; instead, someone else did. She had begged and pleaded with him for years to marry her, and he wouldn't, saying he was never getting married. For years Dacosta had hurt her terribly, but still she had hope. Now all hope was gone. He made someone else his wife, his life. La'friska gave up. She no longer tried to contact him. Once when she was visiting down home two years later on her way back from shopping, she stopped by Dacosta's sister Vicky's house just to say hello to her. La'friska liked Vicky, and Vicky had been cordial to her. She didn't ask about Dacosta, however, during their conversation about their families, Vicky mentioned that Dacosta lived in Georgia and had gotten married. La'friska didn't comment one way or the other, however she was very surprised when Vicky, looking over at her toddler baby walking around, said, "Is she Dacosta's?" La'friska told her no. Throughout the next seven years La'friska still went back home two and three times a year. She phoned her mother three times a week, just to bring joy into her daily life and to see how she was doing. Her mother would talk to her daughter K'yata over the phone. When La'friska visited back home, her mother took over caring for her daughter, while she ran the errands. How her mother loved that baby. Her mother would also come and visit once or twice a year, and again her mother took charge of her daughter K'yata. La'friska's daughter was just like her grandfather, La'friska's dad. She had many of his ways. Even though he died before her daughter was conceived, still the heritage reflected throughout her daughter. She remembered once when her daughter was a toddler sitting in her stroller with her legs crossed. La'friska was in a store shopping and she looked at her daughter and in her mind's eye she thought of her father because he crossed his legs like that. La'friska instantly reminded herself, "No, it's just wishful thinking. A second later a lady customer in the store said, "look how she has her legs crossed." La'friska had to admit, "it's heritage; I wasn't imagining." As a fact, her mother always called her daughter Granddaddy when her daughter was mad about something. Her mother would say, "Alright, Granddaddy." When her daughter got mad at somebody, she was mad at everybody, because she wouldn't talk to nobody until she got over her mad spell. When her daughter was almost two years old, her father Roderick went through a middle-age-crisis in his forties. He left his wife and La'friska for a younger woman.

Even though La'friska always knew he belonged to another woman, she never told him to leave his wife. She never thought of telling him that. She was content with going on as they were. She was deeply hurt by Roderick's actions. She realized that what little she thought she had from Roderick she really didn't have it at all. For Roderick to have been there for her for years and now when she had his child and needed him he left her, even though she wasn't that much in love with him, she learned to love him somewhat after having their child. Naturally she wanted to be a family. Even though she loved him, the love wasn't in any way as powerful as the love she had for Dacosta. She'd never love any man more than she loved Dacosta. She learned that there were different kinds of love. In all fairness, Roderick still wanted to be involved with La'friska sexually, and he also always wanted to be a father to their child. La'friska was the one who wasn't having it. She got a court order and put him out of their lives. She showed him what she could do to him, being an unwed mother and independent at that. She even declined his child support. She raised her daughter with the help of her family. They were great. Her mother would tell them to help Friska with that baby. Family stuck together. Her mother would also say to her, "Take as good of care of the baby as you can. That's both of our baby." La'friska's mother lived eight years after her father died.

The day her mother died was the worst day of her life thus far. Life had never been the same, and it never ever would be again. A mother's love is so very precious. Her mother was a beautiful and wonderful mom. She always placed her family's needs ahead of hers. La'friska's mother was buried on her birthday. It was a Saturday, to accommodate anyone who wanted to attend. Her brother Joseph told her, "We can change the day of the funeral if you want, so that it won't be on your birthday."

## Thoughts

She told him, "That's alright, it really doesn't change things, so now it doesn't matter."

La'friska knew that things would never be the same again. Nothing would bring their mother back. La'friska's mother died from heart failure, per the coroner's report. Her mother was seventy-six years old when she died. La'friska's daughter was seven years old. Her daughter weeks later wrote in a book of La'friska's that was La'friska's mother's. La'friska brought the book back as a momento of her mother. Her daughter,,unbeknownst to La'friska at the time wrote in the diary, "On February seventh my grandmother died. I was sad but I got over it but I am still sad but I know she wouldn't want me to worry. I thought grandma would never die." When La'friska read the sentence I thought grandma would never die, La'friska felt the same way. Even though all their life her mother always taught them when God gets ready for me it's my time to go. Whenever her parents talked about someday when it was their time to die, La'friska only spoke for herself and listened to them respectfully. It went in one ear and out the other, or she'd tune them out because she didn't ever want to think of them dying or leaving them. It would hurt too much. Then eventually they did die, first her father, then eight years later her mother. With both parents gone, life was terribly devastating for La'friska. No one not even her sisters and brothers knew how hard she was grieving. When her father had died she at least she still had her mother. She was the backbone and heart of the family. Her mother then became father and mother to them. Even to La'friska's daughter, her mother would say to her, "I have to be bother granddaddy and grandmother,"and she did a terrific job too. Her mother would say to her daughter, "Key'atta what do want for your birthday?" Key'Atta would say, "Fifty dollars, or she'd say a hundred dollars." Her mother would give it to her. When her daughter was three years old her mother kept her for two months during the summer. La'friska's mother didn't like to hear her cry or see her get spanked or punished. Her mother would say give her another chance. Even her sisters did the same, saying not to beat her and to give her another chance. Her daughter was a beautiful, sweet and affectionate baby. Everyone of all races loved her. Some even told La'friska they were going to kidnap her. Even as La'friska threatened to move back home, Key'Atta's father Roderick told her that she better not let her play out in the yard. Key'Atta was the splitting image of her father. Plus she also had her grandfather's ways. Mainly his talkativeness.

With the death of her mother La'friska needed a shoulder to lean on so for the next five years. She was somewhat involved with a guy named Lodi. She never loved Lodi and she never lied to him about her feelings because she simply didn't want too. She was an honest person. She knew how real love felt and she had been hurt too much from Dacosta and Roderick. She didn't believe in stringing a person along. Lodi was married but separated. After Roderick, La'friska refused to ever become involved again with a married man. With Lodi they went to the movies and dinners. La'friska even paid his way on three cruises. Lodi treated her with respect. He constantly told her that he loved her. She didn't love him but she didn't want him to keepharping on his feelings for her. It was a turn off to her even sexually. She wouldn't let him call her honey. She'd say don't call me that. Again, she didn't love him so she didn't want him using such an endearment word on her. Lodi did what she wanted. He tried to please her. He hoped her feelings would change but it didn't. La'friska believed Lodi wanted her because she was the only woman in his life who never asked him for money or anything else.

Plus, she'd taken him on three fabulous cruises, and most of all because it's true that one wants what one can't have. In Lodi's case, he couldn't have her. As mentioned, she let Lodi into her life because she was grieving hard over her mother's death. One incident in particular that freaked La'friska out was that it almost two years since her mother's death at eight o'clock on a Friday night and the phone rang. The voice on the line sounded like her mother's. She became so happy, thinking, mama your not dead and I'm coming for you. Then she realized it was her aunt which was her mother's sister. All she knew was she was gonna get her mother moving, God knows what, the high heaven, earth or whatever else, she was coming. Her aunt Miranda's voice was like a sound from the grave. It took her nearly five years to really come to closure with her mother's death. During those five years, she functioned normally, working, raising her daughter, etc., but she was hurting and missing her mother. She wouldn't go back home unless it was extremely important. It took her brother getting his doctoral degree and her aunts Miranda's funeral for her to go back home. She phoned her sisters but she wouldn't go unless she had to. It was September 1992 La'friska was talking on the phone with a coworker who knew a psyhic advisor. The coworker's name was Rhonda . Rhonda told her, "Let's go see this psyhic." La'friska really didn't believe in them, but she was hurting and needed some hope to help her hold on. La'friska wanted love, a man. Yes she still loved you-know-who just as much as ever. She'd never stopped loving him, even though she made herself stopped wanting him. She'd heard he was separated and had two kids. Also, her sister had told her when she went home for her Aunt Miranda's funeral that she had seen Dacosta in court for child support. Her sister also said, "You'd both make a good couple now that you've both gained weight." La'friska didn't get her hopes up or think much of it.

Yet even so, in the back burner of her mind, she still loved him, but no one else knew, that not even him, because the day she learned he married someone else she knew that she'd never bother him again. His actions spoke loud and clear; he

## Thoughts

didn't want her. She wasn't the woman he wanted. So she left him alone, even during the eight years which her mother had lived after her father died; when she would be home she never tried to contact him. La'friska, as much as she loved Dacosta, she never wished he was her daughter's father, because a father's love is so very special, and she knew how much her own father loved and adored her, and she loved and adored her father too.

There are some things in life like the natural parents that can never be reduplicated in La'friska's eyes. Also she knew how hard she tried to have Dacosta's baby through those fifteen years. She guessed it wasn't meant to be with her and Dacosta. Besides, she loved her daughter very much and enjoyed being a mother. Her daughter was treated and raised like a princess. As a true fact, her baby's nickname given by La'friska's friends was little princess. They'd say, "How's princess doing?" La'friska guessed she gave them the idea of calling her baby princess, because being a new mother and all alone one day a few weeks after the baby was born her friend Lysander phoned. It was early afternoon and La'friska had all day been busy with her daily routine caring for the baby. Washing and sterilizing bottles, making formula, etc., plus housework, that when Lysander asked, "How is the baby?"

La'friska was tired and she looked over at her baby sleeping peacefully in her pink canopy crib and she said, "Oh, the princess is lounging." La'friska said that because the baby was sleeping, while she on the other hand had work to do. Plus she knew that when she did get ready to lie down to take a nap, with the house quiet the baby would wake up. In September of 1992 La'friska and Rhonda went to the psyhic . La'friska said to the psyhic,"I have this old boyfriend down South; am I ever going to have a life with him?" The psyhic did her stuff and then said, "No, not at this time." The psyhic's saying not at this time made her think, "If not now, and I still have to wait for the future on him, then even if I want him, I wouldn't want him because I'd try and make myself not want him even though I know I'd be lying to myself. I'd give myself the satisfaction of getting even with him." So when the psyhic said those words it was like something sunk into La'friska's mind. She'd never had him anyway. It was time to forget about him and live her life. Even though her heart was disappointed and sad, she was still hurt, and she said to the psyhic "I guess you don't get what you want in life." The psyhic said "Let's see there is someone else out there for you" the psyhic did her thing with the cards shuffling them, going into her trance. She told La'friska things about this man who was for her. La'friska listened but she really didn't care at that point; after all, she was just told that she'd never have a life with the guy she really and truly always wanted. Also, she didn't much believe in psyhics.

## Mattie F. Gaskins

After going to the psyhic, La'friska didn't really think about the things she had said, forshe always met men who wanted to or tried to date and get with her. She put the psyhics words aside, not believing in them. She continued being a great mom to her daughter, worked at her job which was somewhat interesting at a catalog warehouse, and in general existed from day to day, in everyday life. A few weeks upon going to the psyhic, La'friska met this man, but at the time it didn't occur to her. She still tossed the psyhic's words aside, not believing.

# Chapter 4
# Pa'Tony International Playboy

A few weeks later upon being at the psyhic's, La'friska was in the Laundromat. It was early in the night, and she was drying clothes and folding them, when in came a handsome stranger. There was something familiar about him, and even he said the same about her. They both felt that they had met before, and they couldn't figure it out right away. Usually she didn't respond to strangers so talkatively. There was chemistry between them; she definitely felt an attraction. They talked a while and he wanted directions to a particular street. He explained that he didn't know the area. While they continued talking they both kept trying to figure out where and when they had met. Finally La'friska was the one to figure it out first. They had met almost three years earlier in Liberty Park in Jersey City. At that time, she had taken her daily exercise walk on the bike trail for an hour, and upon returning to the parking lot, as she was getting in her car, a stranger drove up asking for directions back to the turnpike to get to New York. Again, he was so very handsome and debonair looking. There were chemistry vibes between them, but she turned hers off, thinking to herself, as fine as he is, I know he must have women flocking all over him, and he must have one special woman at least, whether he's married or not. She reiterated directions to this handsome stranger, and he gave her his business card and said to her, "Call me; maybe we could have lunch someday." She took the card but she didn't answer back whether they could or not because she thought to herself, with his looks and style, he could be a playboy. She kept the card for a while and eventually threw it out and she never phoned him. She hadn't given him her phone number; she didn't really know him. He was a complete stranger no matter how handsome, suave, and debonair he was. She just didn't go out with total strangers. She had to know about them or have been around them, getting an idea about who they were before she trusted them. So when La'friska described the meeting in Liberty Park, he remembered and agreed that yes they both had definitely met before, and it was interesting and something how now they meet again under the same circumstances, him needing directions again. Of course, she supplied him with the necessary information. He also said he had to check on his tenants and see what was happening, adding you know how tenants can be; she agreed. Again he gave her his business card. This was in October. When she got home she tossed the card into her desk drawer and thought nothing of it except to put it with the rest of the cards, because you never know about life. That's why she kept business cards. From time to time when she needed more space in the drawer, then she'd go through the cards and narrow down which business ones she'd keep; having the upkeep of a house, she needed phone numbers on hand. After the Thanksgiving Holidays in November, La'friska was cleaning house. She dusted the desk and went through the business cards. When she came across the handsome stranger's card, she remembered and thought for a few seconds. "I never did call him for lunch because he's still probably a playboy. So she just looked at his name on the business card. Other than that he was extremely handsome, no big thing. She felt he was out of her league with his looks and charm. She knew good-looking men would give you their behind to kiss, thinking and knowing that with their looks they had life like that because there would always be some woman or women to take the place of another to give them what they wanted. With this stranger's sex appeal, he didn't and wouldn't even have to try; the world was his oyster. Therefore, she just read his name on the card, and for some unknown reason she kept the card, putting it back with the other business cards. She also thought, "I threw away the first card he gave me." In December, she went on grand duty jury one day a week for six weeks, and her time was up after the New Year. Before the beginning of the holiday season which was before Christmas, La'friska made a resolution that it was time to come to terms with her mother's death. It had been almost five years, and she needed to stop grieving so hard and put closure in her mind to her mother's death. She needed to stop the hurting part. Even though her mother all her life had taught and given them strength to accept whatever God's wishes were, it nonetheless still hurt her very much her mother being dead. The Christmas Holidays were always the worst for her, because she missed both her parents. For her daughter's sake, La'friska had to make herself endure the holidays after her mother died. Now she needed closure within herself, so she knew it was time to move on after five long years. Also, her best friend Lysander, knowing about the psychic's predictions, although she herself didn't believe too much, but she was always a positive person, forever giving her hope and encouragement, said, "La'friska, remember, this is your year." So once again the new man story began. It was the first week of the New Year, Janurary 1993 to be almost exact. It was a few days after New Year's on a Monday night after six o'clock p.m. La'friska was in the very same laundromat folding clothes on the table, and she looking around at the different people in there, some alone, others in couples, and she thought to herself, they say you meet men in laundromats, single men, and she thought, could mine one day be in here. She wasn't looking for him that night. She was just going about her business not caring if or not a man for her ever came in there. Then, boom, all of a sudden she thought to herself, that guy has a T in his name. She remembered his name from the card when she was eliminating them in November 1992. The psychic had told her that there was someone else out there for her. The psychic said, "He has the letter T in his name. He is connected to another state. He is well off financially." Now La'friska recalled the psychic words. This handsome stranger's name was Pa'Tony DeGrossly. The T was in his first name, Pa'Tony. Remembering this and his handsome face, La'friska thought to herself, I wish I could see him. Even though she still had his business card, she didn't know if or not she'd call him. She didn't dwell on him any longer. The next day which was Tuesday after getting off from work La'friska went directly to her sister's house picked up her daughter and took her sister to the supermarket. When she was taking her sister back home, she had to stop for the traffic light, and fate intervened. The angels, God, destiny, or whatever, but who should walk across her path but the handsome stranger himself who she'd thought about the night before, less than twenty-four hours ago. He was standing at his car getting something and locking the door. Well, La'friska was not about to let the opportunity pass her by, especially when less than twenty-four hours ago, her wish was to see the stranger, and now right before her eyes he was delivered. She yelled out to him, "Hey, I know you," and she was smiling. He was smiling too, and she could tell that he really wasn't sure who she was. So she told him, "We met in the laundromat a few months ago, plus we also met in Liberty Park a few years ago before that; both times you wanted directions. Then from the expression on his face she knew that he remembered her too.

    He said, "Pull over so we can talk." By now the traffic light had changed for her to go.

    She didn't want to hold up traffic, so she said, "I have your number."

He said "call me tomorrow." The next day, which was on a Wednesday, she was on final grand jury duty, which ended at 11:00 a.m. When she got home she phoned the stranger, Pa'Tony. It was around twelve noon. They talked for fifteen or twenty minutes, getting formalities out the way. Pa'Tony asked if she'd have a drink with him around seven o'clock, and she said yes. He said that he'd phone her that evening. When he did phone, it was after eight o'clock. She gave him directions to her home, and she proceeded to wait for him. He arrived one and a half hours later. She was watching a Disney movie, Beauty and the Beast; this was one of her daughter's tapes. Her daughter was back in her room sleeping peacefully, looking like her father Roderick. It was a fact that she looked more like Roderick asleep than when she was awake. Her daughter was home because Pa'Tony called her later in the evening instead of earlier. Therefore, she realized it was getting late and she wouldn't wake her child, up rousing her out of her sleep and bed. Now, had he called her earlier, she'd have had her sister on standby to babysit. It was after nine thirty when Pa'Tony finally arrived. When he walked through the front door of her house, not her apartment, the house itself, at the front door he kept looking around saying, "I've been to this house before; I know this house." Of course, she thought to herself, he's giving me a line. She really believed this until Pa'Tony kept staring around and then he said, "I dropped my sister off here; some girl upstairs braided her hair." Well, La'friska was shocked; he wasn't lying after all, because her tenant upstairs did braid hair. Pa'Tony continued talking, saying, "It was two years ago." By now they were walking through La'friska's apartment door. Once inside, she sat on one sofa and he sat on the other sofa opposite her. They were smiling at each other. He finished watching the movie with her as they sat conversing. La'friska had on a long lounging burgundy robe with pink isotoner slippers. Pa'Tony kept watching her shoes and he said, "Your feet are small. I like your shoes." She didn't bother to tell him that her feet were a size ten, which to her was big. She learned he was a stock broker as well as a musician. He had seven sisters and brothers. His parents were divorced, but his mother remarried, and she lived in Denver, Colorado. She was also a nurse. His father was a military man in the army, and now he was a lawyer. Pa'Tony himself had lived in Boston, Massachusetts, New York, and New Jersey, and also many other locations because of his father's military years as he was growing up. He said that his father made sure all seven of them went to college. She told him about her family spread out over different regions of the United States. She explained the terrible loss of both her parents, especially her mother. They talked for two hours. Pa'Tony, impressed with her feet, wanted her to actually walk on his back. Of course she wouldn't because she knew what her weight was; she wasn't lightweight like

## Thoughts

Sherman Hensley on the Jefferson, therefore she wasn't about to walk on his back and injury him. Pa'Tony told her the sister he brought to her house lived in Denver, Colorado and her name was Alexis . That she was visiting that year and she saw this girl up in the square with her hair braided and she liked it wanting hers braided and they got in a conversation . This girl gave his sister her phone number and his sister came to this house to get her hair braided. He dropped his sister off and he went upstairs with her to make sure everything was alright for her safety. He returned hours later and picked her up. La'friska was amazed that she had missed out on knowing he had been in her home upstairs, because he was someone she wanted to know better. She didn't lie to him. She told him about the psychic predictions. He then was amazed, although he too ddidn't believe in them. However, La'friska on the other hand was getting her hopes up very high. Thinking, he's been to my house before, is this fate? Our destinies finally crossing, bringing us together. As Pa'Tony was walking out of her apartment door, he could see into her bedroom, and when he spotted her beautiful bedroom he was impressed with her canopy bed decorated in pink. Her bed was queen sized pecan wood made by Drexel. She got lots of compliments on her bedroom set from everyone as they entered or left her apartment. The bedroom was so obvious if the door was open. When he spotted her bedroom, he said, "May I?" and she motioned her hand to let him know yes he could enter. He did and stood at the bedroom door entrance. He was very impressed with her room. He walked out of her room and she proceeded with him out into the hallway. When she had the door opened for him to leave and as they said their goodnights, he kissed her directly on the lips and she kissed him right back. The kiss was good, and as they stood prolonging the kiss, Pa'Tony had her in his arms and she felt him touch her breast. She didn't draw any attention to his actions because she wanted to pretend it didn't happened; and also she was highly embarrassed that he had done that. After the kiss was over with, they said goodnight, and she closed the door as he left. La'friska was happy and at work the next day; she told Rhonda about Pa'Tony. Rhonda was thrilled for her, giving her hope and encouragement. When La'friska returned home from work, she couldn't wait for her tenant Jacqueline to come home from work. When she did come, La'friska met her in the hallway asking her if she remembered braiding a woman hair two years ago from Colorado that they'd met up in the square. Jacqueline told her yes that was true. La'friska explained how she had met this guy last night who said he had been here two years ago with his sister and she wanted to make sure he wasn't giving her a wrap line. Jacqueline again said it was true and she also said his sister had told her he was married to a Jamaican girl. La'friska recalled Pa'Tony saying his wife was Jamaican and they were separated. La'friska thanked

Jacqueline for telling her. Two days later, on a Friday, Pa'Tony phoned her. She was in the kitchen preparing dinner. She was surprised and very happy to hear his voice, that same night, he came to see her. It was after nine o'clock, and her daughter was asleep in her room. She and Pa'Tony sat in the living room watching television and talking. Later, they had music on the stereo. It was her favorite singer, Mr. Jon Lucien; no one else in this whole wide world could ever out-top him, for her he was that talented and oh so very good. Anyhow, she and Pa'Tony were getting to know each other. They talked about his Raheem who lived with the son's mother. He didn't talk too much about his ex wife or wives. He had told her days before when they were getting to know each other that he was married three times. She didn't know if or not this was true, having that many wives. As they both sat on the same couch which he had sat on the other night, they began kissing. His kisses were sweet and good and got better and better. She tried to put a stop to them because she knew what that kind of kissing could lead to, and besides, she didn't get sex that often, and she wasn't overdoing the kissing part because then she'd want and need sex. She wasn't going to give it up to him so soon; not this night. Yes, she and her body wanted to, but she wanted to have him around longer, for him to keep coming back. If she gave it up right away she'd look cheap and disrespectful. She wanted him to know that she was about more than that. Besides, her daughter was asleep, and she sat standards and morals for herself and her daughter. As they continued kissing in each other's arms, it was so good and natural, but he wanted much more; to be exact, he wanted sex, and he tried very hard to get it. He was cunning and conniving. He pretended that he wanted to see something in her bedroom. She was no dummy, but she let him go in, and she waited in the door entrance. He sat on the bed pretending to check out the mattress comfort, and he called her over. Eventually, she went to him, and he pulled her to him and he started kissing her, and when he had her turned on he rolled her over onto the bed underneath him. She tousled with him until she managed to get up. She kept saying, "No, my daughter is asleep in her room." Saying that only made him say "She's asleep; we won't disturb her." La'friska said "no" she meant it and walked out of her bedroom. Later, back on the sofa kissing, hugging, and fondling, she was still saying "no" but her body was saying "yes," because by then Pa'Tony didn't stop with the kisses. He was touching her breasts and sucking them, this was really turning her on; that's why she'd learned through the years not to engage in a lot of heavy foreplay unless she was ready to have sex. She'd tried to prevent this from happening with Pa'Tony, but he wasn't having it. He had to keep trying. At one point he pulled her into the bedroom and pushed her on the bed. Again she tussled with him until she somehow managed to get up. After that, she didn't let

## Thoughts

him fool her anywhere near the bedroom. He stayed with her until after eleven-thirty. When she kissed him goodnight in the hallway, he took her into his arms and they kissed each other passionately. Afterward, she didn't want him to leave so soon, so she just laid her head on his chest and clung to him, and he wrapped his arms around her and held her so tenderly. Eventually they let go of each other and he left. She then went to bed thinking of Pa'Tony, reliving the night. She wanted to have sex with him.

It was after four in the morning and her body was on fire for sexual release from Pa'Tony. She told herself, I can't lie to myself anymore—I want him. As she lay there, she reminiscenced about being in his arms. She knew his arms were really the turning point, because when he held her in his arms he made her feel like a child. She just wanted to be held. His arms felt so good and natural like it was making up for all the pain and hurt she'd experienced in her life. During the following days she fantasized about him. Their kisses and being held in his long arms.

A week later he came to see her again. This time she had her daughter at the babysitter for the night since she had special plans for Pa'Tony. He didn't know it yet, but tonight she was going to give it up to him in reality, making him think he had seduced her. She had made her mind up that Saturday morning in the early morning hours as her body blazed with desire for him. Yearning and burning for sexual healing. Mr. Pa'Tony arrived after nine o'clock that night. He was a vegetarian and didn't eat much. He didn't eat at all, but he did drink orange juice. As they watched television and listened to music, they talked constantly, getting to know each other. La'friska loved music, and him being a musician traveling all over the world made his life very interesting and exciting. La'friska had traveled extensively too. Through the years she had already been on five cruises and was departing in five months for her sixth cruise. Even her daughter had been on three of them with her. Once, her brother Joseph and her daughter when she was almost four years old went with her. At that time her mother was alive and she feared for them, taking her granddaughter at such an early age. Her mother reinforced for them to watch that baby. On her third cruise her sister Bonnie and her daughter joined her. That was an exciting cruise because they went to the ports of Mazaltan, Carlos San Lucas and Porto Verlata. These were all ports that the Love Boat went to. La'friska loved Porto Verlata in Mexico. There was a restaurant that started on street level and went down into the ground three more levels with open windows and a terrace that you looked out directly onto the blue sea to feel the open air breezes of the water. It was so romantic. That place always stood out in her mind; she said one day if she was with the man she loved, she wanted the two of them to visit there together. As they relaxed to the music, they kissed, touched, and caressed each other. Finally, Pa'Tony took her hand and pulled her into the bedroom. Once in bed, as he took her into his arms, it felt so good that she just laid there holding onto him. In his arms she was always fascinated and felt like a child just wanting to be held. When she had been held enough, she tilted her head, looked at him, and they began a long, delicious kiss. Sex between them for the first time was exciting and he made her want more of him. They made love off and on for two hours. She reached a climax, but she could tell that he hadn't.

In January, they went to a restaurant in Rutherford, N.J. at a famously known restaurant. Pa'Tony, being a vegetarian, didn't just eat at any restaurant since he was a finicky eater. They had discussed her birthday which was in February. He wanted to feed her banana cake. Just days before Valentine's Day, she ordered a Valentine's Day arrangement and had the florist deliver it to his office. She had the florist write on the card, remembering 2-13, signed banana cake. The night of her birthday she still hadn't heard from him. She didn't know if he was coming or not. He had to know about her birthday because she made sure of that by sending his Valentine gift to the office. She was home in bed and reading a book. She was dressed in a long flannel-print gown and it was just before six o'clock. Later on, she was planning on taking a long, luxurious bath to prepare for his arrival. The doorbell rang and she looked through the peephole before answering. She saw this cake with a candle lit on it and she then recognized his face and reality hit her. It was Pa'Tony. She wasn't ready for him yet. It wasn't six o'clock. When she let him in, she said, "I'm gonna kill you." She was delighted to see him but also she wasn't ready. She'd bought a lounging pajama set just for this occasion. She was embarrassed since she was in a flannel gown and she had cut the long sleeves off into shorter sleeves. As she was telling him she was going to kill him, he was laughing and kissing her, saying, "Happy Birthday." She wanted to change her gown, but he didn't want her to. As she sat on the sofa, she sat on top of him. He liked that the gown was easily accessible, and she had no panties on. She took a picture of her cake, and she then she put on her new lounging set. He didn't want her to change, so she just kept the top on, exposing her thighs and legs. True to his word, he fed her banana cake. She took the whipped cream off of the cake and put some on her nipples and he sucked it off. They had foreplay using the whipped cream. From that moment on she realized what you could do with whipped cream. In reality, as this story is being told today, it's Pa'Tony's birthday, July 26. When Pa'Tony left after twelve-thirty that night, he rang the doorbell before pulling off. He had her birthday balloons in the car. He couldn't bring the cake, ice cream, and balloons in at one time. So now he remembered he left the balloons.

During the next few months, they had many dinners. She would drive to New York City and pick him up from work. She thought he was the man for her. She'd

## Thoughts

fallen for him. Of course, she didn't love him as deeply as she loved Dacosta. In the spring she drove him to his flight lessons in Caldwell. Some of those times, his nine year old son Raheem would be with him and she would babysit while Pa'Tony took his two hour flight lessons. Sometimes she brought her daughter along if his son was coming. She'd take the kids to the Livingston mall. They'd play games in the video arcade. If the kids weren't with her, she'd go shopping herself at the different malls. After his flight lessons, and if the two were without the kids, they'd go to dinner or just go riding. She always drove. Pa'Tony never drove his car.

She'd gone back to the psychic twice since meeting up with him again. She asked the psychic if Pa'Tony was the one. Both times the psychic couldn't be sure, saying he was a cuspy one and she couldn't tell. Well, La'friska was sad and disappointed. The psychic had gotten her hopes up telling her there was someone else out there for her who was her soulmate. Pa'Tony had all these qualities she told her about, and now she couldn't tell her anymore. In February, a month after she had gotten involved with Pa'Tony, she had to hurt Lodi's feelings and tell him she was involved with someone else. Lodi wasn't surprised since they no longer had a relationship. So he sensed something was wrong. Lodi couldn't understand how she could have such strong feelings for someone she'd just met and yet he'd been around for five years and she had no love for him. La'friska told Lodi, I know how love feels. I never lied to you about me loving you, and you know this. I don't believe in lying when love is so free and unconditional. Lodi had no choice but to accept her wishes. Even though she no longer saw Lodi, he'd phone her once in a while to see how she and her daughter were doing. Lodi had been respectful to her daughter in those five years. If she'd had a school problem, Lodi would accompany her to the school, especially her daughter's father Roderick wasn't around to go with her. Her daughter liked Lodi. Pa'Tony knew about Lodi because she told him. She didn't lie to him. She told him what she thought of Lodi, and the respect and support he'd given her through those years, but that she'd never loved Lodi and Lodi knew this. La'friska said, "I'm moving on. I now want you." Pa'Tony didn't believe she loved him. La'friska knew Pa'Tony didn't love her, but she wasn't going to give up. She kept hoping he'd fall for her after fate kept placing them together. She thought maybe it was their destiny. So she waited on him. Pa'Tony lived on the same street her daughter's school was on. He'd even been to her house before. They kept meeting up, and when he held her in his arms, his arms fascinated her, making her feel like a child just wanting and needing to be held to ease the hurt and pain. She'd tell him, "Leave me your arms." She'd jokingly ask, "Could I cut your arms off so I can have them to hold me when you're not here."

He'd laugh, saying how funny she was. She didn't try to be funny; she just spoke the truth as she knew it. Their involvement wasn't a weekly thing. In the beginning he'd phone every couple of days, weekly, or every other week. During the months it was cooling down on his part. She now phoned him more than he phoned her. Although, he'd say call me at such and such a time, and she would, even it was on her lunch hour. Pa'Tony's voice, even over the phone, was so velvety smooth and sultry. La'friska, just hearing the sound of his voice, would instantly have her spirited lifted and her day brighteed. The man was and magnetizable. With a man like him, woman could loose their minds, forget their hearts. Pa'Tony was always charming and witty. In his business attire, being a stockbroker, he was immaculately dressed and very distinguished. When she'd be in a restaurant sitting opposite him, he'd look so distinguished that she wanted to eat a piece of him. Of course she never told him this because to her, his head was probably already swollen enough, knowing how fine he was. He told her how women came onto him. Although she was no dummy, La'friska also knew he hit on them. After all, that's how she came about meeting him. With him being a traveling musician, especially on weekends, she knew and realized there were forever opportunities and chances for him to meet more and more women. Still, she hoped she was the one for him, even though he said he was separated and had been married three times. He didn't talk about his wife or much about his son's mother except that she left him with a one year old baby and joined the army. He said she didn't phone him for ten months. He had to raise the baby, and three years later she came back wanting the child. He said he went through a lot with her. She accused him of child abuse just so she could get the child back. La'friska saw a photo in his wallet of Pa'Tony looking over his son's shoulder smiling as the little boy, age three or four, was doing his homework. Pa'Tony said he was at school picking him up and someone took the picture; he was looking on proudly as his child worked. In June, La'friska's cruise departed. She took her daughter with her. She tried to get Pa'Tony to come instead, but he wouldn't, saying he had to work. On the cruise she was lonely for him, because cruises are so romantic, especially by night watching the moon and the stars, with the wind blowing through your hair and whipping your clothes around you, strolling on deck, lounging inside the cabin, especially with a port hole or window to look out and seeing the colorful water, other ships, land off in the distance, and especially at night; with the darkness outside you can look out seeing the moon and the stars. If the lights are off in your cabin and your curtain is drawn from the window, it's so romantic, and to be with the one you love is awfully thrilling and exciting. She thought, if I had Pa'Tony here with me, we'd never leave the cabin. On the cruise, one of the ship waiters in the dining

## Thoughts

room tried hitting on her; his name was Gregory and he was handsome and was Jamaican, and married, with his wife at home. La'friska had taken her own portable radio and cassettes, and of course her favorite artist's music, Jon Lucien. Jon's latest cassette was Mother Nature's Son. Her favorite song on there was Lonely for You; she loves that song. She played it thinking of Pa'Tony; she was lonely for him At the end of the cruise she gave the tape to Gregory because he didn't seem to know who Jon was. During the cruise she also saw Gregory talking off-ship with another female passenger who was apparently traveling with a white man in a wheel chair. At night, the same female would be walking in the casino alone, playing the slot machines. So when La'friska saw Gregory off-ship dressed in regular clothes instead of his ship uniform, she knew he was hitting on this female. La'friska didn't care one bit, because her mind and body wanted Pa'Tony now. Gregory didn't stand a chance, although one morning Gregory stopped by her cabin; her daughter was there, and later her daughter went to the video arcade. Gregory and she talked about themselves. She told him about Pa'Tony and how she felt about him. As they were talking, Gregory tried kissing her, and she immediately put a stop to it. She was not a shipboard fling, so she had him leave her cabin. When the cruise was over, before departing from the ship, she said good byes to the waiters and the maître-d in the restaurant; she was saving the best for last, meaning she was going to take Gregory for a surprise. She gave him the Jon Lucien tape and she kissed him on the lips goodbye. He was happy and wanted her address; she gave it to him. When she got home from the trip, naturally she phoned Pa'Tony, letting him know she was back home. She brought him a travel bag off the ship from the gift shop, plus other trinkets. She told him about her trip. He wanted to know if the men we hitting on her, and she didn't lie to him. She confirmed they tried hitting on her, but it didn't do them any good; she also told him men hit on her no matter where she went, and that it was up to her to decide whether she wanted to be bothered or not, and she never bothered with them because she learned that when a man spends money on you, especially when he buys you gifts, he thinks you owe him something back, especially sex. She was always independent; whatever she wanted, she bought it for herself, and even if she didn't have all the cash right away to pay for it; she would save up until she did have it, or she'd put it on layaway. She was also the type to cherish her man and buy him things because she wanted to, for example, with Roderick; even though he was married, she wasn't trying to break up his marriage. She never referred to him as her boyfriend or even thought of him as her boyfriend. Besides, she was very much in love with Dacosta and was waiting on him to marry her or either to have his baby. Back to Roderick, yes, she spent money on Roderick too. She gave him money here and there and brought him little trinkets like cigars and pipe tobacco, newspapers, and gave him gas money. Now Roderick, on the other hand, because they worked at the same job, would bring lunch for both of them every day; her way of thinking was that they were helping each other—that's called one hand washing the other. Now with Lodi, he really didn't have much of anything because he was either laid off or just made minimum wage, and she paid for their outings to movies, theater plays, and dinners. On Sundays she cooked dinner and fed him, plus she would take him home with a doggie bag; she also would give him a few dollars for spending money. Once when Lodi was really down on his luck, she took him groceries. Plus she always wanted to travel, and she was getting older, thirty-seven years to be precise, and all her life she wanted to travel with the man she loved. She'd never had that chance, so now with Lodi around, plus she financially had the money, she paid both of their ways. This is also why she believed Lodi said he cared so much for her; because she wasn't self-centered with money. Even Lodi would say, "La'friska what you have done for me, you are about something." At one point Lodi actually shed tears, wishing his mom was alive so one day he could afford to take her on one. The only thing La'friska was self-centered about with Lodi was her love. Again, she never loved him, and she had sexual involvements with him if and when she needed it. As for Pa'Tony, she now loved to buy little trinkets that he needed for survival. La'friska saw right from the start of their relationship that he had a problem with time. He was never on time. He always kept her waiting, and to her it should have been the other way around; her keeping him waiting instead. She'd say to Pa'Tony, "You couldn't be on time for your own funeral." He'd laugh. When he had his flight lessons, in her shopping she bought things for him like an A.M./F.M. stereo radio clock, refillable ink pen set, etc. Also an old-fashioned washboard; she brought him this because this in talking in conversation about how she grew up washing clothes in a washboard; he was fascinated about a washboard, so in her travels she found one and brought it for him. She also brought him a mop and ringer bucket for the floors; as a fact, she had Lodi come with her to the store when she bought it because Lodi rode with her to show her how to get there; yes, Lodi would call her sometimes to see how she and her daughter was doing. Lodi was that type of person; he could be a good friend, helping in time of need. For Pa'Tony's birthday, she bought him a microwave oven that cost five hundred dollars; he picked this out himself. When she told him that she was buying him a microwave, he insisted on going with her to the store. The winter months were so cold, and Pa'Tony was cold-natured; she brought him five sets of pajamas, which were expensive, because he only wanted one-hundred-percent cotton, and then he needed tall size. Weeks

## Thoughts

later, their relationship cooled down on his part; he didn't phone her as much, but yet she hung in there, waiting and hoping. He would make plans with her and then stand her up. He wouldn't even phone to cancel, or even days or weeks later he'd give her an explanation for standing her up. She had his office toll-free number, and sometimes she'd phone him; some of those times he acted like he was pleased to hear her voice, or then again they didn't talk very long because he had some kind of business to attend too. She wanted to spend the holidays with him, but he said being a musician he worked on weekends, holidays, or whenever he could. He named well-known celebrities he'd worked with. Once at his place she saw a video taping of a concert he did in Japan with Hubert Laws and others. It was a year and a half when she got tired of the cold treatment he was giving her. She phoned him, and when he heard her voice, he hung up on her. At first she thought maybe we got disconnected; then she phoned back and asked, "Did you hang up on me?"

He said, "What if I did?"

She hung up on him and was very hurt. He didn't phone her back. La'friska for almost two years didn't phone him, and he didn't phone her. She was hurting.. She tried very hard to forget him, even though she had walked away from him; still, she couldn't forget him. There was always something to remind her of him. She knew he couldn't have forgotten her, because he had so many things she had bought him; that had to remind him of her. Yet he still didn't phone. One night she and her daughter were shopping at the supermarket, and her daughter came over with this boy, and it was Pa'Tony's son Raheem. He had grown since she had seen him two years sgo. If her daughter hadn't said, "This is Pa'Tony's son," she'd never have recognized him. He'd gotten so tall and big, and he was also a very handsome young man. La'friska was touched that he'd asked her daughter, "Where's your mother?" and he came over to say hi. Seeing his son only made her want to see him, just to hear his voice. She hoped his son would mention he'd seen her and that Pa'Tony would phone her, but he didn't phone. La'friska was lonely and hurting for him, so she began to work on writing this story again. She hadn't worked on writing this story in over ten or maybe twelve years; she just put it aside. Now she began again; some chapters she rewrote, but then she didn't get very far. She was distraught and so hurt that she felt like with her luck, she was wasting her time. That her book wouldn't get published, or even if it did get published, it wouldn't be a bestseller. For she had bad luck. Always in love and never having that love reciprocated in return. She was tired of trying at love. When she first got involved with Pa'Tony, she really thought, "Finally, he must be the one for me," after all those signs bringing them together again and again, she thought and felt it was their destiny to be together; even though the love she had for

Pa'Tony was not as deep as the love she had for Dacosta. She would never, no not ever, love anyone else as much as she loved Dacosta in her whole entire life throughout this world and eternity forever more. She was entitled to have some kind of love too, so therefore she kept trying, but things never worked out. She always picked the wrong man to love. She'd always been there for Pa'Tony; if he needed her to pick him up because he had car trouble, she did, even if she had to wake her daughter up at night and take her sleeping along with her to get him and help him out. When he was sick and phoned her, she took him to the store to purchase what home remedies he needed. Whenever she would say to him, "I love you," he'd say, "Stop your lying," to her; it became apparent that he didn't want her to have that type of love for him. After seeing his son, months later she phoned him and his voice sounded happy to hear her. He even asked if she'd like to pursue a relationship with him again. She said, "I don't think that'll be wise not at this time." She wanted to say yes so badly, but she didn't because she wanted him to want her and pursue her. So his final words convinced her he wasn't really serious he'd only been teasing her. He said, "You be well." She wanted to cry, but she held up and wished him well also. Afterwards, she cried; how she longed for him, wanting to be with him. She fantasized about him; at that point all her pleasures were make-believed. She wanted to feel his arms about her. He had a love-making position technique that was triple X-rated that he would use on her, and it turned her on. After which, she climaxed and her body would be in spasms from the release so great. Pa'Tony was kinky and wild. To her it seemed he got turned on from torturing her. She'd be crying for him to stop, but he'd just keep on until she'd just keep moaning and crying for him to stop. It was three months later that she phoned him again, and she point blank said to him, "I want to have dinner with you." He laughed happily and said "Okay." That same night they had dinner at their favorite restaurant. They didn't mention the hang-up phone calls. They talked and he confirmed that his son had told him that he'd seen her. Sitting across from him, he was so distinguished looking. They came back to her house for a few hours. When he took her in his arms, she laid there reveling in the joyous feeling of being there again after waiting so long. They made love and she was content, but she could tell that she didn't turn his body on the way he turned hers on. She also knew love had much to do with turning a person on. When you love someone, you get turned on easily. It's when there's no love for that person that the other person has to work very hard to finally get the person turned on. She'd personally been there herself, so she truly knew from experience. After that, they kept in touch for maybe once or twice a month. She'd phone him; if he wasn't in or available to take her call, she'd leave her name. Sometimes he'd phone back, whether it was the same day, or days later, or even weeks. She didn't make any demands. He still made dates with her and wouldn't come or wouldn't phone to explain. He just did what he wanted. When and if he wanted her to buy him something, especially when his birthday came, he'd make a date with her and keep it, because he was getting something out of it. She knew he was using her big-time. He didn't buy her anything when her birthday came. Oh sure, sometimes he'd say, "It's to late now to get you a cake." Half of her birthdays he didn't even phone her. Sometimes he lied, saying, "I didn't get no answer."

She'd say, "I was there."

Sometimes she lit into him, calling him a liar, and he'd say, "Prove it." He was sometimes bored and restless for whatever reason. He'd call her up and whether they went out or stayed in, he'd be miles away in his mind. She'd ask him something and he'd ignore her, and then all of a sudden he'd sexually attack her, or he'd sing her a song if he didn't want to answer her. He had mood swings with a personality of Doctor Jekyll and Mr. Hyde. Once she played him a Phyllis Hyman cassette tape, the Living in Confusion song, and as they were driving she pushed the tape in and said, "I saved this for you." He sat there and listened to the song, and he said, "My ears clogged up I can't hear a thing," and they both burst out laughing. With Pa'Tony she was for real and truly living in confusion. One minute he would act like he cared for her some, and then later his attitude and his actions said otherwise. La'friska would say to him, "Actions speak louder than words." She learned not to give him an ultimatum, because she once did that, and with his no uncertain terms and attitude, he told her, "You take that and give it to the other guy." She never made that mistake again with him. He was hard on women; he'd say, "A woman belongs two places: in the kitchen and the bedroom." She could tell that he didn't care much for his son's mother. Sometimes he talked with so much intelligence. They'd talk about children in general, and he'd say, "Children are loaned to us; we have to let them go. We nurture them, and then our job is done; we must let them go. Not have all these custody battles over them, or even try to control them when they are grown." La'friska would think to herself, that makes sense. She wanted to marry him and have his baby, and he knew this. Like the story of her life, Pa'Tony, like Dacosta, didn't and wouldn't always make love to her completely. He didn't get easily turned on by her, and she worked so hard on his body to please and to turn him on. He got more turned on when he was physically hurting her by biting, her whether it was on the lips, her breasts, or her back side. He was so kinky and wild. She had to fight him off from certain positions, but that didn't stop him from constantly trying again and again. By then, she'd be tired and want to stop. She wanted to please his body, but she also knew that she didn't, because he wasn't easily turned on by her; maybe because he really didn't want her. She was having her doubts, thinking is he all used up because he's been with other women, or I'm not the woman he wants, that's why I can't turn him, on even worse, she began thinking as kinky as he is about a certain position, is he gay, I wonder. Then she'd think, I don't know if he's gay or not, because I can't tell, and I believe he likes women too much. Yes, he likes women, but he also wants the women to chase him. He always says "call me." She'd say, "what time," and he'd tell her the hour. She was apprehensive about phoning him after he'd hung up on her. She never forgot that incident; it was always in the back of her mind when she'd phone him. Half the time, she'd phone when he told her what hour, and he wouldn't be there; she'd think, is he playing a game with me?

Pa'Tony was very abusive to her in another sexual way. They'd be in the restaurant eating and he'd softly say to her "La'friska, you wanna suck my penis," or he'd say, "You want me to do you." She would be so embarrassed but she didn't let him know how much. He was abusive by kissing, touching her body, and he'd even suck her breasts. He'd have her body so ripe and heated with lust and her hopes built up that they were going to have sex later that day or night. Then she'd have to take him home, with him saying he had to take care of some business, or that he was expecting a phone call from his father. He invented all kinds of excuses. He'd say, "Maybe I'll see you later when I'm finished." Or sometimes he'd definitely say, "I'll come to you late tonight." Over ninety-eight percent of the time, he never came, and he didn't phone for weeks or months, with no explanation. La'friska would be crushed with hurt, still yet she hung in there, enduring his cold ,deliberate treatment. She endured for another four years. Sometimes she saw him maybe once or twice a year, even though they'd talk on the phone a few times throughout the year. She stopped buying him gifts, especially expensive birthday gifts, since he never brought her one. The only thing he ever brought her was the cake, ice cream, and balloons that first year. Half of the time he paid for their dinner, which wasn't, that expensive because they went to the same restaurant. Of course, there were those few times they dined in New York. He only ate limited foods, and he said he didn't eat meat. At least he never ate meat when they were together. Once he phoned her and asked her what she was doing. She replied, "Eating." He asked her what was she eating, and she replied, "A ham and cheese sandwich."

He said, "La'friska you can't be eating meat and kissing on me." Pa'Tony was definitely proud of his good looks. Although a few times he agreed with her that looks weren't everything. She would also say, "Using one's common sense makes them wise, and with book educational learning, one becomes more wiser and intelligent." Many times, they had great serious intellectual conversations.

## Thoughts

From January 6, 1993 to September 20, 2000, La'friska was living in a state of confusion with Pa'Tony. She wanted him. She thought he was for her since she'd never had the love of any man, especially Dacosta, whom she wanted and loved to death. But Dacosta had married someone else; he didn't want her. So she tried to move on with her heart and life, thinking with fate and all those signs that Pa'Tony was the man fate wanted her to have. But again, she was denied love. She had learned in those almost eight years with longing for Pa'Tony and waiting on him that life wasn't fair. That fate, the gods, or whatever, can really screw with your mind. That for some people in life, whether male or female, there is no mate for them to be with to share their lives. The people who are lonely and alone have to make up for the couples who are united and happy together. She learned and now knew fate could really fuck a person good and big-time without giving them any penis sexual release. With Pa'Tony she knew from the start he was out of her league, but she was going to give it all she had because she was having fun and she wanted him—hoping that he'd eventually want her too. During those almost eight years, he never spent the night at her house or allow her to spend the night with him. She'd ask him to stay the night, and he'd have some excuse. Once or twice after she'd brought whatever he wanted that cost hundreds of dollars, he's say, "I have to give you a night," but he never did. La'friska wanted so much to spend the night in his arms; to awake in the morning with him, especially on weekends, when they'd be off from work, but again, on weekends, being a musician, he'd say, "I'm just a black man trying to make it in America." She knew he worked hard and long hours. Some days when she'd be talking to him on the phone at lunch, his phone line would be buzzing, and he'd say "The market's gone crazy today." She'd heard how stock brokers got frustrated and stressed out; now she believed it, and being a musician only added more fuel to the burning fire. Pa'Tony knew and thought that he was God's gift to women, and then some; that he had it like that, and he did. From her viewpoint, no matter how good looking he was and no matter how much money or education he had, there was no excuse for treating women the way he treated her. Making dates and not showing, or canceling them. He thought he was so cool and suave, saying, "I'll call you with further instructions." She had never met his family or friends, and he'd never met hers. Months later, before she walked away again from him in the year 2000, she asked, during their conversation, "Why don't I get to meet your friends?"

He said, "Why don't I get to meet your friends?" She knew that he was throwing it back in her face, plus he was also conning her. She really did want to share his life and his world, yet he wouldn't let her. Sometimes he acted like he cared for her a little bit, and then he'd pull away like he didn't want to get to close to her. He knew he could depend on her. Sometimes she'd say, "I'll never forgive you for—," now whatever it was, she was referring to such and such, he'd say "You always do." He never drove his car; she always had to do the driving. That's why when he'd attack her with his Jekyll and Hyde personality mood swings. She'd be so defenseless driving her car. She didn't know if he thought that he was to good for her, or that she wasn't good enough for him. That she wasn't rich enough or educated enough or even pretty enough for him. As the last four years went by, sometimes he didn't have sex with her for almost a year, or she'd see him once in six to ten months, even though she might have talked to him on the phone sometimes every month or two. With him she was never sure of what would happen next. He phoned when least expected and he wouldn't leave a message on her answering machine most of the time. Then again he'd say "La'friska this is Pa'Tony, it's now (whatever time the hour would be), and he'd say the time and that he didn't like talking to machines," and that he'd call back later or he'd tell her to call him when she got in. They hadn't had dinner in over a year and a half. She'd taken him to purchase his new car, a Passat; that was over a year ago. The time he did come to her house in his new Passat, he stayed looking out the window watching his car; as a matter of fact, he could hardly screw her for watching his car. Pa'Tony should have had money with being a stock broker, musician, and a photographer, yet he always wanted her to buy him something that cost hundreds of dollars. He acted like he didn't have money at all. La'friska eventually made herself face the facts—that he didn't want her, and that if she brought him whatever he asked for, then he'd spend some time with her. She now needed him to in return spend something on her. It wouldn't have mattered how inexpensive the gift was, especially a birthday or Christmas gift. To her it was the thought that counted. He was all about himself—self-centered. Pa'Tony, with his possibly money, handsome good looks, and his educational intelligence—all these qualities, yet he was dumb with using his common sense when it came down to his treatment of women; so sad, what a waste of a man. After all the times she'd come to him, night or day, when he needed her because of his car problems. It was the principal of the thing. She wasn't talking about the money she spent on him; she did that on her own. He couldn't have made her. She learned with all she gave him: her love, endless time, and money; she got nothing in returned but heartache, loneliness, misery, and a painful hurt. To her, love should make you happy, not constantly hurt you. The last time she asked Pa'Tony to spend time with her was in September 2000, when it was a celebration time for her. She was celebrating her anniversary date of her job, and he was to have dinner with her that night. In the past, they had done this. Pa'Tony never phoned or came that night, and what's worse, he didn't phone her

## Thoughts

for three and a half months— bn which time she had made up her mind to walk away completely and never go back with him, because all he'd ever done was hurt her, and she was overly tired. Also, she finally realized that fate can play tricks and games on you. Also, the angels, or our father in heaven, was helping either. It was way past time for her to give up on Pa'Tony, and so be it, she did no phone calls ever again. There's a saying in life; when one door closes, another one opens. Maybe in her case it was true, and maybe it wasn't. It was almost two months later in November 2000 when fate intervened again in her life after twenty-two years; who entered her life, heart, mind, body, and soul, none other the only one Mr. Dacosta Tiawan Gahenne himself. Hallelujah.

# Reunited with Dacosta

It was almost seven years since La'friska had last been down home to South Carolina. After the death of her mother, she didn't come down home unless she really, really had to. It had to be extremely important for her to come, even though two of her sisters still remained there. Through the years, she'd phone them or write to them. The death of her parents was still too traumatic, especially her mother's death. Remember, it took her five years to bring closure to the death of her mother. It was a holiday weekend and she went down home to see her sisters and their families. It was on a Sunday in the month of November 2000 about 1'oclock in the evening when LaFriska saw Dacosta after 22 very long years.Let's back up to two days earlier, which was when she arrived down home that Friday morning; she didn't know that hours later, the urge to see Dacosta would be so strong. She knew that he was divorced, and she was told he didn't seem to have anybody—even though she didn't believed the part about him not having anybody; not the Dacosta she knew. The urge to see him was so real and strong that she told her nephew Lamar to tell Dacosta she wanted to see him; this was on a Saturday night. The next morning, which was a Sunday after a late breakfast, she and her sisters who had traveled with her, they all went out in the country to their parents' home, because now they stayed in hotels or motels mostly when they came back home. Her nephew had been to Dacosta's house earlier that morning and relayed the message to him that she wanted to see him. Dacosta said he'd be coming about twelve-thirty to her nephew's place. She visited with her sisters and their families. It was so good to see all of them. She was happy, content, and having fun. Her sisters who were traveling with her stayed awhile, and they left to go back to the hotel. La'friska stayed behind just to see Dacosta. It was after twelve-thirty and she was still at her sister Vicky's house talking with her when her nephew came to get her because Dacosta had come. She went with her nephew in the car, which was only two blocks at the most. She wanted to see Dacosta and she was so nervous, scared, and anxious all at the same time. She hadn't attempted all those years to see him, and he made no attempt to see her. Even though through the years her nephews had told her that he asked about her. She'd eight years before from listening to a psychic's prediction phoned his sister and asked about him. She still knew his sister's phone number from past remembrance, and she wanted to know if she'd changed the number, which she hadn't. So, talking with his sister she learned that he had two children and that he was separated from his wife. That his trailer home had burned down. La'friska told his sister to tell him if he wanted to he could call her. Well, he never phoned her, so she figured he didn't want to be bothered with her. She never phoned his sister again. Even during her conversation with his sister, she never told her if or not she still loved him. To La'friska, he had married another woman and had children with her; that action said it all. There was nothing else he could ever again do to hurt her more; the damages had been done, which were irreparable. La'friska's anxiety and nervousness stayed with her as she got out of the car and walked over to him. He was looking through a family brochure of her sister's retirement party and her four-year-old grandniece was standing beside him. He looked up and saw her and they both smiled and reached out and embraced each other in a hello hug. To La'friska, he was just as handsome as ever. He'd gotten heavier weightwise, but then, so had she. The anxiety and nervousness she'd been feeling now evaporated. She was so glad and very happy to see him again after all those long twenty-two years. They were surrounded by others in the yard, his cousins and family members and friends. Dacosta seemed and acted happy to see her also. They tried to talk, but his cousins and her nephews they all were putting their two cents in, trying to get the two of them to go off and be alone. Her nephew offered his car for them to drive. His cousin tried to give them his house key, plus offered them money for gas. She and Dacosta were somewhat embarrassed, but they had fun laughing at the others pushing them together. His cousins cracked jokes, telling her, "Don't hurt him;" she knew that they meant sex-wise. Standing beside Dacosta, he whispered only for her ears what he wanted to do with her sexually, and she was happy he wanted to do that to her, because he'd never done it to her before. His whispered words meant oral sex. She could tell he had changed somewhat. Dacosta wanted them to leave, and yes, she wanted to also, but she didn't want to borrow someone else's car. Plus, they had finally gotten her sick sister outside. She didn't want to leave her sister right away. So when Dacosta said, "Friska, let's go somewhere," she said, "Later," and explained about her sister getting out of the house. She asked to see pictures of his children, but he said he didn't have any in his wallet. Naturally, she had pictures of her daughter in her wallet and she showed them to him. He said her daughter was pretty and that she had La'friska's facial features. Not wanting the others to hear to hear what she was saying because it was only for his ears, she softly whispered, "You gave someone else two babies."

Dacosta said, "Friska, we couldn't have any; we tried." He was drinking a Budweiser beer and eating a barbecue sandwich. He looked like he needed help with his food, so she held his beer while he ate his sandwich. She wanted to wrap her arms around his now protruding stomach. She was getting turned on from just the sight of him. Dacosta stayed for an hour; he was riding with a cousin because his driver's license was revoked, and had been for years, but he was due to get them reinstated that same month. La'friska told him she'd come to his house at five o'clock that evening. They kissed goodbye, and when he was inside the truck to leave, her nephew was holding him up from leaving by giving him a pep talk, telling him, "You're going to be in the family."

Dacosta called out to her, "La'friska, come get him." She went over and her and Dacosta smiled, laughed, and talked a few minutes, confirming she'd be to his house at five o'clock. He asked if she knew the way, and she said, "I'll find it." Even her nephew heard and he also told her the way, because it had been over twenty-two years since she'd gone to his house. When he was getting ready to finally leave, she wanted to kiss him so badly that she said, "Give me a kiss," and they both leaned forward and kissed. Dacosta kissed her lips like he couldn't wait for later. She also kissed him likewise and she didn't care others were watching. His lips were so soft, sweet, and good, just like twenty-two years ago. She went back to the hotel and prepared herself luxuriously for him. She took their rental car and left for his house. As she got nearer, her anxiety returned because she wanted to see him so much. She was hoping nothing went wrong, but fate wasn't going to make it easy for her. She thought that she knew the way, but she took a wrong turn and stopped at two different houses for directions, but no one would come out, and there was cars at both houses. She told herself, they don't know me and I'm black with a new 2000 car and New York license plates, plus the fact those were white folks' homes; again, she knew they were in there. She didn't get out of the car, but she blew the horn a few times so when no one would come out she knew it was time for her to leave because she didn't want any trouble. She was getting impatient and desperate. She almost phoned her nephew on her cell phone, but then she told herself, no, I'll do it. So she persevered, and when she stopped at the fourth house, a woman came out, and La'friska thought to herself, that she looks like Dacosta's baby sister Shar. La'friska told the woman, "I'm trying to find Dacosta's house. He's expecting me."

The woman said, "That's my brother; he lives on the farm. I don't know if he's home."

La'friska said, "He's expecting me; I saw him earlier."

Shar said, "I'll take you there."

Well La'friska was so very happy. His sister got into her own car, and she drove, making one stop in the road when she saw someone and she asked them if Dacosta was home. La'friska couldn't hear all of the reply, and his sister drove on for a minute and then she stopped and, leaning out of her car, his sister, pointing toward a road, said to La'friska, "Take that road and it'll take you onto his house." La'friska thanked her and she proceeded, following the road, and then her familiarity came back because she'd been to his house several times before, though that was over twenty-two years ago. She drove in the yard, blew the horn, and a man came out.Dacosta had told her earlier that he had two roommates; one was his cousin Henly, and she knew him because they all went to school together. She told the man that she was looking for Dacosta. The man went back inside and out came the only man in this life for her—Dacosta himself. She was so thrilled to finally reach him, because back there she was desperately panicking from the anticipation of finally being with him again.

Dacosta got in the passenger seat and said, "You smell good." Of course she knew she did because she'd pampered herself with expensive shower gel, lotion, and Fendi perfume. They talked about if she had a hard time finding his house, and she explained how she'd stopped at the other houses, and finally the last house was his sister's. Dacosta was looking so good, and those two kisses earlier made her want and need more. He was talking and she couldn't take it anymore; she said, "Shut up and kiss me." He smiled and leaned over, kissing her. She kissed him back greedily, because this was what she'd wanted for hours. They kissed and he touched her breast. He said, "Lets go somewhere." She asked, "Do you have a condom?" and he told her, "No." She told him to find one, and he told her, "Let's go to the store." They drove to the store and then to a motel. It was around seven o'clock when they got to the room. He said, "Let me go inside first before someone knocks you in the head," and he went in first. As she walked by him going into the bathroom, he grabbed her and tried to throw her on the bed. She tussled back; knowing they had time, she didn't want to rush. She got up and Dacosta said, "You're strong." They got into bed and he kissed, touched, and sucked her breasts.

## Thoughts

La'friska knew she still loved him very much. She had never ever stopped loving him. His lips were still so soft and sweet tasting; he had her blanking in and out of this world. He even performed oral sex on her. This is what he whispered earlier that he wanted to do to her. He'd never done that to her before. The years had changed him. As a matter of fact, he said so himself that he was fifty years old and learned to eat pussy. Having him do that to her body felt so good. After twenty-two years, she was now where she'd always wanted and needed to be. He was the only man she'd really ever truly loved. After performing sex on her, he wanted her to reciprocate on him, and she wanted it too, but she didn't because other thoughts were on her mind. Like, "I want this to last, being with him tonight." She thought she had time. Hours yet to still be with him, and mainly she thought of the AIDS virus and not knowing these twenty-two years who else he'd been with. Dacosta told her that unless she performed the sex act on him, he wouldn't be able to get his body back erect again. Earlier when he'd tried to throw her on the bed, he was good and ready then. Now he was getting old and couldn't do what he used to do. She hadn't know this at that, moment because if she had she would have gladly seized that moment to once again feel his hard penis inside of her. Again, she thought she had time. So they kissed and touched and caressed each other—especially her. She couldn't and wouldn't keep her hands off him as they laid there kissing and talking. They had never before talk that way. Dacosta said things she'd been waiting all those years wanting him to say to her. He said, "Now I know you were the one for me." He said that twice that night in their conversations. She was so happy and glad to finally hear him say those words, hoping he meant them. When she explained how much he hurt her by going with Kim and those other girls, but especially Kim, he told her, "Kim was a city girl and I knew she would put out sex." La'friska told him she too would have given him sex, because she loved and wanted him that much. He also indicated that he didn't have sex that much with Kim. Of course, she thought to herself, she didn't believe him, since she saw how he treated Kim like he really cared for her. She told him about the Sunday he phoned her and said he only wanted her pussy, laughing at her with his friends and cousins in the background listening and laughing at her. Dacosta told her that he could have been nicer. No wonder I didn't have any luck; now I know why. As they continued talking, they were both so serious, and a few times La'friska was so emotional from his words that she'd moan with pain and relief saying, "Don't make me cry." She'd even wail, starting to cry as she stared in his face and eyes. She'd never seen his brown eyes so clearly. His eyes were beautiful, and she asked him, are those your eyes, thinking they could have been contacts lenses. He said yes they were his own. As she looked into his eyes; he was kneeling on the floor suffering from gas and La'friska was lying on her stomach at the end of the bed facing him. She had her hand gently touching and caressing his back, and he kept saying, "That feels good." Again, she couldn't or wouldn't keep her hands off him. Dacosta said, "I've never talked like this before; it feels good." Dacosta told her that he had feelings for her. As a matter of fact, he said this at least three different times in those hours they were together. La'friska didn't comment, since she was again hoping that one day those feelings would eventually turn into love for her. He also told her he didn't have anyone, nor did he want anyone. He told her that there was a woman he'd messed with, but now she was preaching. Later, La'friska learned this same woman had come to his house after he'd left her at her nephews. He told her she came on business about a hog. He also said he wasn't gay or anything. She asked him what did he do about sex? He said, "Sometimes I buy it, go in my room, and you know what, beat it."

La'friska thought to herself, "He buys it and here he could have mine for free." She told him again, "You gave some woman two babies."

He said, "Friska, we tried and we couldn't have any." She told him he married someone else and not her. He said, "Kids should have a father and for ten years; I tried to make it work." He said he didn't have his father because he lived in Philadelphia. When he was nine years old he went to see his dad. At that time his father had someone else. He told her earlier out at her nephew's place that she shouldn't forget home. She should come home because her parents were good and wonderful people. La'friska told him about her parents' death, especially her mother's, which was too painful and hurtful. That's when he told her about when he was a nine-year-old boy and went to see his father. She asked him if he had cheated on his wife, and he indicated that he did and that his wife must have too, since she remarried six months after they divorced. La'friska didn't ask him if he had loved or still loved his wife. She didn't want to feel the pain if he had said that yes he had loved her. Dacosta would stare at her and say, "Old Friska," and he'd smile, and he did that many times throughout those five hours they were together. He told her that Brandi Fletcher, who was his cousin and had been her best friend, had told him that she wanted to fight Kim over him. La'friska told him that wasn't true and that she'd never fought over any guy and she wouldn't unless the person attacked her first, and what she'd done was sent word to Kim that she wanted to see her, and when they met, she said to Kim, "You didn't have to lie about going with Dacosta, and don't ever say anything to me again." She didn't think he believed her because of the way he said, "You wanted to fight that girl." Dacosta said, "When you said, 'Dacosta, tell me you love me,' did you think I was going to tell you no? I was scared and said, 'Yeah, Friska, I love you." She learned that

## Thoughts

his brother Peter had seven children and was still unmarried. While at her nephew's house, she asked him about his mother, and she told him she was happy for him that his mother was still alive. His sister Vicki had died almost a year ago. He was hurting from her death since they were so close. La'friska was hurt when her nephew had phoned almost a year before telling her his sister Vicki had died. She liked Vicki and had been to her house and talked on the phone with her. She would always remember her words when she met La'friska's daughter. Vicki didn't ask right away, but later as Vicki was looking at her daughter, she asked was she Dacosta's. La'friska responded, "No." La'friska told Dacosta, "I wanted your baby, and she should have been yours."

He responded with, "I haven't been much of a father, and she's better off without me." They were content just lying next to each other talking.

Earlier when they'd had sex, La'friska's emotions took over, and as he was moving inside of her she stared into his eyes and said, "I still love you." He didn't say anything. As they continued talking, he said, I must have changed to lay here talking like this, and it feels good. I've never done this before." She told him that she really wanted to clarify things about his brother Peter, because one time he accused her of messing with his brother. She said, "I like Peter; he's your brother to me—he's always been my brother in law. Peter was always a respectful gentlemen with me. He even gave me hope where you were concerned. He'd pass by and say, 'Dacosta said he loves you.' Of course, I didn't believe him, especially not with your actions toward me." Dacosta coughed a lot, saying he had the smokers' illness. He couldn't remember the name of the word it was called. He asked her, "Why do you want me?"

She said, "Because I still love you and I want you."

He replied, "I'm all washed up, and I'm a broken man."

She told him, "I still want you." At one point she rolled underneath him and he entered his penis inside of her body and they were both staring into each other's eyes. She cried out moaning in pleasure when his penis was inside of her. She felt like she was drowning down into a sea of the abyss. She loved him so very much. They kissed, touched, caressed, and did a lot of foreplaying while making love. Of course, neither of them climaxed, but they enjoyed each other. They were both older now and couldn't do what they use to, and the day had taken both of them by surprise. He hadn't know she was in town, and she didn't know if he'd come to see her. Her biggest excuse was she had waited so many long years for this that she didn't know how to let go and love him. She could tell he was getting sleepy by the sleepy look in his eyes, and he'd nod off every so often. She told him he looked like he needed some sleep. She really wanted to spend the night with him at the motel. He didn't ask her to, and she didn't volunteer to ask him to stay with her. So they left the motel and she took him back to his house. On the way, she kept thinking, "This is it. I won't see him again. Tomorrow I leave to go back home to Jersey." It was very dark and quiet as they drove. He said, "I'm sorry I kept you this late. I don't want something to happen to you. I don't want people saying, 'Dacosta kept her out when she came down here.'" At his house sitting in the car she gave him her phone number and address. She also told him anytime he wanted to visit her in Jersey he had an open invitation. He said he'd call her and when he came to Philadelphia with his buddy he'd stop by and see her; that sometimes they came up at holidays. She was now staring at him for life because she didn't know if and when she'd see him, so she was storing up memories of his face. They eventually kissed goodbye and she left. Driving back to the hotel she was somewhat dazed, in a tranquil state. She was sorry that she didn't seize the moment with him and had sex right away when his penis was erect, and she was so very sorry that she didn't perform the oral sex act on him. She thought, "If I ever again in life get that chance, I'll seize the moment; I won't let it pass me by." She went to bed that night in a dreamy, dazed, tranquil zombie trance-like state of mind. She kept reliving in her mind the time they'd spent together, hearing him say all those things to her. There was a song stuck in her mind and heart; "Sade's Tattoo." She kept hearing in her mind for fourteen years. He said I couldn't look into the sun. She saw him laying at the end of my gun. "Hungry for life and thirsty for the distant, I wear it like a tattoo." As a fact, this song played when she left Dacosta's house. To La'friska, those fourteen years were the twenty-two years without seeing or hearing from Dacosta. La'friska left back for her home in Jersey; she wasn't the same. No one knew what she was going through inside and out. She was in deep turmoil. Once again she now wanted Dacosta just as much as ever. All those years she'd just pushed her love on the back burner, or whatever words that'll describe her feelings, because he was married to someone else; she knew she didn't have a chance. She now knew no matter who he was or wasn't married to didn't and wouldn't stop her love for him. She'd tried through those twenty-two years of not having any contact whatsoever with him to forget him, even though she went on with her life, and had someone else's baby and raised her child by herself, of course with the help of her wonderful family. She'd tried to have a life with Roderick to help raise their child. Forget Lodi; there was never any kind of love there on her part. She liked and respected him for showing respect and kindness to her and her child, but again, there was no love for Lodi. She only existed at living life. Now with Pa'Tony, she again tried hard for almost eight years, but again, Pa'Tony treated her worse than any man ever had. Temporarily reminiscing of

## Thoughts

the twenty-two years without Dacosta in her life was an empty void. She really did have no other choices, now twenty-two long years later. Two weeks after returning home to Jersey, her need and want for Dacosta made her again write him a letter. To be exact, her final ever letter, and she told him that in the ending of her letter. She told him that she wasn't trying to push him or chase him again, but she did want him to know again how she felt about him, and to understand. She told him how much she had enjoyed seeing him and that she loved being with him. She said that she was very sorry for not seizing that special moment making love with him, and that if he ever again gave her a chance, she would take that moment for all it was worth holding on for dear life; she'd seize the moment. She asked him to please give her that chance, that if he didn't want to come to her and if he wanted her, then she'd gladly come to him. She told him when she'd said the other week that she still loved him that she really and truly did meant it and still did; that if he'd now give her that chance, she'd proudly and gladly take him, no matter how broken of a man he was, being washed and worn out, as he put it. She didn't see him that way. She said, "If you meant that, saying now you know I was the one for you, it's not too late. You can still have me, because I love and still want you. I beg you to take this chance. Think about it, because life is too short and I've waited and wanted you almost all of my life. Let's live out the rest of our lives together. I want to love you, and I also need you to want me too. I want to be your world of joy and share your life with you. Again, I want you to want me to so we can share the rest of whatever life we have left on this earth. To share whatever may come our way, through good times and bad times, joys and sorrows, trials and tribulations, etc." La'friska also told him years ago, "When I gave you a key to my necklace, the inscription on it read, 'He who holds the key can open the door to my heart.' Darlin,g whether you forgot about that key, lost it, or threw it away, it's still true you are the only one who can open the door to my heart. Do it for me and for you; us together." She told him if he didn't want to leave the South and live up North, then she'd leave the North and come to him, that she didn't care where they lived as long as they were at last finally together. She said, "Let me refresh your memory; over twenty-two years ago, in another of my letters to you, I told you that I didn't care if where we lived we was surrounded by deadly reptiles, of snakes and alligators and crocodiles, just as long as we were together. Well, darling, that's still so true. I must really mean it because I'm terrified of snakes I have bad nightmares about snakes at least once a month. I wake up moaning and half of the time I turn the covers back making sure there's no snake in my bed. Tell you this, if I had to kill a snake to save my life or someone I loved, I would do it, and then I might would have a heart attack, but then I'd tell myself, 'fool, you are still alive; you did it, you defeated the snake. now why give yourself a heart attack." Back to the letter, she told him THAT no matter what, they could work out something to be together, whether it was temporary or permanent. La'friska reminded him that no matter what, he always had an open invitation. She mailed the letter to her nephew to give to Dacosta. She knew Dacosta received it, because her nephew told her so. She trusted her nephew Lamar. Dacosta told her nephew twice that he was going to call her, but he never did. As the months went by, still no word or call from him. She didn't know what was going through his mind. Even if his answer was no, she still would have accepted it and even left him alone forever, never bothering to contact him again. She was in turmoil, wondering why he wouldn't get in touch with her. Then God and fate step in intervening. Dacosta knew about these incidents, and still yet he didn't contact her. She had to return down home for the death of her Aunt Elanie's funeral. She didn't try to contact him because she knew that he was aware of it. She kept hoping he show up, but he didn't. After returning back home to Jersey, she sprained her ankle and was out of work for weeks recuperating. With both of these traumatic and devastating experiences when she needed his comfort to give her strength, he wasn't there for her. He didn't know that since being reunited with him, she was contemplating still trying to have his baby now at her age, but once again fate stepped in and took that idea away from her, because she had to have surgery, and even Dacosta didn't help out because he wouldn't phone her for her to tell him what she still wanted. He'd said that he wasn't much of a father to his kids; here she would have given him another chance with her. So before going under the knife and having surgery, she wanted and needed to hear his voice. She told her nephew to tell him before she went under the knife that he could call her, but again he wouldn't and he still didn't. Three weeks later God stepped in again because her sister Victoria died. She didn't want her sister to die, and she loved her sister very much. Her sister was a wonderful and loving giving person. This reflection of her sister was shown by all the people attending her funeral. People came from miles around; all except one who should have, which was no one other than Dacosta. He didn't come, and she needed him for strength and support. Grieving from death and the pains of surgery, he wasn't there for her; he didn't even show respect for her dead sister, and he should have, because he'd taken her to her sister's house in the past; also, he'd seen her a few months ago, plus, years before when he was in court for child support payment. So by him not reaching out to her, especially at a time like this when she needed comfort, support, and strength, she was to hurt by him again. He let her down, so the day her sister was buried that same night she buried Dacosta too, even though he was very much alive. She had to face facts; that he still didn't want

## Thoughts

to be bothered with her. La'friska walked away from him by not bothering him. She was deeply hurting, devastated from both pains of grief and unrequited love. La'friska again tried even harder to get over wanting him; it didn't work. She was doomed. Even though she made herself stop fantasizing about him, she still thought of him, but she'd tell herself, "He's dead to me, because he didn't really care about me or want me unless it suited his purpose." It wasn't until exactly fourteen months later that she and Dacosta just happened to unexpectedly meet at a club hangout when she was down home again for another family funeral. When Dacosta saw her, he seemed and acted happy to see her. They talked, and he confirmed that he'd gotten her letter and that yes he should have answered her back. They hanged at the club for a while and had a dance or two. They spent the night at his house. She lay in his arms. It was positively wonderful. She really needed his comfort tremendously, because she was mourning the death of her brother Junior. Yes, La'friska got the chance to seize the moment from fourteen months before. To finally make oral and passionate love to him. Dacosta in return did likewise to her. At one point, she stared into his eyes and softly said, "I love you."

Dacosta said, "I know." They held each other throughout the night. She hardly slept as she lay there holding him lovingly \while he slept contentedly snoring. She lay there listening to an all-night oldies music radio station. Those hours in time were exquisitely nostalgic, and fate was somewhat cruel when it played a Stevie Wonder song from twenty-four years ago on a night when she'd stayed at his sister's house lying beside him in his bed. The name of the Stevie Wonder song was "I wish." All too soon the morning came and La'friska knew the magical time had ended. They parted sweetly, both kissing each other lovingly. Once again, she had a love hangover from being with him, even though she was painfully mourning the loss of a loved one. She wrote him thanking him for the wonderful night she spent with him and the comfort he gave her that she needed at that time. This time he wrote back confirming he'd gotten her letter and hoped that she was doing all right. Even though his letter was only a few lines, she was shocked and thrilled that he'd written her back. For the next three and a half years they kept in contact with each other by phone, and once a year on her vacation she would go back down home to see and be with him. Things had changed somewhat, some for the better, others for the worse—meaning Dacosta still made dates with her and he never showed up. Now if and when he wanted and needed money, he'd be there. Also, he was right about his being older now and unable to do what he used to; this being sexually. He constantly told her that he wasn't gay or anything; that he just didn't want it. Of course, when they were together she would never stop trying to turn him on and change his mind. Sometimes he'd kiss hug and foreplay with her, but then he'd stop, saying, "maybe later," but later never came—even if she'd again initiate. She remembered one year on her vacation when she did her best work trying to turn him on sexually that he got up and left, and he didn't returned until hours later, and he never gave her an explanation as to where he'd been all that time. Although, when he left her he did say that he was worried about his cousin and roommate because they didn't get along and they weren't answering his phone calls. So he stopped her from performing oral sex on him and he left, wearing her strap sandal shoes and driving her rental car. She was so worried about him, not knowing whether something had happened to him because he'd been drinking and doing a little smoking drugs. She wondered if he'd made love to someone else after she'd halfway turned him on. When he returned three hours later, he just got in bed and lay there over on his side of the bed, not even touching her or anything. La'friska thought to herself I leave in a few hours catching a flight back home to Jersey. Finally she said out softly "I'm tired of leaving you." He said, "It'll just be for a while longer." They both knew in a year that she'd be retiring and moving back to South Carolina. She softly said, "I love you." He said "I know."

La'friska couldn't take it anymore, so she said, "Do something about it."

He said, "What do you want?"

She said, "Hold me in your arms." When he didn't move, she said, "Come and get me." He did come, and he got her. They lay there like that for a few minutes then he said, "I can't sleep like this." She just rolled out of his arms back to her side of the big bed. She just lay there not even thinking, because no matter what she did, she couldn't win for loosing . She gave up and eventually sleep came. Four hours later when she dropped him off at home standing out in the yard saying goodbye, unexpectedly he reached out and touched the cleavage in her dress between her breasts. Neither one said a word, although she thought to herself, "He's playing with me. I thought he didn't notice my dress, and out of nowhere he's fingering my cleavage. Besides, he knows I'm now leaving for home in Jersey; we won't be seeing one another." They both had decided that they'd live together when she retired, and he told her that if things worked out with them, they'd get married in a year. To her it seemed like sometimes he'd be getting close to her, like he was beginning to care more, and then he'd pull away. She knew he was deeply hurt from his ex-wife, even though he didn't talk much about her. He said he wanted her to make it with her new husband. He also wasn't that close with his children. La'friska often thought, "Why can't he love me like that?" Then she'd remind herself, "That was then; it's over with between them. Maybe now it'll work out for us. We've both had a life with others, and we have children with others. We're now older hopefully much wiser, because life does goes on." Yes, on with

## Thoughts

life went. As usual, Dacosta would phone saying, "Wire me three hundred dollars; I need to buy hog feed, etc." She'd do it, even if it was on a Sunday afternoon and she had to run all over town to find a Western Union that was open. He would lie so sweetly, saying, "You are the best friend I have." She knew it was a line for him to get what he wanted. He also said, "I love you, but I'm not in love with you." It was four months before she was due to retire that she came to her senses about moving in with him. She remembered how he'd treated her all through her life, and even now half of the time, so she realized and knew that she couldn't possibly take the chance on living with him. Giving him money to help fix up his house the way she liked it. She thought and knew, "With that much money I could have my own home halfway paid off. Not to mention, what if one day he put me out; then I'd have no place to go, plus I'd be out of a lot of money." She also knew that she had to have a place of her own so that if her daughter fell on hard times, she'd have a roof over her head and a home to come to. She was a good mother and had always taken care of her child first and foremost. Therefore, she couldn't and she wouldn't take a chance that he could kick her out, and even if her child needed refuge he'd not want her there at his house. Even with his own children, she couldn't trust the fact that someday they'd want to return back home. She knew how she'd raised her daughter and taught her values and principles. Also, she knew that when your own children see you doing things for your spouse's children who aren't kin to you, that's when your own children feel left out, knowing you're doing things for someone else's children and not your own. So when she did tell him that she decided to get her own place after all, he said that was for the best. Finally retirement did come, and she left New Jersey. Dacosta came up; finally she did get him up. He drove her back to South Carolina. When they left Jersey, it was very sad for her, because she was leaving behind her daughter and sister, whom she loved so very much. As fate would have it, she had to put her feelings aside, because the weather was very bad. It was windy, with downpouring rain, and she had to direct Dacosta with the right directions. It was now all about their own survival; the visibility and rain were so horrendous that they had to get off at an exit on the turnpike waiting for the rain to slack up. Sometimes the rain visibility was so bad that she thought to herself, "If I was doing the driving, I'd stop and wait it out," but Dacosta just mainly kept on driving. During that twelve hours' drive, time quickly flew by. She loved being with him; she had waited all her life for this time. When you're happy, my how time flies by and gets away from you. They were in and out of the bad weather for hours, and eventually it cleared up. They had great conversations. Sometimes she had to laugh at his ideas and his ways of thinking; he was comical. She'd never heard nor ever thought that anyone would say they wouldn't die for their mother. She thought most people would kill for their mother. Dacosta's reply was, "Mama done live her life." Again, she thought a mother's love for her child was so precious and the bond between them so strong. She also thought that if somebody had a bother, her mother, what she would have done to them. She'd have been on the first and fastest thing smoking. Come hell or high water train, plane or bus, and she couldn't stand riding the bus that far. If she couldn't have gotten on those vehicles, then she'd have driven her own car. Although she did recall over thirty years ago when she once took an express bus to down home to be with him. Now that bus ride wasn't so bad because it was an express bus, and her mind was full of Dacosta, thinking of him. Otherwise, the local bus stopped; too much picking up and discharging passengers. The ride could be a nightmare. Back to their driving down, once arriving back home in South Carolina, she was very busy settling into her new home. Plus, Dacosta kept her on the road to the three different Veteran's Hostipals. She was his transportation and chauffeur. He was into rehabilitation for alcohol and substance abuse, plus he was now sickly and applying for his disability. He now had the Sarcoidosis lung disease. He told her he suspected he'd gotten this lung disease from the job he'd worked on for almost twenty years, and that he couldn't prove it. For the next three months, the routine was almost the same. On weekends, he'd come on Friday nights and stay sometimes till Monday morning when he left to go to work. Even if he left on Saturday morning to do chores or whatever, he'd return back at night. She fixed elegant meals for him. He made breakfast in the mornings. He was a big eater; he loved food. When he was at her house, he constantly ate and watched television. He wasn't drinking alcohol or beer anymore. It seemed the rehabilitation was working. She also helped by no longer buying beer or alcohol for him. She was content and happy being with him, although she'd have been truly ectatic if he'd make love to her. It now seemed he didn't too much care for her kissing and hugging on him, especially if and when he was watching television or sleeping. He'd groan and pull away from her. She was hurt by this action, and she'd leave him alone, that is, until the next time she'd try again. She knew he was worried; about his job mishaps and also the summer weather was excruciatingly hot. She asked him how he was making it working in the hot weather in the fields and driving trucks that had no air conditioning. He'd say that he was managing. She knew that by him not drinking anymore, plus the heat, that things were taking a toll on him. She remembered one night in particular, which was a Sunday during the middle of the night, they'd awoken and he was in a talking mood. She thought to herself, he should be trying to sleep, because he has to go to work in the morning. She listened attentively and patiently as he kept talking about his job's mishaps,

# Thoughts

and just life in general. Eventually, morning came, and off to work he want. She began to notice how his attitude and mood swings had changed. Several times, he complained about her driving when she took him to the Veteran's Hostipal. One incident in particular she came back at him and put him in his place. When she replied, "It's just like a man to tell a woman how to drive." Well, he was surprised at her outspokenness. He must have thought to himself and realized how much he needed her to transport him back and forth to the different Veteran's locations. He then said, "I'll shut up." She thought to herself, the way he said that, he's mainly talking to himself. She'd never before talked to him like that. The argument was dropped. They found the place he needed to be. On the way back home he told her about the party his family was having in a week. It was a yearly thing. He told her to stop at the supermarket. While he went inside shopping, she stayed in the car. Even so, their argument was dropped and never mentioned again; what she didn't know was that stemming from this event, a dramatic change was coming into their lives. She was now very thrilled about going to his party. She got to see his family and friends, some which she hadn't seen in over thirty-five years. On the day of the party, he phoned early that morning and told her to go to the store and bring him seventeen pounds of rice. When he said this, she thought to herself, "Rice doesn't come in a seventeen pound bag; I'll have to get a twenty pound bag," and that's exactly what she did. She took it to his house. He'd already started cooking in the wash pot his signature chicken and rice dish. Again, he reminded her to be on time for the party that afternoon. Back home she prepared herself, wanting to look extra special for the occasion. In her life, as fate would have it, she was the last one to get to the party. It was in full swing. The lawn was full of cars and people. As she approached, he saw her. So did others who watched. He was in a conversation with some guy. Beside him was his brother Peter and their mother. She'd seen his mother a few years back, but hadn't been introduced to her. Dacosta had played a game on her at that time. She'd been on vacation and had picked him and his cousin Hank up. What happened was, as they drove by, this woman on a riding lawn mower blew the car horn and then he backed, back up to where she was. He said a few words to this woman, such as, "Hi , how are you doing, etc." He talked over her to this woman because he was in the driver's seat. It wasn't until they drove off that he said, "Well, why didn't you say something?" She sprung around quickly look at him and said, "That was your mother?" He laughed at her and she said, "I'm gonna kill you." That only made him laugh even louder. Even his cousin Hank was laughing from the back seat. Now at last, over forty years to finally meet her. To La'friska, it was truly thrillingly, wonderful. Again, as she continued to approach, Dacosta was engrossed in his conversation with this guy; she didn't know who he was. He still kept on talking. When she finally stopped at them, she smiled at Peter standing beside his brother Dacosta. She said hi to Peter; to her she'd always had a fondness for him. She rememberd how he'd lie for Dacosta at school as they passed by in the hallways. Peter smiled back and said, "Have you met momma?" It was then that their mother turned and looked at her and said, "This is the one who went to Germany?" Well, La'friska was surprised his mother still remembered that. La'friska said hi to his mother and confirmed that yes, she went to Germany. His mother then said, "That ole crazy nigger." La'friska didn't ask what she meant by that remark, but she wondered to herself. Dacosta then turned to her and asked if she had trouble finding her way. She confirmed yes that she did. She gave him a gift bag with a card, bath robe, and bed slippers. At the party she mainly stayed by his side, standing around talking with whomever remembered her from school. She told Dacosta to fix her plate to go, and he did. He fixed her a big plate because he knew that she didn't eat anything at the party. She enjoyed herself and she stayed over three hours. When she left he walked her to the car. She asked him to come to her house that night. He said if he could and that he didn't know because the party would last into the night. They kissed each other goodbye. If the others at the party were watching them, they couldn't help but see this kiss. Back at home she ate her plate of food and it was very good. She laughed out loud remembering what Dacosta's mother had said to him when she looked at his rice and chicken. She said, "Did you leave any pepper at home?" His rice dish did have a lot of pepper in it. Dacosta didn't come that night. The next week at nighttime he phoned and asked her did she want some peanuts? She said yes, and she wanted to see him. He told her the weekend. When the weekend came he never showed up. She hadn't seen him in three weeks. Finally one night she phoned him and when he answered the phone she just bluntly said, "Do you have a problem with me?" He was apparently surprised at her bluntness, and he softly laughed and said, "Man, I need a break." She was hurt by his words. Now she knew why his behavior was strange and that she hadn't seen him in weeks. So hurt by his words, she then said, "I'll leave you alone." She said goodbye and hung up. After that phone call, those words he said to her were way too much. It was finally the turning point of her love for him. All she'd ever done was want and wait on him, loving him no matter what. Giving him money unconditionally. Being his transportation and chauffeur for three months, taking him back and forth to the different veteran's hospital locations. It seemed he used her to get what he wanted, trying to get his disability. She didn't know what he needed a break from her for. After all, she only saw him on weekends and when he had a doctor's appointment and he needed a ride from her. The turning point made her see the truth finally. He wasn't in love

## Thoughts

with her; a second chance at a relationship totaling over forty years. She became angry at him and mad at herself. She was mad with herself because she'd allowed him all her life to had have control of her heart, body, and mind. She got even madder with herself because she should have told him off a long time ago. He wasn't all that after all; yes, he was still handsome and sexy, but greatly overweight. He couldn't even give her sex anymore; his body was so burned out that his penis wouldn't and couldn't harden. Believe you me, she really and truly knew about his penis erection difficulties, because as hard as she tried for years doing her best work to turn him on, that is when he'd let her, and here's the kicker, which is icing on the cake—the night in the motel when she was working so very hard giving him oral stimulation sex, he stopped her in the midst and left to go God knows where because she didn't and still doesn't know. Apparently, between the women, alcohol, and drugs throughout the years and years had finally taken a toll on his manhood. Even so, he carried himself outwardly with high self esteem for other's to see. She knew better the for real deal; it just wasn't and isn't so. Truthfully, he was impotent. La'friska was now to done trying to get him. She knew that if by chance he ever called her again and wanted to see her, that she'd tell him no, that she no longer wanted to be bothered with him. She really and truly finally meant this. Even if by some miracle God had intervened telling her to give him the chance, she would have say no, telling God she didn't believe it because after all those years he didn't care by now; why would he start now? Her hurt was way past too much pain and heartache. Years upon years, almost all of her whole entire life. It was two months later that fate and the cosmic forces stepped in; tax preparation time had come. She kept waiting for her information to come. When it didn't, finally she phoned her retirement office and was told it had been sent to his address. She had no other choice but to phone him and ask about her mail. He told her that a letter had come for her three weeks ago, but that now he couldn't find it; someone had moved it. He said that he'd look for it and give her a call. She gave him time; a week went by and he still didn't call, therefore she again had no other choice except to call him. This time she called his cell phone number, but he didn't answer. An hour later he phoned asking did someone call his number. He didn't even recognize her home phone number anymore to have asked that question. She asked had he found her letter, and he said no, that someone had moved it, and couldn't you get another." Well, that was the last time she ever phoned his house. The nerve of him. He had her mail for three weeks and wouldn't pick up a phone and call her to come get it. Even after she called him asking about her mail, waiting for another week for him to get back to her. Yet he still wouldn't call her. This action confirmed to her that he wanted nothing to do with her. It's a Federal crime to tamper with someone else's mail. So be it. It is what it is. She went on with her life. Birthdays and holidays passed, and year after year and yet he never phoned her. True to her words, "I'll leave you alone," she didn't contact him either. Her will power was very strong, and she was finally determinde to stop chasing after him and to leave him be. Through the years, fate many times tempted her mind and heart by letting her meet up with his sisters, cousins, or friends. She didn't and wouldn't let it get her down or affect her to much. She again kept reminding herself that fate was playing with her heart and mind. She'd learned years ago how cruel fate was and could be. Therefore, she was no longer going to let fate or Dacosta have this control over her. Yes, she still loved him just as much as ever, and in her heart she also still wanted him, but she now knew it would or could never be, because it didn't take over forty years for love to come from the same person. If it hadn't come by now then it most likely wouldn't. La'friska did believe that Dacosta loved her some, but like he always said he wasn't in love with her. All those forty-some years she loved him more than she loved herself. Now it was way beyond time for her to begin to love herself. After all, the greatest love is learning to love one's self. With his words ringing in her ears, heart, and mind—"I need a break"—she many times wondered what she had done to him for him to say that, plus stayed away from her all those years never bothering to explain why to her. Those words really opened her eyes and made her see, realizing that she deserved better than that. That he wasn't now good enough for her. The shoe was now on her foot; the tide had changed. Over forty years ago, on a Sunday afternoon, he'd said those words, "I'm to good for you." It was a way long time ago, and he was young and dumb. He hadn't grown up and experienced life. He had an excuse then, but not now, because time had flown passing by. She had proven her love over and over again. It was time to let go. She told herself that she should've never looked back in his direction, because she still wasn't the one he wanted. She thought to herself, "For all I know, he could still be in love with his ex-wife or even have someone else in mind." She knew that life doesn't stand still; it passes on by, and quickly at that. That none of us knows what tomorrow will bring or even take away from us. She several times thought about going to see Dacosta's mother and letting her know how much she did and still loved him. She wouldn't do that because she knew it had to be over for her. She had to forget him, plus she didn't want to upset his mother in any way. Also, his mother had nothing to do with what went on between them, and besides, La'friska had an old-fashioned belief about love. If Dacosta had wanted her to meet his mother, he would have introduced them long ago, and besides, he had two different chances in the past to do so. His first chance was before he went to Germany; they were outside in his mother's yard and he went inside the house and she stayed in the car. The second chance was a few years back when she was visiting on her summer vacation and he backed up and talked with her as she sat on her riding lawn mower—and at the time, La'friska didn't know that was his mother. So again, she resolved to leave his mother alone; it had to be over because it was for her own sake and good, therefore it must be. She had tried and tried and still couldn't make him want her. For almost three years now, they hadn't said a word to each other. Fate again intervened; it was mid July on a Sunday afternoon, 6:00 p.m. exactly. She was sitting on her porch and Dacosta drove by; he didn't speak. She knew he had to come back past her because there was no other way out; it was a dead end road. She wanted to run back inside the house. She didn't want him to think that she was looking for him. She reminded herself, "This is my porch and I'm not running hiding from him." Besides, she wanted to see if or not he'd speak to her. Five minutes later, he passed back by her house. As he did so, he didn't stop his truck, but he did slowed down and yelled out the window and said, "Hi, La'friska." She yelled back, "Hi," and before she knew it she again put her foot in her mouth. She said, "Come over here and let me tell you off." He laughed softly and said, "Maybe next time," and he kept on going his way. She had just now given him the opportunity to talk with her, and yet he declined. Her family members had told her before that he wanted to talk with her, yet he made no move to get in contact with her. To make matters worse, the truck he was driving was one she'd seen several times in her area, but she didn't know it was his truck until her family members told her. Yes, in her mind Dacosta Tiawan Gahenne was more than a piece of work. For three years he'd been sometimes working or at other times joyriding in her area, yet he didn't or wouldn't stop by and see her. She'd always been there for him; didn't he even care how she was doing healthwise, if nothing else? That Sunday in mid-July when she caught a glance of him from a distance and they'd said those words to each other was and would be the last and final time they spoke alive. Eight months later, Dacosta died after a brief illness from an aneurysm. When La'friska first heard of his death, she didn't even cry, and she didn't plan on going to his funeral. Of course she still loved him just as much as ever. She thought, "Maybe now I can and will get over him, because he's dead." Two days after hearing of his death, something came over and upon her; finally she went to see his mother. His mother was home alone while his family members were making funeral arrangements. His mother reminded her again about her being the one who went to Germany to see him, and also when she asked her if he was dropped on his head when he was a baby. La'friska had forgotten about asking her that over forty years ago. La'friska finally told his mother how very much she had always loved him, and would forever. That she had loved him more than she loved herself, and she had to give up trying to get him because he was still hurting her too much. She told his mother how much she'd always wanted to meet her and how much she loved and admired her. La'friska told his mother that he didn't have to have been by himself; that he could've had her, but he didn't want her. His mother also told her that she'd been thinking about her that morning, thinking her name was Gloria. His mother also said people were calling from Maryland wanting to be honorary flower bearers at his funeral. La'friska was glad she'd gone to see his mother, because she knew other than his family that no one else in this world could love him more than she did. She changed her mind about going to his funeral. First she went to the mortuary to view his body. She needed to see what he looked like. She hadn't seen him up close in almost four years. At the mortuary she was the only person there viewing his body. When she stood looking down on him, yes, she still loved him so very much. She softly said, "Dacosta, this is the end of us." She was daze-d, but still knowing reality. She wanted to ask him why did he stay away from her all those years, but she didn't because she didn't want the mortuary attendant hearing her conversation. Plus, it seemed unreal. She was hurting and in a trance-like surreal state of mind. She didn't stay long, and after she left, she wanted to return back to the mortuary and say to Dacosta, "Why did you stay away from me?" In church at his funeral she knew no one, other than his immediate family. She didn't even know what the kids looked like in person aside from seeing them in the obituary. No one could possibly had loved and wanted him more than she did. At the funeral, no one comforted her other than her family members who took her there. She was hurting just like everyone else, but still, those who did recognize her and knew about her and Dacosta said nothing; some even acted like they didn't see or know her. Throughout his service, there were two girls sitting behind her crying; she never turned around to get a good view of them, and she wondered who they were and what he meant to them. Dacosta was well liked by everyone. He could be a good friend to all others, it seemed, except to her, the person who loved and wanted him the most. His funeral was very large, and she'd even read the mortuary Facebook page where people posted nice things about him; people as far away as California. As in her life, fate would have it even in death at his funeral, fate was still very cruel and hurtful to her, because a female classmate of Dacosta's was there; the one who, over forty-some years ago, had gotten a letter she'd written to him. This girl had given the letter to Dacosta's cousin Brandi to return back to her. This girl, who's name was Nyra, even had the audacity to laugh when she did that. La'friska figured it was because Dacosta must have been talking to her sister. After all, her sister was the one who was his date for that social dance. Now even in death at his funeral, this

## Thoughts

same classmate of his participated in the proceedings, being an honorary flower bearer. La'friska wondered if this girl herself had something going on with him at some point in time. Also, La'friska now didn't know what this girl looked like after over forty years, and she looked trying to figure out which one was her, and she never did; it was a mystery. What a hellish turmoil La'friska had to endure. When La'friska had her last and final look down on Dacosta in his coffin, she gently touched his red necktie and she kissed his forehead. She would have kissed his lips for all the world to see, but she didn't, because she remembered how he'd pulled away from her many times when she kissed on him. She didn't know if or not he'd want her even now at his funeral to do so. As she kissed his forehead she never murmured outloud, but inside her heart and mind was saying, "I'll love you infinitely forever." She stared so hard and lovingly looking down at him, knowing this was the last time she'd ever see him. She had to remember his face. She still didn't cry, and she walked proudly away from his coffin. At the gravesite burial as she stood watching his cousin, Franklin recognized her and he never said a word, but he smiled at her and she said hi. After the burial she went home. Back at home she recalled the past four years and how she thought that if he died before she did, that she wouldn't go to his funeral. Now she knew that she'd been lying to herself. She had to see him being put in the ground. Five days after his burial, she returned back to the cemetery. At his gravesite, being the only live person there, she asked him why did he stayed away from her all those years? What did she do to him? Why did he need a break? She'd made no demands on him. What happened after the party? Everything changed. Also, she finally said to him that he wasn't all that. That she now knew that she deserved better than him. He wasn't good enough for her. Yes, she'd always loved him, but she had to let go of him, because he really didn't want her. Saying those words, she felt better. Even though he was dead and couldn't hear them, she felt better finally getting to say them to him. To have even more closure, she took a road trip to drive the pain and hurt out of her heart and mind. The road trip required her alertness and concentration. She wanted to live, and she had a lot to live for. Her tears finally came down upon her, but still she pushed on driving. She reminded herself that for almost four years she hadn't seen or been with him; that even though he was alive all those years, he was still dead to her because she had finally made herself stop wanting and chasing him. Now in reality he was dead and gone, never ever to return back to earthly life. She didn't think he would've died so soon. He wasn't fifty nine years old. During those long hours of driving, upon facing the true facts about their relationship, she had to accept the reality for being what it was. She told herself to stop grieving so hard. She'd done her very best to get him. Over forty–four years of wanting, waiting, and praying, and yet her prayers weren't answered. That God knew her heart and mind and he hadn't helped her to get Dacosta. During those forty-four years, she had hopes that Dacosta would someday give her a chance; that he'd return her love and want her. Life had now shown her it wouldn't happen. The reality was that Dacosta never really loved and wanted her. Even in the beginning of their relationship, he was only pretending. Impressing his cousins and friends. Trying to be a Casanova and boasting his own ego. After that, his actions through all those years proved over and over again that he never really cared. Still, she cared, hanging on hoping, wanting, praying, needing, and desperately loving him, even though his actions proved otherwise, speaking louder than words. Even after twenty-two years of being reunited with him, she thought, hoped, wished, and prayed that she and him could finally be together. They were now both older and hopefully much wiser. Through the years she'd learned to never say never, because we don't know what can and will happen. Only now, in this case of her and Dacosta, she now knew the facts and had to accept the harsh reality of her life. All hope was forever gone of a life with him. She'd never share his life, and he'd never be her world of joy. La'friska drove on, continuing her psychological therapy journey to restore her wounded and devastated heart and mind. Her body still ached and longed for his touch, lips that were so soft and sweet drowned her in a sea of abyss knowing she'd never, not ever again in life have it. Oh how her heart, body, mind, and even soul bled for him. She had to deal with it because his earthly life was over and he was not never ever coming back. She had to accept closure. He was dead. Like she said to him in the mortuary, "Dacosta, this is the end of us." Surely and truly for real, Dacosta Tiawan Gehenne, you were infinitely loved by the girl who became a true woman, La'friska Tashanti.

# Epilogue

Time waits for no one. In some and many instances, it quickly moves on by getting away from all of us. Right now I'm personally referring to myself. Five years ago I had an ideal of what the ending of my story *Thoughts* would be. I just hadn't put it in writing or had fate prove it at that time. The pointed hour, date, and time has finally arrived at last for destiny. During those two years before Dacosta died, I tried many times to conclude writing this epilogue, but to no avail; my words and thoughts just wouldn't flow and come together as I wanted them to. Also, my mind wouldn't push the writing ideal. So therefore I took a rest period from trying to write. I've never had any writing and training class experience. Besides, I don't know if or not this book will ever be published, because I have no contacts with the right connections that'll help me. I'm not some celebrity or star. I'm just an average, ordinary, unknown person, and more importantly, I've never been that lucky in life. In my lifetime, I've had much pain and difficulties, and the good and blessed part is, I preserved and overcame those hurdles and obstacles. Whether or not my book is or isn't ever published I'm very much proud of myself for trying. It's taken over thirty-nine very hard and too-long years to finally do it. Therefore, I'm contented with myself knowing that I tried. I also hoped and believed I had time to someday finish this epilogue. As the writer of this book, a lot has happened to me in these past years to change my life forever. I now know that it's time for me to get my affairs in order and try to make things happen, because, again time "don't wait for no one." So I'd better wake up to the harsh reality. Now it's time to complete the finale. It's now been five years since Dacosta died. First and foremost, for clarification, there is in reality a Dacosta and La'friska, whether it be these two in this story or other twos somewhere in life; let's all remember that life happens to everyone, all of us. Only the writer of this story really knows what's true or false, although some and many events in this story are both fictitious and autobiographical. In the prologue of this story when La'friska said, "Where has time gone in my life?" well, her conclusion is that only she herself let it pass directly on by her. Also, fate played a great very big hand in it. Fate being a force much stronger and more powerful than her. These past years, she's learned much about fate; that fate is and can be very cruel. Life isn't fair, especially for some people, but regardless of the facts, one must deal with it, whatever comes their way. Life is full of trials and tribulations, because no one knows what tomorrow brings or takes away from us. Looking back over her years of life, La'friska believes her purpose in life is to write this book. There's a myth saying that in life everyone has a certain talent or gift. Well, La'friska now realizes her gift is feelings and writing, even though it's taken her more than half a century to finally figure this out for herself. Yes, math was always her worst subject, except for the multiplication part—that she was a wiz at, only she sometimes didn't put the decimal point in the right place. What a waste of years; why has La'friska been so hurt by love? The answer is because she loves too deeply and she always picked the wrong men, giving them way too much, such as her body, money, time, and mind. Too much control over her heart. In all the years of her life, why hasn't she found the love she so desperately wanted and needed?" Well, La'friska can only answer that to a point, which is she should have let them go and move onto the next one. After that answer, the only other answer is only God knows and he isn't verbally talking. Eve, woman, was made from a man, Adam's ribcage, to keep man company, which was why God made woman Eve. Yet in this world, many upon many are very unlucky in love. They go through life looking, waiting, wanting, and needing to find love, but, they never do find it. In La'friska's opinion, the unluckly ones who don't have love make up and equal out to the lucky ones who are fortunate and blessed to have or have had love. Everyone can't be happy. That's just the way life is and love goes, because there's no guarantee; the one you love is going to love you back. For love has many definitions. It's beautiful and joyous and oh so good when it's returned, but when it's unrequited it's very painful and miserable, for love is truly a hurting thing. Love will make a strong person become weak and vice versa a weak person strong. To be love is life's foundation. The final analysis of love is joy and pain. Rewriting this story has also resurfaced much hurt and anguish for La'friska, remembering things that she'd forgotten through the years and blocked out of her mind. The hurt was still just as strong

## Thoughts

and painful as ever. Those forty-six years hadn't diminished any of the hurt; not at all. Matter of fact, it hurts even more because now La'friska knows there is no hope for her. Dacosta is dead and buried; her road ended. She no longer wants or is she looking for love. For her, love is overrated, even sex. In her opinion, from learning experiences, a man is good for two things, starting with reason number two: he's very good at fixing mechanical thing or things in general, and the number one, from her viewpoint now, not wanting to offend anyone, her point is a man is good for sex. In her opinion, sex is number two, because when you, a woman, want sex from your man, he's not there to give it to you because he's too busy giving it to someone else. La'friska would have had a much easier and better life if she hadn't loved too deeply, because all throughout her life that same loving caused her unrequited and deep turmoil within herself, problems in more ways than one, which started in her adolescent years throughout her whole entire adulthood life. Problems mentally and emotionally that caused turmoil inside her mind. She didn't discuss these problems with anyone; instead, she kept it to herself. She loved Dacosta more than life itself, or even herself, and so when he broke up with her in her adolescent years at age sixteen years old, when he on that fatal Sunday afternoon forty-six years ago phoned her and told her off in front of his cousins and friends, that had a very traumatically devastating effect on her socially, emotionally, and mentally. The hurt destroyed her heart and mind. When he told her off, her cousins were at her house, but they didn't hear what was going on, and she didn't tell them. Even though she was in shock and terribly hurting, she had to act like nothing had been wrong. She kept that pain and hurt to herself, never telling anyone, and it backfired on her mind, spiraling way out of control. She hurt so badly that she began to think that if someone hurt her mother, what she'd do to them. She had thoughts of how she'd retaliate revenge on them, getting even with them. Again, no one knew the turmoil she was going through inside of herself. Outwardly, her appearance was fine. It was years later that she discussed these thoughts with a doctor and he explained about obsessive compulsive disorder (OCD). La'friska learned much about OCD. In her case of battling all those thoughts and images, she thought that she was evil for having them to begin with, and she was very afraid that she would act on them. She learned that that was why she'd get upset, because she did know better. She was not to act them out and not to dwell too much on trying to reason them out when they came into her mind. When she heard the doctor say that, she realized this was true, and she instantly became relieved and well on her way to controlling her own type of OCD. What La'friska had to learn, we all, meaning everyone of us, is that no one of us are exempt from having thoughts. We all have them at some point in time, whether the thoughts are happy, sad, good or bad, evil, and dangerously harmfully wrong; the crux is everyone has thoughts. The point is not to act upon them or be afraid of them, letting them put fear into us or trying to reason them out for ourselves; just again let them come through our mind and let them go on away. Let me leave some examples. A total stranger you see could have on a beautiful outfit, and you admire it, thinking, that looks good on her, I like that outfit, I wonder where she got it. Another example is, she has nice hair, or, I like his suit, he is so sexy and good looking. Now, on the other hand, if someone makes you angry, mad, or upset, you might think to yourself, I want to knock the hell out of them or even tell them off. Ending this story, it's been a very long thirty-nine years of errors, trials, and much tribulation; what wasted years, and such a horrendous and harrowing experience from La'friska's stand and viewpoint and thoughts. Love is supposed to comfort you and to make you happy, but not in her case, for she loved Dacosta too deeply and he hurt her so much and badly and painfully in earthly life that now her only thought where he was concerned was when her life was over and her judgement day came, and should she and Dacosta be in the same place, whether it' hell or heaven, she just wishes, hopes, and even prays very hard to God that Dacosta and her never, no not ever again, meet. Even if by chance of fate he and she are about to come face to face with each other, when they do meet, La'friska wants both of them to be looking in different directions so they won't and don't ever see each other. Never Anymore. The End.